Preface

Throughout the Second World War, but especially during its closing stages, Germany's aircraft designers came up with unusual solutions to some very specific problems.

In particular, the urgent need to strike at bomber bases in Britain, shoot down the bombers coming from Britain, gain air superiority over the likes of the Spitfire and Mustang, make do with fewer material resources and do all of the above as quickly as possible, seems to have inspired some very creative thinking.

The first three parts of my Luftwaffe: Secret series each focused on a particular thread of aircraft development in Nazi Germany during the war years – jet fighters, bombers and tailless aircraft. In each case, rather than relying on existing works by other authors, I endeavoured to base my work on original source material – German documents captured by the Allies in 1945 and reports made by the Allies of interrogations and other contemporary intelligence work.

The result has, hopefully, been a somewhat clearer picture of the framework of requirements, competitions and contracts surrounding the development of some of Germany's most famous, or perhaps infamous, 'secret project' aircraft. I was by no means the first to attempt this – quite the reverse. Ever since the end of the Second World War and the Allies' diligent efforts to haul away huge quantities of 'secret' documents from Germany, there have been writers and historians who sought to piece together details of exactly what aircraft designs, advanced or otherwise, the German aircraft companies had been working on.

With this in mind, I had thought that every sketch, every drawing, every crumpled piece of doodled-on scrap paper from every designer's wastebasket (the ubiquitous and in some cases infamous 'napkin waffe') had already been found and published years ago. But it seems I was wrong – there was and is still more to be discovered.

As I went about my research among the 'usual suspects', I would frequently happen upon drawings and documents that were wholly unexpected – seemingly unheard-of versions of well-known German wartime aircraft, clear drawings of aircraft proposals whose existence had been the stuff of mere hints and rumours, straightforward reports which offered explanations of previously inexplicable designs.

Indeed, while researching each of the first three titles in this series I discovered some 'projects' which appeared to be previously unknown and some which, though known, appeared to be little understood.

In some cases, the designs exist only as drawings or even sketches. In others, they exist only as textual descriptions – the associated drawings having apparently been lost or destroyed. For still others, there are full reports which seem simply never to have previously been reported on. This time there is no broader narrative linking the featured designs together other than the fact of their obscurity.

At the end of each previous Luftwaffe: Secret title, I included a section called 'Unknown!' – a not-so-subtle reference to the old Reichdreams Dossiers created by Justo Miranda and Paula Mercado during the late 1990s and early 2000s. But whereas Miranda and Mercado used their five volumes of 'Unknown!' as a clearing house for a jumble of British, Italian, French, American and even a few German projects, I subtitled mine 'Postwar discoveries, misinterpretations and mysteries' and used it to critically examine some of the dubious or little-known German projects referred to by various historians over the last 70 years or so.

I examined designs such as the so-called Blohm & Voss Ae 607, the Heinkel VTOL fighters and the Messerschmitt 'animal names' types but also managed to include a few of my own discoveries – such as a Henschel P 135 looking very different to how the design is usually seen, and the Swaty S.8.

Even before I started this section, I knew I had far too many entries for it. In fact, I had intended to include 20 pages of 'Unknown!' in Luftwaffe: Secret Wings until I realised that this would leave too little room for the eponymous 'wings'. And so I conceived this title as a means of drawing together a collection of both entirely new discoveries and details of known projects I had not seen published anywhere else.

In writing this publication, I wanted to be candid about the status of the 'projects' I was presenting. Where very little information was available, I wanted to try and make that as clear as possible. You should not expect, therefore, to find all the answers concerning everything you see within this volume. Neither will you find any ambiguous 're-draws' or unlabelled 'speculative' drawings, which may or may not represent the features of an original drawing (you will not find them in any of my previous Luftwaffe: Secret titles either).

The modern colour artwork commissioned for and included in Luftwaffe: Secret Designs is intended to stick as closely to those original designs as possible and is clearly labelled as artwork. Where it has been necessary to 'speculate' about the features of these designs, particularly where the original exists only as a single-view drawing or undetailed sketch, I have attempted to explain the nature of that speculation.

My aim here then, rather than to offer a broad narrative, is to showcase and comment on material which has lain largely undisturbed for the best part of a century and which might otherwise have continued to languish in the shadows for many decades yet to come.

There can be no greater thrill for the dedicated researcher than the discovery of something 'new' – and I hope I can share a little of that feeling with you as you read this publication. ●

006 **Known unknowns**

008 **Arado 'Dreieck'**

012 **Arado ÜS-Flugzeug**

014 **Arado E 208**

018 **Arado Ar 233**

024 **Blohm & Voss BV 138, projects P 81, P 84, P 85, P 86, P 94, P 110, P 111, P 112, P 144, P 145 and BV 238 Seefernaufklärer, Dornier P 93/Do 214 and P 173/Do 216, Heinkel He 120**

036 **Dornier P 209, P 215, P 231, P 232, P 238, P 252 and triple jet fighter**

042 **Dornier P 144, P 149, P 150, P 151, P 153, P 155, P 222, P 223, Do 317 and Do 417**

052 **DVL jet fighter**

056 **Focke-Wulf Grosstransporter**

062 **Gotha P-60.007**

066 **Gotha oddities**

072 **Guided weapons**

076 **Heinkel P 1076**

082 **Henschel P 75, P 87, P 90, P 108, P 122, P 130, P 135, P 136 and Hs 132**

Contents

ABOVE: Messerschmitt P 1079/17 attacking a
USAAF Manta Aircraft Corp fighter.
Art by Ronnie Olsthoorn

FRONT COVER:
Zeppelin pulsejet fighter
shoots down a Soviet Lend-
Lease Bell P-63 Kingcobra
east of Berlin. Art by Ronnie
Olsthoorn

INSIDE COVER:
Dornier P 144 (top) and
Do 317. Drawing circa
1939/40.

GW00702992

AUTHOR: Dan Sharp
DESIGN: Lucy Carnell - atg-media.com
REPROGRAPHICS: Jonathan Schofield, Paul Fincham and
Angie Sisestean
PRODUCTION EDITOR: Pauline Hawkins
PUBLISHER: Steve O'Hara
ADVERTISING MANAGER: Sue Keily, skeily@mortons.co.uk
PUBLISHING DIRECTOR Dan Savage
MARKETING MANAGER: Charlotte Park
COMMERCIAL DIRECTOR: Nigel Hole

PUBLISHED BY: Mortons Media Group Ltd, Media Centre,
Morton Way, Horncastle, Lincolnshire LN9 6JR.
Tel. 01507 529529

THANKS TO: Steven Coates, Zoltán Csombó, Calum
Douglas, Chris Elwell, Hamza Fouatih, Dan Johnson,
Luca Landino, Paul Martell-Mead, Ronnie Olsthoorn,
Alexander Power, Kay Stout, Daniel Uhr, Stephen Walton
and Tony Wilson

PRINTED BY: William Gibbons and Sons, Wolverhampton

ISBN: 978-1-911276-62-3

094   **Junkers EF 116**

100   **Lippisch P 15 Diana**

108   **Messerschmitt Me 109 Zw, Me 309 Zw and Me 609**

116   **Messerschmitt Me 163 with canards**

118   **Messerschmitt P 1079**

124   **Messerschmitt Schnellstflugzeug**

128   **Zippermayr's Pfeil Flugzeug**

130   **Zeppelin pulsejet fighter**

MORTONS
MEDIA GROUP LTD

Known unknowns

Projects without pictures

Some of the most enigmatic German aircraft designs of the Second World War are known only through textual descriptions – no drawings apparently having survived. This state of affairs has, in some cases, led artists to attempt 'speculative' drawings of them...

MESSERSCHMITT ME 334

```
                    Fernschreiben                    708


    Herrn Urban - Berliner Büro

    Ich bitte Sie im Amt zu klären, wie der Auftrag der 163 mit
    Otto - Motoren gedacht war. (Me 334). Die neuen Entwürfe ergeben
    ein vollkommen neues Flugzeug. Damit wird der Arbeitsaufwand ein
    Vielfaches von dem betragen, was ursprünglich veranschlagt war.
    Ich kann die Arbeit an diesem Vogel nicht verantworten. Ich
    bitte bevor Sie Schritte im Amt unternehmen die Angelegenheit
    M mit Herrn Seiler zu besprechen


                                    gez: Messerschmitt


    Augsburg, 19. Februar 1943
    Mtt/Gü         , gez? Günther
                   (Günther)
```

ABOVE: A note from Messerschmitt dated February 19, 1943, concerning the Me 334.

At the height of the antagonism that grew between Me 163 designer Alexander Lippisch and his boss Willy Messerschmitt, in February 1943, Lippisch drafted designs for new piston-engine and jet-propelled fighters based on the aerodynamic form of the Me 163. The jet version was the P 20 but the piston-engine version apparently received a Reichsluftfahrtministerium (RLM – the German air ministry) designation as the Me 334.

Part of the problem between Messerschmitt and Lippisch was the latter's tendency to take projects directly to Reichsmarschall Hermann Göring without Messerschmitt's knowledge. Messerschmitt would only find out later what his colleague had been up to. This would seem to be what happened with the Me 334.

Unusually, Lippisch did not write about the Me 334 in either of his books and never seems to have mentioned it elsewhere either. But a note exists, signed by Messerschmitt himself and dated February 19, 1943, which discusses the project.

He wrote: "I ask you to clarify in the office how the order of the 163 with Otto engines was intended. (Me 334). The new designs result in a completely new aircraft. Thus, the work will be a multiple of what was originally estimated. I can not answer for the work on this bird. I ask you to take steps in office to discuss the matter with Mr Seiler."

Mr Seiler was probably Messerschmitt AG director Freidrich Seiler, and the note seems to suggest that Messerschmitt himself was deeply unhappy that a piston-engined Me 163 was being worked on due to the amount of time and effort it would take to make it.

It would appear that the matter was dropped just over a month later, on March 26, when Seiler told Lippisch that his department Abteilung L was being dissolved. Lippisch resigned and left the company.

Although re-draws or perhaps speculative drawings have been printed, it would appear that no original drawing of an Me 334 has ever been published.

FOCKE-WULF STRAHLJÄGER (ENTE)

On December 1, 1942, Focke-Wulf worked on calculations for a new tail-first or 'canard' fighter powered by the BMW P 3303 turbojet.

Work on the P 3303 had evidently begun in 1940 or earlier and between April 21 and June 1, 1942, it was given the official designation BMW 018. Clearly, Focke-Wulf did not get this message and even by January 20, 1943, was still referring to it as the P 3303.

A BMW report entitled Einbaumappe 109-018, dated June 1, 1942, gives the engine's overall length as 4.75m and its weight as 1740kg. By comparison, the Jumo 004 was 3.86m long and weighed only 719kg.

With these specs in mind, the Strahljäger (Ente) must have been a fairly substantial aircraft to accommodate it. However, there is no drawing and beyond these basic facts nothing more is known about it.

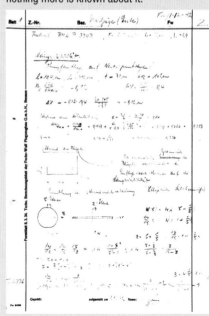

ABOVE: The first page of the three-page document on the Strahljäger (Ente).

BMW OJ-X

BMW produced a report on August 8, 1944, entitled Möglichkeiten der weiteren Jäger-Entwicklung or 'possibilities of further fighter development', which compared the performance of the Focke-Wulf Ta 152, fitted with the company's own BMW 801 R, against that of the Messerschmitt Me 262 with either the BMW 003 A or Jumo 004, the Horten 8-229 with either the BMW 003 A or Jumo 004, and something called the OJ-X.

The introduction says: "By comparing the performance of various fighters with gasoline engines and turbojet drive it is possible to investigate whether the new development of a jet engine of the gasoline engine design based on an 18-cylinder double star of 3000hp is justified against the possibilities offered by the jet drive."

So, was it worth developing a massive 18-cylinder piston engine when working on jet engines might be more worthwhile? To represent "the most advanced Otto engine fighter design", BMW used something it called the "Otto-Motor-Jäger X (OJ-X)" which "would be superior even in high altitudes to the Me 262 in the form available today. It would, however, need even more development time".

Germans at this time often referred to the piston engine as an 'Otto' engine after German engineer Nikolaus Otto, who invented the first four-stroke petrol engine in 1861.

The BMW report found that a "properly designed" jet fighter could exceed even "the performance of the best gasoline engine fighter by far. Only in terms of flight times and ranges at medium speeds, is the Otto

		Fläche [m²]	Streckung [b²/F]	Zelle mit Ausrüstung u. Besatzung [kg]	Kraftstoff [kg]	Triebwerk [kg]	Waffen [kg]	Startgewicht [kg]
Ta 152 mit BMW 801R		19,6	6,2	1592	450	1950	528	4520
OJ-X mit 3000 PS	Normal	30	6,5	2740	1000	3000	800	7540
	mit Zusatzkraftstoff	"		2840	2250	"	"	8890
	mit 2× BMW 003A	21,7	7,3	2100	1350	1240	810	5560
Me 262 mit 2× 1600kg-TL		"	"	.	"	2480	"	6740
	mit 2× 1600kg-TL u. Zusatzkraftstoff	"	"	.	"	2180	2260	"	7730
	mit 2× BMW 003A	53	5,6	2 160	2 300	1240	800	6 500
Horten mit 2× 1600kg-TL		"	"	.	"	2480	"	7 740
	mit 2× BMW 003 A und Zusatzkraftstoff	"	"	2 260	3 400	1240	"	7 900

ABOVE: The BMW OJ-X fighter compared against the Ta 152, Me 262 and Horten 8-229.

engine fighter more powerful, especially in medium and low altitude. Since the OJ-X's manufacturing and development effort seems to be greater and a longer development time will be required, especially for the special-purpose propulsion engine, such a development could be superior to the Horten jet fighter in only a few special cases. Not recommended.

"The most suitable fighter design proves to be a

Horten flying wing fighter with two jet units". And "the development of a special type of air-cooled 18-cylinder double-star engine for pressure propellers cannot be supported".

Tables show further details of the OJ-X, such as a wing area of 30sqm, similar to that of the Ta 154, so it was presumably more than just a set of stats but there is no accompanying drawing.

BLOHM & VOSS P 214

The lengthy series of projects produced by Blohm & Voss's designers has long been a source for speculation, particularly since very few of those projects were ever actually built. Lists exist which provide a very brief description of each project but one of the most enigmatic is the company's penultimate design – the P 214.

The only known evidence of it is a series of five sheets: two text and three graphs dated November 20-24, 1944. These describe the project as a 'Bemannte Fla – Bombe', with the 'Fla' evidently being short for 'Flugabwehr' meaning 'air defence', itself meaning 'anti-aircraft'. So the P 214 was, in effect, a 'Manned anti-aircraft bomb'.

Given its size – a wingspan of seven metres, similar to that of the He 162 by way of comparison, and a wing area of 10sqm, only slightly smaller than that of the He 162 – it wasn't exactly a missile. It weighed 3600kg, of which 1700kg was fuel. Its empty weight of 1900kg was almost exactly the same as the empty weight of the Me 163, though the latter carried just over 2000kg of fuel and oxidiser for its rocket engine.

No engine type is given but the remainder of the text states: "Flight route: The course of the flight is assumed as follows: The aircraft is accelerated on the ground until the speed has reached 700 or 800km/h, with which it should rise below 45°. The thrust for acceleration on the ground should be equal to the initial thrust when climbing."

This certainly suggests rocket thrust. The accompanying graphs show the P 214 climbing to an altitude of 15km (49,212ft) or 17km (55,774ft), depending on whether take-off speed was 700km/h or 800km/h, in just under two minutes. Descending flight then began, with the total flight time including climb expected to last around eight minutes.

It has been suggested that one or more of the

late-war designs of Karl Stöckel, an employee of the Deutsche Versuchsanstalt für Luftfahrt (DVL) or 'German aviation research institute', is actually the P 214 – but none of these matches the weights and dimensions of the P 214 given in the Blohm & Voss paperwork, particularly his MGRP which consisted of a 5m wingspan glider attached to the back of a very large rocket, giving a take-off weight of 10 tons. For now it would appear that we simply do not know what the P 214 was intended to look like.

ABOVE: The first of five known pages detailing the Blohm & Voss P 214.

VDM INSEKT

As a company designing and building high-performance propellers, VDM worked closely with all the major aircraft manufacturers as well as the engine builders.

As a result, it often had opinions and ideas about what future technological developments were possible. On December 2, 1944, VDM engineer Konrad Mielke wrote a three-page outline of a new aircraft design he had been working on which mechanically imitated an insect in flight.

The textual description of what the aircraft was intended to look like is vague, except to say that it had multiple propellers and was capable of ascending vertically, remaining motionless in the air and attaining high speeds during level flight. It seems to have been something like a modern day drone with various rotors working simultaneously but there is no known image of it.

ABOVE: The covering sheet of Konrad Mielke's description of the VDM Insekt.

The flying triangle

Flying wings had been a focus of Arado's project work as early as 1935 but these efforts were soon abandoned as unworkable. However, something happened in 1943 which would prompt the company to revisit them.

There seem to have been numerous instances of the design team at government-owned Arado being used as a stalking horse for industry. When a requirement was issued to the private companies, such as Heinkel, Messerschmitt and Focke-Wulf, Arado would be quietly asked to see what it could come up with to meet the same requirement.

Sometimes the resulting design made Arado a competitor for those companies, but on other occasions it simply served to represent what might reasonably be achieved. Projects such as the E-470 transport/bomber, E-580 single-jet fighter and E-395 jet bomber seem to have resulted from this process.

In early 1943, Alexander Lippisch approached Hermann Göring with a proposal for a twin-jet flying wing aircraft capable of flying 1000km, reaching 1000km/h and carrying a bomb load of 1000kg – the P 11. It was a project he had started at Messerschmitt in the autumn of 1942 and which he had taken with him when he left the company in April 1943. Göring went on to tell others just how much he wanted a '1000 x 1000 x 1000' aircraft and this resulted in the Horten brothers coming up with their own proposal to meet the spec – a tweaked version of their H IX, which would later become 8-229. Even Focke-Wulf, in October 1943, investigated the idea, though its approach suggested that '1000 x 1000 x 1000' performance might be more easily achieved with an airframe of conventional layout.

A month earlier, however, Arado project engineer Hans Walland had begun to draw up designs for a twin-jet aircraft of a comparable size to the P 11. Like the P 11, but unlike the Horten and Focke-Wulf designs, Walland's flying wing had a single central tail fin. And unlike any of the others, its planform was that of an isosceles triangle – a pure delta wing.

It was to be powered by a pair of

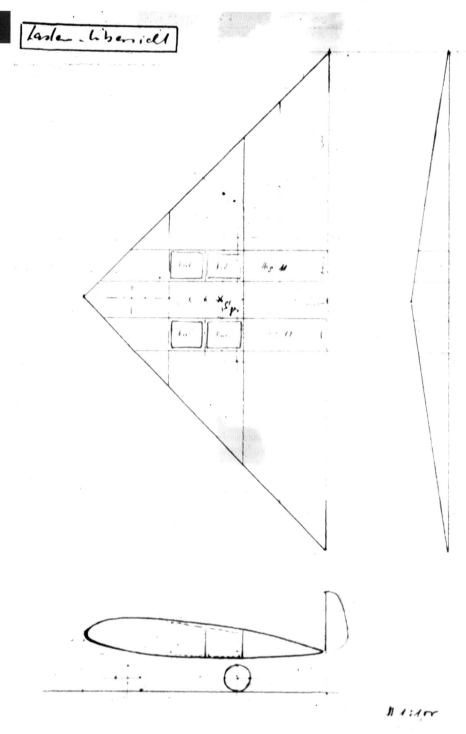

ABOVE: Sketch of Arado's triangular twin-jet aircraft, drafted by Hans Walland in September 1943.

Heinkel HeS 011 turbojets to the rear of the airframe with its fuel tanks positioned in the middle around a clear space at the centre of gravity. The tanks appear to be positioned directly in front of the turbojets themselves, so whether air from the engine intakes would go above or below them is unclear. Presumably the clear space represents the aircraft's 1000kg bomb bay.

Walland's triangle sat on a tricycle undercarriage and while the drawing does not show a cockpit, it is reasonable to assume that a cross placed towards the leading edge of the wing in the centre is where it was intended to go.

By September 1943, Arado had already been engaged for several months in designing its series of large flying wing jet bombers – E-555. The shape of these designs was what the company referred to as 'knickpfeilflügel' or 'creased arrow wing' and was far removed from Walland's

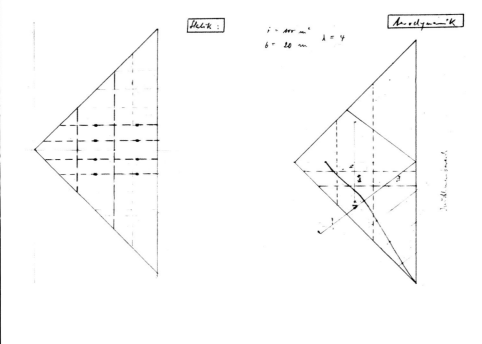

FDA = 3

Figure 3.- Suspension of the wing in wind tunnel.

EDA = 2

Figure 4.- Suspension of the wing in wind tunnel.

ABOVE: Triangular models tested by the DVL.

ABOVE: Further sketches by Walland showing the triangular shape of his design.

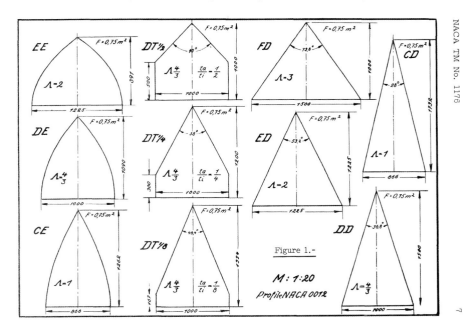

ABOVE: Wind tunnel shapes tested by the DVL during 1943, seen here in a postwar NACA report.

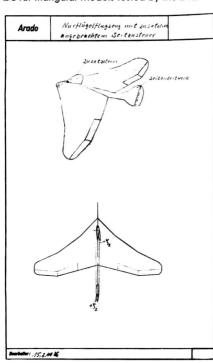

ABOVE: The state of Arado's flying wing design by February 1944, from a patent application. The company evolved the wing shape but struggled to find a form of rudder that would provide adequate stability.

regular triangle form. So what could have prompted a design that deliberately stepped away from the curves and refinements of other Arado projects?

During the Second World War, Germany had access to 78 wind tunnels – 19 of them suitable for use in high-speed research. This both allowed and encouraged German scientists and engineers to test a wide range of different aerodynamic shapes to determine which might have advantageous characteristics for future aircraft designs.

Some of these shapes must have seemed outlandish even at the time but they were tested anyway to gather baseline data. In September 1943, the DVL published a report entitled Prüfbericht über 3- und 6-Komponentenmessungen an der Zuspitzungsreihe von Flügeln kleiner

Stockung (Teilbericht: Dreieckflügel) or 'Test report on 3- and 6-component measurements on a series of tapered wings of small aspect ratio (partial report: triangular wing)' by Lange and Wacke, Untersuchungen und Mitteilungen ('Investigations and Communications' or UM) Nr. 1023/5. This effectively assessed the aerodynamics of pure delta wings in flight and it is not inconceivable that Arado, which received the same aerodynamics reports as every other aircraft manufacturer in Germany via the ZWB (Zentrale für wissenschaftliches Berichtswesen or 'Central Office for Scientific Reporting'), saw and acted upon it.

Evidently Arado designers' notes were filed in date blocks from, say, April 1943 to September 1943, and the only known evidence of Walland's triangle

or 'dreieck' project today comes in the form of a few basic sketches and pages that were captured by the Allies in 1945 jumbled up among pages from other reports and projects from that date block.

It seems unlikely that a triangular aircraft could have been made to work given the limited technology available in Second World War Germany, even with a tail fin to add directional stability, but nevertheless it indicates that the '1000 x 1000 x 1000' proposal put forward by Lippisch was more significant than has perhaps previously been acknowledged. ●

Arado 'Dreieck'

September 1943

Artwork by Luca Landino

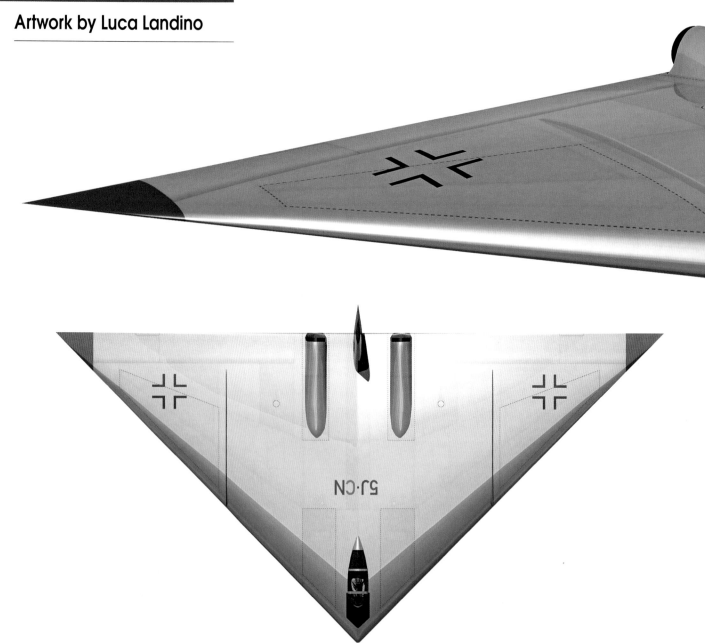

COMMENTS

The sketch which provided the basis for the Arado 'Dreieck' design shown here is short on detail and its dimensions had to be worked out using the size of its HeS 011 jet engines, a known quantity, for scale. The result is a clean-looking triangular single-seater very much in the vein of the other known 1000 x 1000 x 1000 projects.

Going supersonic

Arado Überschallflugzeug

While much of the Arado projects team's attention was focused on advanced versions of the Ar 234 during 1944, in September of that year Hans Walland worked on the design of an experimental aircraft designed to break the sound barrier.

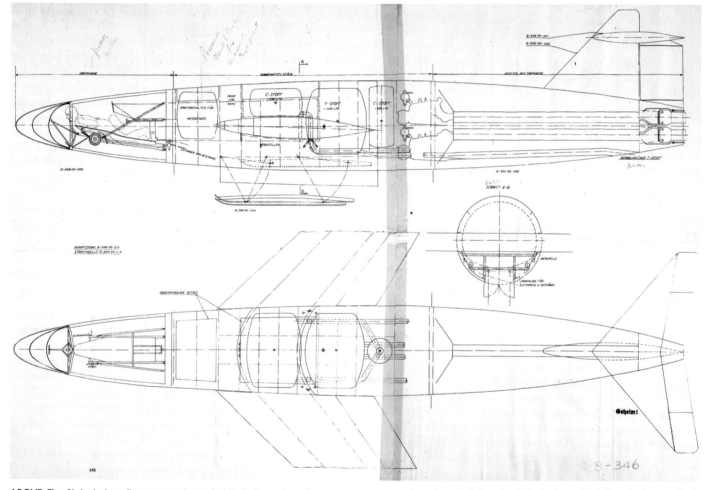

ABOVE: The Siebel aircraft company based at Halle in eastern Germany commenced work on building the DFS-designed 8-346 rocket-propelled supersonic research aircraft in November 1944. Two months earlier, Arado had been working on a competing design which was reportedly similar in its overall dimensions called the ÜS-Flugzeug – 'ÜS' being short for 'Überschall' or 'supersonic'.

Documentation on German wartime plans to build a manned aircraft capable of going supersonic is sparse but it does exist. Alexander Lippisch's wind tunnel experiments on his P 13a ramjet-powered rammer aircraft certainly suggested to him that it ought to have been able to reach Mach 2 but whether it would truly have been capable of this is unknown.

However, it would appear that during 1944 both Arado and the Deutsche Forschungsanstalt für Segelflug (DFS) or 'German Research Institute for Soaring Flight' worked on competing designs for

an Überschallflugzeug or 'supersonic aircraft'. Walland's report on his company's effort, dated September 15, 1944, is entitled 'ÜS-Flugzeug' and begins: "Task: It will be investigated to what extent the supersonic speed can be reached and exceeded, with an experimental aircraft with swept wing and rocket-thrust system with a launch weight of seven tons, of which 4.2 tons is fuel." It was proposed that the aircraft would be towed to an altitude of 9km (29,528ft) before being released for its high-speed run.

The report goes on to state that performance figures had been calculated

to offer a better picture of the altitude, thrust and fuel quantity necessary for the mission – some of the data borrowed from the known performance of projectiles.

These tended to suggest that 9km was too low and that going higher would result in reduced air resistance, although more fuel would be consumed by the aircraft in climbing to that altitude from a starting point of 9km. Altitudes of 15km (49,213ft) and 17km (55,774ft) were studied but there was a lack of clear documentation available to determine exactly what level of resistance the aircraft would meet at those heights.

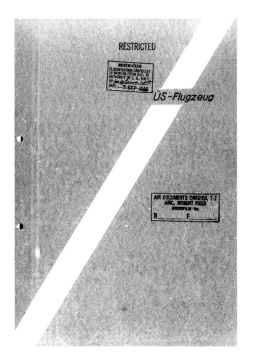

ABOVE: No drawing of the Arado ÜS-Flugzeug outlined in this report, dated September 15, 1944, appears to have survived.

However, Walland wrote, it could be assumed that at an altitude of 15km a Walter engine with 2000kg thrust – presumably the HWK 109-509 as fitted to the Me 163B – would be insufficient, "so the installation of two rocket engines will be required and the expected difficulties with the centre of gravity must be accepted. The test times for the on-board flight diminish in the extreme case to half (about two minutes). In general it turns out that about half of the amount of fuel available at the start is consumed in climb from an altitude of 9km to 16km".

The aircraft's fuselage could be made

ABOVE: The first page of the Arado report on its ÜS-Flugzeug design, a competitor for the DFS/Siebel 8-346.

lighter and fuel load could be reduced, but this would "mean a corresponding reduction of the experimental flight time". The pilot would lie prone on his front but with his head up – a position in which he would be able to withstand acceleration of 12g for between three and four minutes, 17g for a short time, and up to 26g for under 1.2 seconds.

The Arado ÜS-Flugzeug was expected to be able to fly at Mach 2 for around two minutes and Walland reported that the DFS supersonic design, designated HS-8, with similar external dimensions,

would only be able to achieve the same performance for about one minute.

There is no drawing of the ÜS-Flugzeug appended to the report file, and no dimensions are given for it either, but it seems likely that the DFS design was chosen over it and received the RLM designation 8-346; Siebel then being awarded a contract to develop and build it. Anecdotal evidence gathered by historian David Myhra from former Siebel employees in the late 1980s suggests that Siebel received the 8-346 contract in November 1944 and between then and May 1945 the company worked on three airframes – two for research flights and one for stress testing. None of them were complete when the war ended.

Like the Arado ÜS-Flugzeug, the 8-346 was powered by a pair of liquid-fuelled Walter HWK 109-509 rocket engines and had a prone-pilot cockpit. Its wings were swept back 45-degrees and it was to land on an extendable centreline skid. According to CIOS Evaluation Report No. 149 it was designed to be carried up to 10km and released, before its engines were switched on and it was propelled up to an altitude of 20km (66,000ft). At this height, it was expected to achieve a top speed of 2000km/h (1250mph) – somewhat less than the top speed projected for the ÜS-Flugzeug.

Siebel's facility at Halle was captured by the Americans in May 1945 and a number of drawings and documents relating to the 8-346, but not all of them, were handed over. In July, the Americans withdrew and the Soviets moved in – capturing the remainder of the 8-346 drawings and documents, not to mention the three incomplete airframes and the Siebel staff who had worked on them. Meanwhile, Arado's failed supersonic competitor, the ÜS-Flugzeug, was forgotten. ●

ARADO GROSS-TRANSPORTER

Another unusual design from the pen of Hans Walland at Arado was the Gross-Transporter. On April 1, 1943, Walland drew up a size comparison chart for transport aircraft ranging from 60 tonnes to 145 tonnes in weight. These are compared against the 20-tonne Ar 432 in the right-hand column. The accompanying sketch shows the outline of an Ar 232 B in the centre with at least three outlines of gigantic aircraft overlaid on top of it.

During late 1941 and into 1942, Arado

had worked on a project to determine whether a large transport aircraft design could provide a suitable basis for a bomber, a project designated E-470. And in the intervening year or so, it had enjoyed some limited success with its battlefield transport, the Ar 232.

The Gross-Transporter appears to be a wedding of these two designs, with the smaller variants retaining the Ar 232's tail boom while the larger variants exhibit the E-470's twin boom layout. Around six weeks

after Walland produced this drawing, on May 23, 1943, Arado put out another report proposing an 'Einfachtransporter' or 'easy transporter' based on the same basic design principles as the Ar 232. With a wingspan of 45m, the four-engine Einfachtransporter looks somewhat similar to Walland's 60-tonne 41m wingspan Gross-Transporter.

In the end, Germany did build some truly enormous transport aircraft in the form of Junkers' Ju 390 and Blohm & Voss's BV 238 but Arado's designs came to nothing.

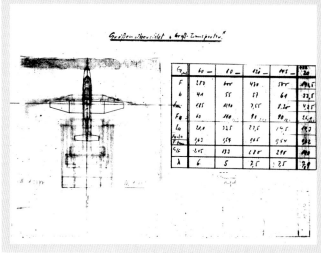

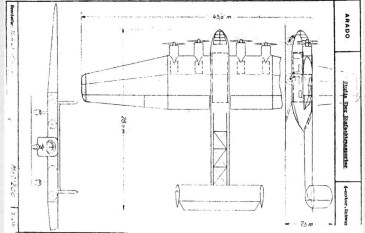

The new beginning

Arado E 208

During the early years of the Nazi regime, in the midst of enforced nationalisation, Arado nevertheless managed to come up with a compact and modern-looking aircraft design which would provide a firm foundation for the Luftwaffe's standard wartime trainer.

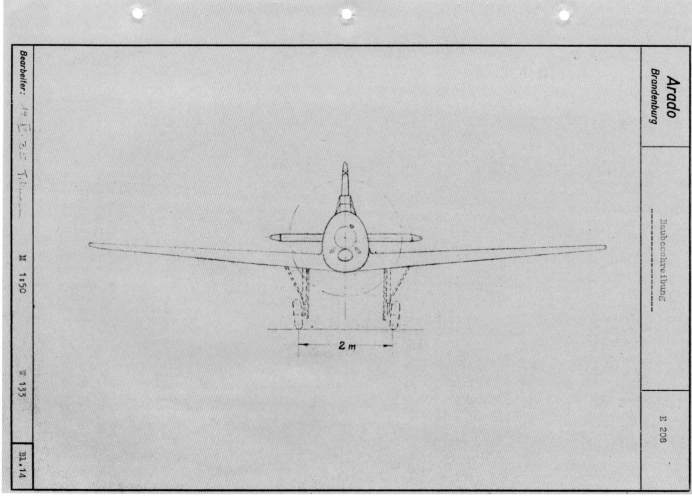

ABOVE: Forward view of Arado's E 208 trainer from the original report – one of the few images clear enough to publish without enhancement.

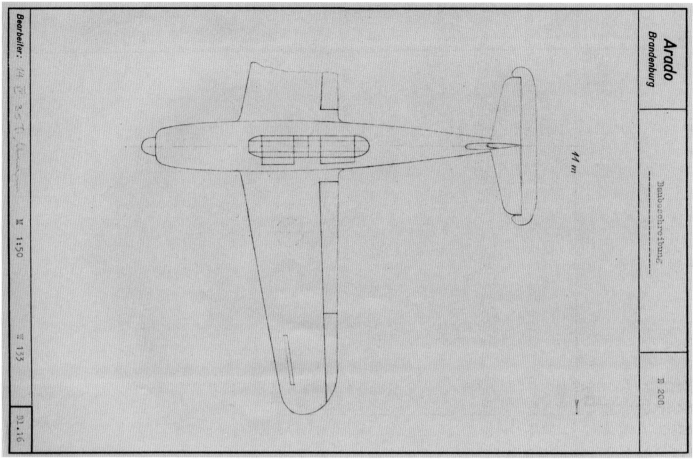

ABOVE: Top view of the E 208.

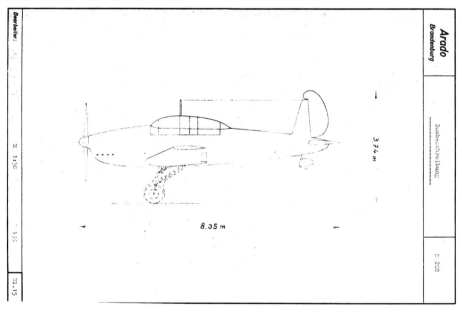

ABOVE: A side view of the E 208 in generic trainer form. The original version of the drawing, similar to the one shown above, is faint to the point where it is almost impossible to discern details.

A rado underwent a seismic shift in 1935. When the Nazis seized power in 1933, they brought with them ambitious plans to accelerate the re-armament of Germany at a time when most of the nation's aircraft manufacturers badly needed the work. What would become the Luftwaffe was being equipped with its first postwar fighters at this point – Arado's Ar 64 and the more advanced Ar 65.

It might seem that winning contracts to supply these aircraft put Arado in an advantageous position, but instead it seems to have made the company itself a target. Even before Adolf Hitler had been named chancellor, the German government had evidently become suspicious about Arado's financial situation and particularly about the dealings of its senior partner Heinrich Lübbe.

Government meddling in the affairs of Arado apparently began as early as 1931 when ailing industrial giant Albatros finally collapsed and Arado was forced to take on some of its senior staff – particularly technical director Walter Blume, who was installed in the same post at Arado in January 1932. A financial audit at the end of 1932 apparently found some irregularities, Lübbe having withdrawn a substantial sum in private capital some months earlier.

Nevertheless, as the process of rearming continued, huge sums of government money were pumped into Arado, swelling the company payroll from 287 in December 1932 to 2485 by the end of 1934. In the space of a year it had become almost a different firm – though still a privately owned one.

Matters came to a head in 1935, not long after the death of Hugo Junkers while under

house arrest and the nationalisation of his company. A similar process then happened at Arado. Lübbe was arrested and forced to sell his shares in the company to the government.

Arado was destined to become primarily a mass manufacturer of other companies' designs, but like Junkers it retained a team of designers and just as the company was becoming a wholly owned tool of the Nazis they came up with what was arguably the firm's greatest success.

On December 14, 1935, the company produced a proposal for a new multipurpose light monoplane advanced trainer aircraft which it designated E 208.

A year earlier, as a still-private company, Arado's Ar 76 had narrowly lost out to Focke-Wulf's Fw 56 in a four-way competition. This contest, also involving Heinkel and Henschel, had been intended to provide a new trainer which could double up as an 'emergency home defence fighter' and the attractive easy-to-fly Fw 56 had taken the full production contract. Nevertheless, more than 180 examples of the Ar 76 were ordered and built. Both the Ar 76 and the Fw 56 were parasol-wing fixed undercarriage types – neither pushed the boundaries of technology particularly far.

By comparison, the E 208 was positively ▶

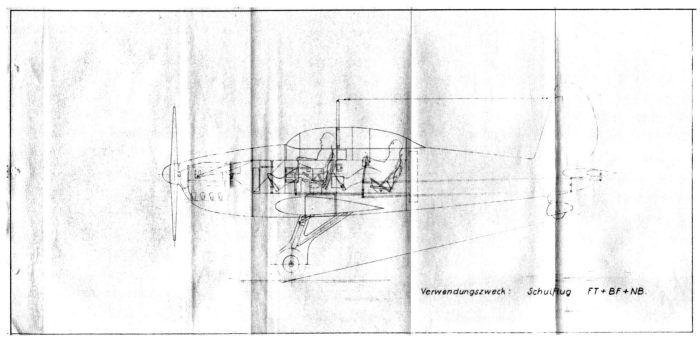

Verwendungszweck : Schulflug FT + BF + NB.

ABOVE: The E 208 as a straightforward advanced flight trainer with the pupil seated in front and the instructor behind.

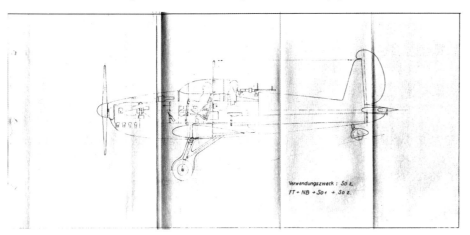

Verwendungszweck : So 2.
FT + NB + So 1 + So 2.

ABOVE: The rear section of the E 208's cockpit canopy could be removed to permit gunnery training – referred to in the caption as 'use SO 2'.

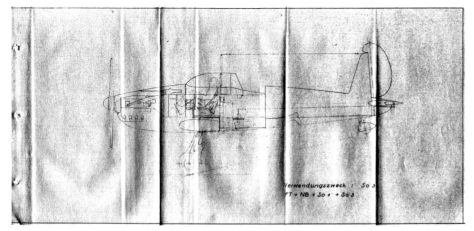

Verwendungszweck : So 3
FT + NB + So 1 + So 3

ABOVE: For bombardier training, there was a clear pane of glass set into the rear floor of the E 208. The trainee would be expected to lie prone while looking through an aiming device.

futuristic with its all-metal construction, low wing, fully enclosed cockpit and retractable undercarriage with tail wheel. And that was just the beginning. The E 208 was designed to be capable of adaptation to five different roles – fighter trainer, aerobatic trainer, gunnery trainer, bomb aiming trainer and reconnaissance trainer.

According to Arado's proposal, other key features were the installation of on-board

radio equipment which could be operated "both from the front seat by remote, and the rear by direct operation, and night lighting," plus a fixed machine gun would be included in the fighter trainer version. In this role "it has not only high flight performance, but also due to the high surface load a relatively high landing speed, to accustom the student to the high landing speed of modern fighter aircraft. For night school flights, which

the student does without a teacher, the tank is only half filled, so that the landing speed is lower. The cab roof of the front seat is equipped with constricting curtains, so that without modifications the model can also be used for blind flying exercises. As a result of the permanent radio facility, the teacher can instruct the student, even if he is flying alone, from the ground".

When it came to aerobatic training, visibility from the front seat was "especially excellent" and in this configuration the rear portion of the canopy would be omitted. The aircraft's weight had been carefully balanced and if the student was flying alone a trim weight of 43kg would be installed and the rear cockpit area covered over with a metal sheet.

The gunnery trainer configuration also omitted the rear canopy and included "the installation of a modern machine gun of various types" with space for three double drums of ammunition. According to Arado: "Due to the favourable position of the tailplane, the shooting angle is large, as are the firing conditions obliquely backwards and downwards. The spatial conditions in the observer's seat allow for a 90-degree field of fire upwards."

As a light bomber, the E 208 could carry six 10kg bombs – three in each of two magazines to the left and right of the observer's seat. There were two bomb sight options available – a conventional scope operated by the observer in a seated position, or a visor on the floor of the observer's position which was operated by the observer while lying down and "since the opening on which the bombing visor is mounted is also intended for the photo-imaging device, it is so large that the observer can overlook a large area of the underlying terrain and therefore can recognise the target very early".

For the final role – reconnaissance trainer – a small generator would be provided to power the camera or "if a hand-held camera is needed, targets can be photographed through the opening intended for the fixed camera without the observer having to take

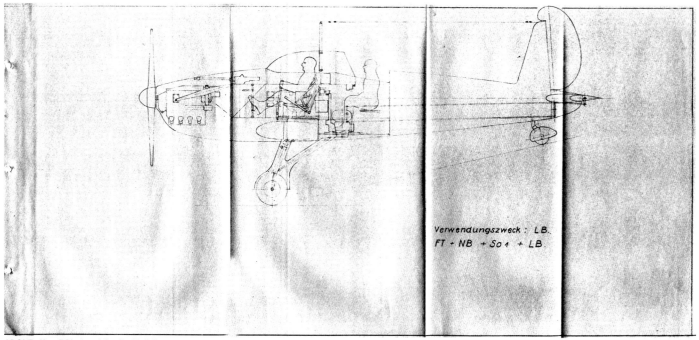

Verwendungszweck : LB.
FT + NB + So1 + LB.

ABOVE: Use 'LB' stood for 'Luftbild' or aerial photography. This was the reconnaissance training version of the E 208.

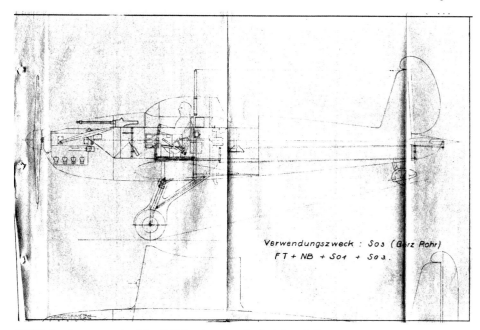

Verwendungszweck : So3 (Görz Rohr)
FT + NB + So1 + So3.

ABOVE: Another example of the E 208 as bombardier training platform, this time fitted with a scope which would enable the trainee to remain seated.

a photo overboard, which is hardly possible at high speed. Again, the large opening in the fuselage provides a good overview of the terrain underneath the aircraft".

Crucially, a single E 208 could perform all these five roles with only minimal alterations – by simply removing and replacing the "special installations" and "making use to the greatest extent of the same bearing plates, fixing points and fuselage cut-outs". A sixth training role was also possible – use of radios – without any modifications since the aircraft came fitted with this equipment as standard.

The E 208 was offered with a choice of two engine ratings – a 237hp Argus As 10 C, for which fuel tankage of 100kg would be provided, or a 345hp engine of unspecified model supplied by Hirth, Siemens or Argus with 145kg of fuel. In either case the range would be 600km with a climb rate which corresponded "to the most modern requirements".

In fact, if the As 10 C was fitted and a high rate of climb was unnecessary, a fuel load of 125kg could be carried – increasing range to more than 900km.

The E 208 proposal was at pains to point out how "the entire flying crew training is to be performed on a single aircraft model" and how "procurement of a series of the same type reduces the acquisition costs and, correspondingly, the direct and indirect association costs – small spare parts warehouse, exchange options, uniform maintenance. Unconditional familiarity of the ground staff and possibly the repair workshop with the model reduce the cost of flight operations".

The author proudly proclaims: "All of these benefits have been instrumental in developing the model. First and foremost, a truly useful aircraft should be created for all uses." And furthermore, "excellent visibility is a major requirement that must be placed on all military-type machines.

The arrangement of the structure with V-shape and arrow shape, the connection of the wing on the fuselage, the formation of the fuselage sections and the arrangement of the tail are so constructed that the blind spots are as small as possible. Great value was placed on good flight characteristics, so the aircraft has the greatest control and good manoeuvrability qualities and can therefore be flown by beginners. In addition to good flight characteristics, excellent flight performance is achieved. As shown by the performance data, the model will not only be equivalent but considerably superior due to its aerodynamically exceptionally favourable shape".

Top speed with the As 10 C was given as 275km/h (171mph) or 318km/h (198mph) with the more powerful unit, and landing speed was 92km/h and 96km/h respectively. Time to climb to 1000m was 4.2 minutes with the Argus or just 2.7 minutes with a 345hp engine. The aircraft had a wingspan of 11m, length of 8.35m and height of 3.74m.

There was surely no denying, back in December 1935, that the E 208 looked remarkably advanced and attractive as a trainer for fighter pilots, if not for bomber or reconnaissance aircraft crews. The E 208 was given the RLM designation Ar 96 and did indeed become the Luftwaffe's standard wartime trainer, although the original design's undercarriage was altered so that the wheels retracted inwards, rather than outwards. Around 3000 were built – making it easily Arado's most numerous in-house product even if its fame in recent years has been overtaken by designs such as the Ar 234 bomber, of which just over 200 were made, the Ar 196 floatplane with around 500 made or the Ar 232 with just 20 or so examples being produced.

Incidentally, the highest volume production version of the Ar 96 retained the E 208's wingspan of 11m, was slightly longer at 9.1m and significantly lower at 2.6m in height. Fitted with an Argus As 410 A-1, producing 465hp, it had a top speed of 330km/h (205mph). ●

Trusting an
to the French

Arado Ar 233

Several years into the Second World War and even with the Americans having sided against them, the Germans had not lost faith in their own eventual victory. If nothing else, Arado's Ar 233 serves to demonstrate this faith – a civilian luxury touring and exploring aircraft designed and developed just as the siege of Stalingrad was getting under way.

ABOVE: Mock-up of the Ar 233 built by French firm SIPA on the outskirts of Paris.

amphibian

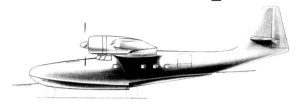

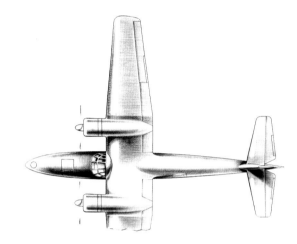

Abmessungen:	
Spannweite	23.70 m
Gesamtlänge	20.87 m
Höhe	6.55 m
Luftschraubendurchmesser	3.50 m
Flügelfläche	75.00 m²

Wasser-Land-Flugzeug
— Ar 233 —

Above: Shaded three-view drawing of the Ar 233 shows the position of the aircraft's floats and wheeled undercarriage when extended.

Although it received a full official designation and sits on the RLM list beside the relatively well-known Ar 232 transport aircraft, very little information has survived about the Ar 233's background. It seems that the project began in 1942 as the E 430 and according to an RLM data chart two versions were initially envisioned – a conventional Bramo 323 R2-powered seaplane with a wingspan of 23.7m capable of transporting up to 10 people and the smaller Argus As 402-powered "E 430 Amphibium", with a wingspan of 18m, which could carry up to eight people.

The RLM chart, which places the E 430 in the same loose category as the Blohm & Voss BV 144, Siebel Si 204 B and Focke-Wulf Fw 206, shows the project commencing in October 1942 but it doubtless began internally at Arado some months earlier. CIOS Item No. 25 File No IV-7 & V-16 Aircraft – Paris Zone, a report on how the French aircraft manufacturers based in Paris worked on German aircraft projects during the war, includes an interview with staff at the Société Industrielle Pour l'Aéronautique (SIPA) who worked on the Ar 233. It states: "The design of this aircraft had been started two years ago." The interview was conducted in September 1944, so the project probably began in July or August at the latest – allowing time for the project to be given the go-ahead for development and for Arado to arrange matters with its 'partners' at SIPA.

Between the publication of the RLM

Above: Wind tunnel test model of the Ar 233 – the bulge behind the engine is a retracted float.

data chart in October and December 1942, the type had gone from being the E 430 to receiving its designation as the Ar 233. In addition, the smaller design had been dropped and its 'amphibious' aspect transferred to the larger 10-seater design. On Christmas Eve 1942, Arado published a detailed brochure on the Ar 233.

Besides the usual drawings and data, it contained several photos of a full-scale

mock-up constructed at SIPA's factory on the Ile de la Jatte – an island in the River Seine to the north-west of the city.

The brochure begins: "Usage: the present draft shows a water-land aircraft for transport, travel and transportation, which is suitable for service in all climatic conditions from the north to the tropics. As an amphibian, the aircraft can be used in many cases, where this would

ABOVE: This scale model of the Ar 233 was hung from wires then blown with a fan to make its propellers spin for the photo – unfortunately this seems to have made the model move, blurring the image slightly.

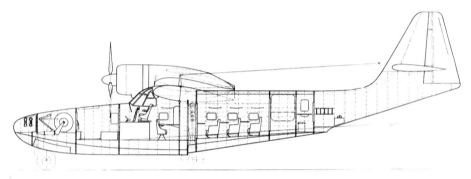

ABOVE: Side view shows the internal layout of the Ar 233.

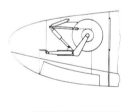
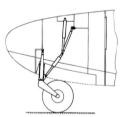

ABOVE: The nosewheel was designed to retract far enough into its compartment that it would be above the water line when the aircraft was afloat.

not otherwise be possible with a pure land or sea plane. In sparsely populated areas, where the construction of airfields would be too uneconomic, a makeshift port should be easy to locate or set up.

"For flights along the coast or from the coast to the interior of the land, the optional approach of land or sea airports can be of great advantage. In emergency landings, a water surface or river allows a far safer landing than unprepared terrain. As a connecting aircraft to ship rendezvous a lot of time can be saved by loading and unloading directly on to the ship. Thus, the water-land aircraft seems despite its weighty chassis and boat hull particularly suitable for the fulfilment of numerous tasks."

The Ar 233 was proposed with four possible internal arrangements in mind – a

10-seater commercial airliner, a four-seater touring aircraft for long-haul flights, a cargo aircraft and as a flying ambulance. The first of these, the commercial airliner, would have a range of 1200km. In the forward section there would be four seats – for the pilot, radio operator and two passengers, one of them seated up high next to the pilot himself and one lower down next to the radio operator. Behind them, through a hatch between the retracted main gear legs, the adjoining passenger compartment would house another six seats. Behind this was a small space for accessible luggage and further back still was the on-board toilet. The remainder of the luggage was to be stored in the bow section of the hull, in front of the pilot but behind the nosewheel compartment.

As a touring aircraft with just four seats,

including the pilot, the aircraft would carry "two additional containers of 400 litres each content, which are located in the outer wings and can be filled with fuel to achieve greater ranges. The capacity of the lubricant reservoir is adapted to the increased range. For longer cruises, a second steering column can be attached. With double controls, the aircraft is also suitable for training". In four-seat configuration, range was increased to 1800km. It is easy to imagine the Ar 233 set up this way as an aircraft ideally suited to exploration in remote areas or for cruising across continents in comfort.

The transporter arrangement brought things right back down to earth however – with the passenger compartment stripped of its fittings and capable of holding loads of up to one ton. The floor would be able to cope with loads of up to 300kg per square metre. Loading and unloading would be via a door in the side of the fuselage and "devices for lashing the loads are provided".

The entry for the ambulance appears to contain a section from an earlier report that has not been updated to accommodate the Ar 233's new designation: "Ambulance with the E 430: the passenger cabin can also be equipped with four beds. These serve to transport the sick or as sleeping places for the travellers."

In terms of strength, the nosewheel suspension was capable of take-offs and landings up to an altitude of 1500m and outside temperatures up to 40°C – an important consideration if the aircraft was to be used in tropical areas. Maximum take-off weight was 9500kg.

In terms of seaworthiness, the aircraft could cope with a swell of up to 1.5m and "the spray water is kept in suitable limits by the bottom shape of the boat. Due to the existing hull height and the far forward hull bow, the cabin is well protected against splashing water. The propellers and buoyancy aids remain splash-free in a moderately moving sea. The floating stability on the water is due to the relatively large support floats. Also, the propulsion properties are likely to be good for the chosen boat shape".

By this time, engine manufacturer BMW's

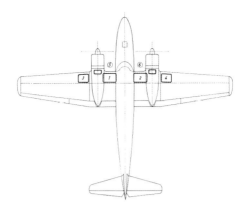

ABOVE: Fuel tanks were kept close to the centre of gravity in the Ar 233 design.

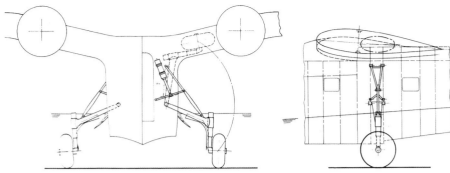

ABOVE: The main undercarriage retracted up into the fuselage sides, with the wheels going into the underside of the wings.

ABOVE: Nose-on view of the Ar 233 mock-up. Closest to the camera is a tow-ring and behind that are markers to show where the Ar 233's forward lamps would go.

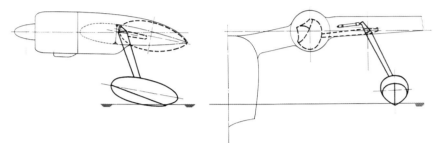

ABOVE: One of the Ar 233's more novel features was its retractable support floats.

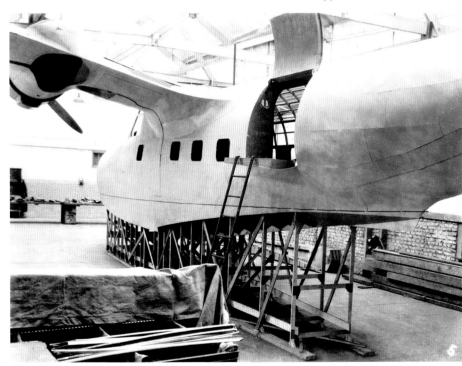

ABOVE: Rear side view shows the port-side main access hatch.

takeover and assimilation of Bramo was complete and the engines are specified as a pair of BMW 323 MAs. The on-board radio system consisted of FuG X P, FuBl II F and FuG 101, running off a generator which also powered a pair of electric fans for ventilation. Heating was provided for both cabins and de-icing gear was in place for the outer wings and elevators. An "extensive list" of maritime equipment was also to be carried.

STRUCTURE, FIXTURES AND FITTINGS
The Ar 233's unusual but not unattractive form was largely dictated by its function. The wing centre piece, which effectively sat on top of the fuselage, was V-shaped with the engines being fitted on the upper ends of the 'V', because "due to the strong V-shape of the wing centre piece, the engines and propellers get a sufficient distance from the water surface". Another novel feature was the way in which the under-wing support floats retracted up into the engine nacelles behind the wing spar. The wheeled landing gear retracted into the sides of the fuselage, putting the wheels themselves into wing root recesses.

As a landing aid, small 'expansion flaps'

were provided and the flaps were designed to yield in heavy seas to prevent water damage.

In the cockpit, the side windows could be opened by sliding them forwards and hinging them outwards, while the front windows could simply be dropped outwards on to the aircraft's long bow section. The cockpit could be reached via a ladder which was hinged to the leading edge of the wing and folded up into the underside of the wing when not in use.

Two handwheel control columns were fitted but the second one was only for use on longer flights and for training. From

these "power is transmitted to the rudders via poles and wires. These first run under the floor of the driver's cab to the landing gear shaft and here they are led upwards. The aileron and flap linkages then continue into the wings, where they run behind the spar. The control to the tail first goes inside the centre wing from side to middle hull. From here, a straight shaft drives on the ceiling of the fuselage to the rear.

"The cover plates are easy to release so that the control line can be comfortably monitored from the cab. The adjustment of the fin and the trimming of the rudders

ABOVE: The passenger compartment featured comfy-looking armchairs for the travellers.

ABOVE: The pilot's seat and a secondary position for an observer, navigator, trainee or passenger. Between the two raised chairs is a hatch leading to the forward baggage compartment.

is done electrically. For emergency operation, two handwheels are provided next to and behind the driver's seat for the vertical fin and rudder. The flaps are hydraulically extended and retracted, with the expansion flaps and the ailerons going along with them."

Within the passenger cabin, in 10-seater configuration, would be six armchairs with waist straps, pockets, side tables, reading lamps and luggage nets. The middle window on each side could be opened and could serve as an emergency exit. The lighting fixtures were embedded in the ceiling and the two electric ventilation fans were positioned at the entrance to the cabin and in the landing gear shaft. The entrance itself took the form of a large door on the left side of the

fuselage, sections of which opened upwards and downwards so that "the lower part thus forms a platform on which loads can be deposited and which makes it easier to dock boats. Opposite the door are installed devices for stacking the luggage and an inflatable boat. Then follows the toilet with hand basin behind the rear room".

When the aircraft was sitting in the water, the upwards curve of the rear fuselage meant that the horizontal stabilisers would remain a good distance away from the water's surface to prevent damage. The retracted main landing gear recesses were also above the waterline which, according to the brochure, "is extremely favourable for the life and reliability of the system. The pulling in takes place hydraulically

via bending struts. As an emergency operation, a hand pump is located next to the right-hand driver's seat. The nose wheel is located in a shaft of the fuselage nose, which is closed after being pulled in by bottom flaps. The main wheels are 1015 x 380mm wide, with brakes, while the nose wheel is 875 x 325mm. It is swivelling and provided with a locking mechanism. The rear bulkhead of the nosewheel space has a lid lying above the waterline, whereby the nose wheel can be maintained while the aircraft is on the water."

The Ar 233's support floats, each connected to the wing with a single steel strut, were hydraulically retracted and the strut itself also went into a recess on the underside of the wing. Each of the two 986bhp BMW 323 MA engines had a three-bladed propeller and was started electrically. Fuel was housed in three "densely riveted" containers in the wing leading edge. Refuelling was to be carried out by climbing up the cockpit

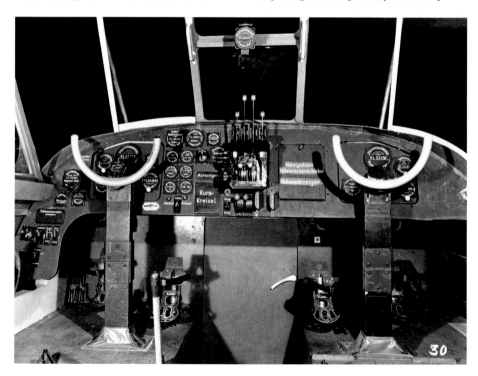

ABOVE: The Ar 233's twin control columns and dashboard as seen with the seats removed.

ABOVE: Radio operator's station in the cockpit – all of the equipment is labelled in both German and French.

ABOVE: The rear end of the mock-up from inside, looking towards the tailfin.

access ladder up on to the wing.

Under 'equipment', the brochure lists a number of handy items that would have helped the Ar 233's occupants when travelling in hostile environments – a detachable sun canopy that could be erected over the cockpit glass, a rubber dinghy, fog horn, emergency provisions, emergency tool bag, boat hook, ground anchor, sea anchor, "leakage protection material", towing gear plus various ropes and other attachments.

The whole aircraft, the brochure notes, had been designed so that it could be transported by rail across central Europe.

MADE IN FRANCE

The brochure makes no mention of the fact that the Ar 233 mock-up was made in France but the clues are there – particularly the photograph of the radio operator's station mock-up where some of the items of equipment are labelled in both French and German.

According to the CIOS report, SIPA "had been told that the maximum all-up weight would be approximately 20,000lb (9000kg), but they considered that it would actually be greater". And the French made mention of another feature not included in the brochure, that water would be expelled from the nosewheel compartment using compressed air.

In fact, work on the Ar 233 seems to have been carried out at three sites in Paris: two SIPA facilities – Ile de la Jatte and 27/29 rue Dupont in Neuilly under SIPA technical director M Volland – and at the Dewoitine Design Office, 11 rue de Pillet-Will, under Dewoitine chief designer M Tourret. SIPA also worked with Arado on the Ar 396, parts of the Ar 234 and Ar 196.

The ultimate fate of the Ar 233 is summed up in just one line of the CIOS report: it "had been suspended in favour of military aircraft". The mock-up seems to have survived the war, along with notes and drawings, but SIPA never resumed work on it. ●

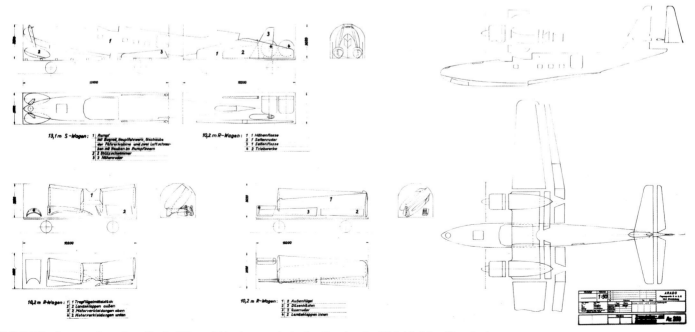

ABOVE: This diagram shows how the Ar 233 could be transported using the standard Third Reich rolling stock.

Chronicle of the Seefernaufklärers

The most successful product of Blohm & Voss Flugzeugbau was the BV 138 flying boat. It was a highly unusual design and entered frontline service only after numerous problems. The design continually evolved and a number of projects arose for its replacement in the role of Seefernaufklärer – long-range maritime reconnaissance.

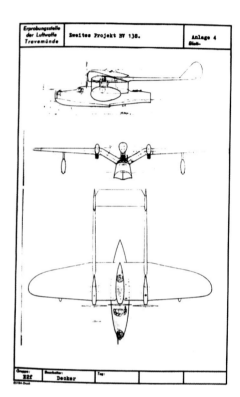

ABOVE: The second project version of what would become the BV 138, possibly the P 14. While it is clearly recognisable as an ancestor of the BV 138, almost every detail is different – such as the gunner's position right on top of the central nacelle and the shape of the underwing floats.

ABOVE: The first prototype of the Ha 138 (later to become the BV 138) differed dramatically from the later production version in having a gullwing profile and an entirely different fuselage.

Every now and then during the Second World War, German aircraft manufacturers and those who worked alongside them seem to have felt compelled to publish a 'history' of a particular aircraft project series. Messerschmitt produced a document detailing the long and complex history of the Me 109 H, Focke-Wulf created an overview of its attempts to design a single-jet fighter, and in August 1943 the seaplane test facility Erprobungsstelle der Luftwaffe Travemünde drafted a detailed account of the BV 138.

Exactly why someone called Decker at E-Stelle Travemünde, near Lübeck, to the north-east of Hamburg, compiled a full report on the background of the BV 138 is unclear. Reading between the lines, it would seem that E-Stelle Travemünde put a huge amount of effort into making sure that the aircraft was eventually fit for service, despite overwhelming indifference from the government and the Luftwaffe, and seems to have been proud of its work in that regard.

The BV 138's Dornier-made competitors are also detailed to a lesser degree but the most interesting aspect of the report is the selection of Blohm & Voss project designs it includes – some of which are otherwise unknown. It also includes all three views of Heinkel's shadowy He 120, a design previously only known

from a side view, and drawings of little-known Dornier projects as well.

The report is entitled Chronik des See-Fernaufklärers von 1933 bis zum heutigen Tage or 'Chronicle of the long-range maritime reconnaissance types from 1933 to the present day' and starts: "The present development history of the long-distance reconnaissance seaplane includes the main points of development, testing and later use and touches the timing of the other military and civilian flying boat development. It begins with the construction of the German Air Force after the seizure of power by the Führer in 1933. In general, the type was initially based on existing civil aircraft and gave these, in some form, a military character."

Fitted with three MG 15 machine guns, Dornier's Wal or 'Whale' flying boat became the first German long-range maritime reconnaissance aircraft in 1933. It weighed eight tons and had a range of 1700km. Later the same year, Dornier began to produce an enlarged 10-ton Wal powered by a pair of BMW VIU engines, rather than the

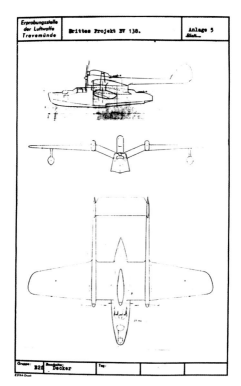

ABOVE: The third project BV 138. Now the fuselage nose has been lengthened and the floats, fins and cockpit are all different. The gullwing profile has been carried over, however.

Fluggewicht   11,6 to
mittl.Reisegeschw. in 0 m   240 km/h
Flugstrecke   2500 km

Fluggewicht   11,8 to
mittl.Reisegeschw. in 0 m   240 km/h
Flugstrecke   2500 km

ABOVE: A rear view of the BV 138 V1 and a view of the V2 taking off.

original version's BMW VIs. This type enabled Deutsche Lufthansa (DLH) to set up a weekly postal service across the South Atlantic – from the African coast to South America. It had a range of 3000km and resulted in a request from DLH in 1934 for a further development of the Wal in 1934, to be powered by Jumo 205 diesel engines. Dornier responded with the Do 18 – effectively a streamlined Wal weighing nine-and-a-half tons and with a range of 3500km.

This aroused the RLM's interest and it was determined that the Do 18 could carry two MG 15s plus a pair of 50kg bombs for a loss of 500km in range. Dornier won contracts to produce both the civilian and military versions. However, in mid-1934 the General Staff issued a new requirement for a long-range multi-engine day and night reconnaissance aircraft. It had to have a forward-firing cannon, a rearward-firing cannon and "many" machine guns covering the area immediately above and behind it. A 150kg bomb load was needed, top speed had to be 280km/h, range was to be 2400kg and maximum altitude 4000m. Specifications were also given for the type's required performance in taking off and landing at sea, manoeuvring in strong winds and towing while on the ocean.

Since the Do 18 could not meet these requirements, and since it had already been ordered, it was regarded as an interim type and both Dornier and Blohm & Voss were commissioned to produce designs capable of fulfilling the requirement in full. Both firms realised that two Jumo 205s were never going to meet the speed and altitude specs, and two petrol engines would be too thirsty, so it was agreed that the projects would have three diesel engines and a target weight of 11.5 tons.

Dornier produced the long and low

Do 24 while Blohm & Voss, then known as Hamburger Flugzeugbau, came up with the short, twin boom, gullwing profile BV 138 (then known as the Ha 138). The mock-up of the latter was ready for inspection by February 1935 but Dornier was overburdened with work on the Do 18 and Do 17 and only completed its Do 24 mock-up in August 1935. The BV 138 was already approved for prototype construction by this time. That same month, DLH "demanded that the RLM develop a long-range 5000km airliner for the North Atlantic Service to keep pace with its development abroad", and again both Dornier and Blohm & Voss were awarded development contracts.

Dornier now came up with the Do 26 while Blohm & Voss designed the BV 139, each with four engines. A further inspection of the Do 24 mock-up in September 1935 revealed that the "weapon side had so many defects that again a change had to be made" and towards the end of the year Dornier successfully acquired a licence to build a Do 24 fitted with Wright Cyclone engines to fulfil an order from Holland, which caused further delays.

The company was now simultaneously building the Do 18, the Luftwaffe's Do 24 Seefernaufklärer, the Do 24 Holland, the Do 17 and finally the Do 26. An assessment of priorities saw the Do 17 and Do 24 Holland ▶

Erprobungsstelle der Luftwaffe Travemünde	BV 138 A und B.	Anlage 7 ~~Blatt~~

Fluggewicht	15,0 to (R-Geräte-Start)
mittl.Reisegeschw. in 0 m	200 km/h
Flugstrecke	3600 km

Fluggewicht	18,0 to (Schleuderstart)
mittl.Reisegeschw. in 0 m	230 km/h
Flugstrecke	3200 km

| Gruppe E2f | Bearbeiter Decker | Tag: | | |

ABOVE: The BV 138 A and BV 138 B. The former was underpowered and overweight. Despite numerous revisions, the latter wasn't much better. Note the four-bladed prop on the central engine intended to cure damaging vibrations.

jumped to the front of the queue and the Do 24 Seefernaufklärer dropped to the back – particularly as the RLM noted that "the work on the BV 138 was very advanced and the design of this pattern in terms of arming and seaworthiness promised much". So, "as a result of this measure, Dornier, the favourite in the construction of flying boats, was virtually eliminated as a competitor in Seefernaufklärer. This gave the young company Blohm & Voss a great opportunity".

At Blohm & Voss, construction of the BV 138 and the structures of the BV 139 and BV 140 were all under way at the same time. The BV 138 V1, without weapons or equipment fully installed, was nevertheless ready for flight trials by the middle of 1936 but "the result of the flights was devastating". The gullwing form offered unusually poor lift, resulting in an extremely high take-off and landing speed. In flight, changing direction sharply could cause severe vibration through the tail booms and a sudden change in the trim position, while "particularly dangerous was the mid-engine gondola downdraft, which brought a significant loss of elevator effect with it".

Blohm & Voss apparently acted swiftly to fix these problems and had done so by July 1936 but "the flight and sea characteristics still left much to be desired". Not only that, "the provisional changes greatly defaced the plane, making it even more difficult to get used to this new pattern, which in itself was difficult. The crease wing could not be taken over due to the bad experiences under any circumstances for the next aircraft. Significant changes had to be made to V2, the main ones being: change of the boat bow and better transition from the front dome to the boat bow. Reinforcement of the boat

Erprobungsstelle der Luftwaffe Travemünde	BV 138 Postflugzeug und Seefernauf- klärer.	Anlage 9 ~~Blatt~~

Fluggewicht	17,0 to (später 19,0 to)
mittl.Reisegeschw. in 0 m	250 km/h
Flugstrecke	5000 km

Fluggewicht	17,0 to
mittl.Reisegeschw. in 0 m	206 km/h
Flugstrecke	3450 km

| Gruppe E2f | Bearbeiter Decker | Tag | | |

ABOVE: Two very different versions of the BV 139, civilian above and military below. Although it is a completely different design to the Ha/BV 138, there is evidence to suggest that it was originally designated BV 138 at a time when the (later) BV 138 was still known as the Ha 138.

bottom, straight centre wing, whereby the outer motors were lowered by 200mm, raising the centre motor axis by 100mm. Better shaping of the mid-engine nacelle. Increase of the span by 1m and enlargement of the flaps. With these changes, it was hoped to fly the aircraft in order and get a series release".

Work on the V2 got started but then ground to a halt "as a result of personnel and manufacturing difficulties" and "it was already recognised that a long time would pass until the creation of a series was possible and therefore increased importance was placed on the Dornier Do 18 series".

With strong doubts having been raised about the BV 138, the Do 24 Seefernaufklärer mock-up was finally approved for construction but work on it continued at a snail's pace.

BV 138 V2
At the beginning of 1937, Heinkel was commissioned to build a mock-up of its He 120 project – a multi-engine flying boat designed to carry passenger traffic across the Atlantic with DLH. It had a range of 7500km and a take-off weight of 27 tons. Meanwhile, "at the same time,

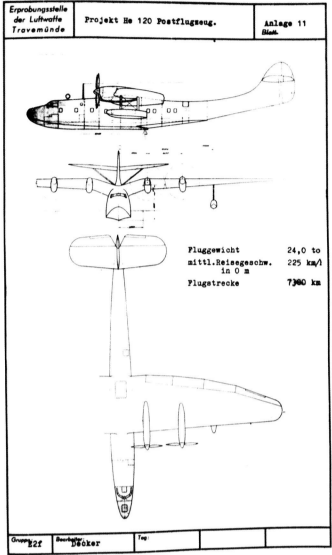

Fluggewicht 24,0 to
mittl.Reisegeschw. in 0 m 225 km/l
Flugstrecke 7300 km

| Erprobungsstelle der Luftwaffe Travemünde | B&V-Projekt 81. Fernaufklärer. | Anlage 12 Blatt |

Fluggewicht 84,0 to
mittl.Reise- geschw. in 0 m 235 km/h
Flugstrecke 12200 km

ABOVE: Heinkel's He 120 was designed as a long-range postal aircraft and a mock-up was commissioned at the beginning of 1937, but the design went no further.

ABOVE: At the behest of Ernst Udet, Blohm & Voss drafted four different designs for large floatplanes. The first was this, the large and heavy P 81. Its defence was primarily left to turret gunners mounted on its floats.

Do 18 production at Dornier was in full swing. The aircraft, with 9.5 tons flight weight, two MG 15s and two 50kg bombs, achieved its range of 3000km and was flying very well. Until the completion of the BV 138 V2 at Blohm & Voss, the Do 18 was delivered on an ongoing basis. In September, the BV 138 V2 was able to carry out the first flights. The changes made had been successful. When flying through the test station at Travemünde nothing significant was found except for high rudder forces".

The BV 138 V2 looked significantly different from the V1, with different wings and numerous detail changes. But before the type could be approved for full production, the original rules of the competition required that it had to be compared against the Do 24. By now, Dornier had managed to get the first Do 24 Holland flying with its Wright Cyclone engines and it performed "fairly well" although its range was well down on that projected for the Jumo 205-powered version at just 2800km.

A comparison between the Do 24 Holland and the BV 138 V2 showed that the Dornier design was better at taking off and landing but Blohm & Voss's creation had a better turn rate in the air and better towing

performance on the water. The Dornier's advantage was largely a result of its more powerful petrol, rather than diesel, engines so it was decided that only a comparison between the BV 138 and a German spec Do 24 could provide the basis for a final decision. Since the German Do 24 still wasn't built, the BV 138 was instead compared against a set of calculated values from Dornier and found to be the superior design – resulting in approval for a pre-production A-0 series.

More substantial changes were required though: the rear was extended by 200mm, the hull step was relocated by 750mm and increased in depth by 200mm, a change in the wing shape, a change in the point where the wings joined the fuselage, reinforcement to the hull, changes to the cockpit arrangement, changes to the steering and rudder linkages and changes to the engine installation. According to Decker: "This required an almost complete redesign of the flying boat and the construction of a foredeck mock-up."

With the Do 24 now an estimated 12 months behind the BV 138 in development, and the BV 138 itself not yet cleared for full production, "the RLM decided to expand the Do 18 series again".

At this point, due to competition

from abroad, DLH "was again forced to approach large-scale aircraft projects in the order of 50 tons. The construction of such flying boats posed new problems for the RLM. The development capacities of the companies were fully utilised for warplane development, primarily for land planes. By contrast, it was the other way around abroad. However, German aviation could by no means be allowed to fall behind in world aviation access. The RLM therefore commissioned the company Blohm & Voss with the pre-development of a 40-ton large aircraft for the carriage of 14 passengers over a 6700km route."

This civilian project was the beginning of what would become the BV 222. In September 1937 the BV 138's new foredeck model was finished and it was approved for construction three months later.

In May 1938, the German Do 24 V1 was finally ready for flight-testing against the BV 138 V2. These tests determined that the Do 24 was still easier to start and land, had better handling in flight, and was better at towing in calm water conditions. The BV 138 had the advantage of better-positioned weaponry, the ability to fly comfortably on two engines, 1000km

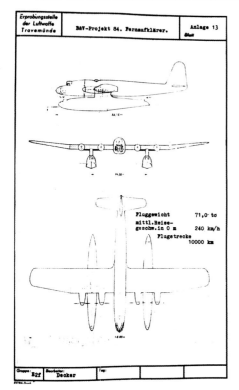

Erprobungsstelle der Luftwaffe Travemünde | B&V-Projekt 84. Fernaufklärer. | Anlage 13 Blatt

Fluggewicht 71,0 to
mittl.Reise-
geschw.in 0 m 240 km/h
Flugstrecke 10000 km

ABOVE: The slightly smaller P 84 maritime reconnaissance aircraft. Again, forward and aft defence is down to float-mounted turrets.

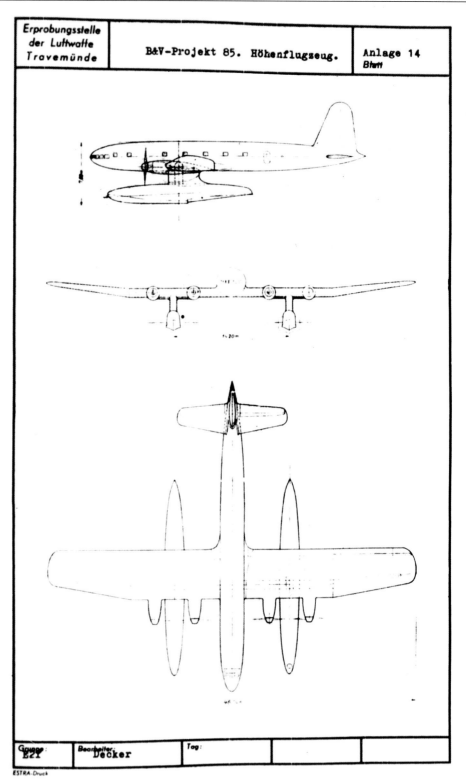

Erprobungsstelle der Luftwaffe Travemünde | B&V-Projekt 85. Höhenflugzeug. | Anlage 14 Blatt

ABOVE: While Udet only asked for military reconnaissance designs, Blohm & Voss was keenly aware of the prospect of potentially lucrative contracts from DLH. As a result, it designed this – the P 85 floatplane airliner.

better range and better towing ability out at sea – plus the 12-month development advantage and "manufacturing superiority".

While making a decision was "extremely difficult" the BV 138 ultimately won because the Do 24 couldn't fly on just two engines. Now Blohm & Voss began to consider a new engine for the aircraft to improve both speed and range – a BMW 132 K, DB 601 G, Jumo 220 G or the diesel Jumo 205 D. The latter could provide a theoretical range of more than 4500km so the others were rejected. Work began in mid-1938 on a batch of 60 production aircraft, four of them fitted with Jumo 205 Cs and two with Jumo 205 Ds.

The first BV 138 A-0s were completed in January 1939 but bad weather and other problems meant that test flying could only commence in June and "unfortunately, the results did not meet expectations. Blohm & Voss also had to make several changes to this aircraft before it could be flown by the E-Stelle".

Meanwhile, "at this time, Blohm & Voss, at the suggestion of the Generalluftzeugmeister [Ernst Udet], engaged in the further development of the remote reconnaissance machine".

B&V P 81, P 84, P 85 AND P 86

The company's response to Udet's suggestion for a much longer-ranged reconnaissance machine than the BV 138 took the form of two floatplane designs – the P 81 and the P 84. The P 81 was very large – somewhat resembling a scaled-up BV 140 with a BV 222 tail, it was 39.5m long, had a 55m wingspan, weighed 84 tons and had a range of 12,200km. Powered by four Jumo 218s – each one a linked pair of Jumo 208s – it was protected by turrets both at the bow and stern of its floats, plus both nose and dorsal turrets.

The P 84 was similar in form to the P 81 but scaled down somewhat. It was 33.75m

long, had a 46m wingspan, weighed 71 tons and had a range of 10,000km. It was also powered by four Jumo 218s. Given DLH's ongoing need for transatlantic passenger transports, Blohm & Voss also presented two civilian designs based on the same large floatplane template – the P 85 and P 86. The P 85, a relatively straightforward passenger aircraft with a cylindrical fuselage, had a 46m wingspan but other details are unavailable from the E-Stelle report. The official Blohm & Voss project list confirms that it was powered by four Jumo 218s and weighed 68 tons.

The P 86, described as a high-altitude

transatlantic passenger aircraft, was unusual in being a double decker – with passengers seated on two levels. This aircraft was 37.4m long and had a wingspan, again, of 46m. Yet remarkably it weighed less than the other designs at 56.7 tonnes.

Dornier was also asked to chip in at Udet's suggestion and evidently presented its P 133, "a flying boat with 6 Jumo 208 engines and a flying weight of 58 tons at 8150 km range". Unfortunately no drawing of the P 133 is known to have survived. None of the Udet-commissioned projects went anywhere "because there were no corresponding tactical demands that

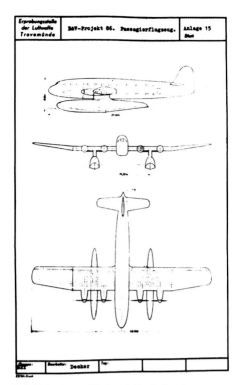

Erprobungsstelle der Luftwaffe Travemünde	BuV-Projekt 86. Passagierflugzeug.	Anlage 15 Blatt

Gruppe:	Bearbeiter: Decker	Tag:		

ESTRA-Druck

ABOVE: The last of Blohm & Voss's four large floatplane designs was the double-decker P 86 airliner. This design was comparable in size to the BV 222 flying boat.

justify the construction of such aircraft, the procurement of the planned engines was not present for the time being and the development effort seemed too large".

Tackling the BV 138 A-0's problems was harder than it first seemed. The various alterations and redesigns had added two tons to its weight and "this unfortunate fact, which was mainly due to the lack of weight control at B&V, now required substantial strength improvements for the current series. The flight characteristics were better compared to the V2 except for a constant rudder shake and excessive lateral and elevator forces. The water properties had deteriorated considerably. At take-off and landing, the boat tended to jump so that it could not be released for the series production without modification".

The aircraft could only take off with its fuel tanks 57% full, reducing its tactical usefulness considerably. At the outbreak of war in September 1939, the Luftwaffe's only Seefernaufklärer remained the Do 18 – which was too poorly armed to fly missions against England. A fully functional BV 138 was urgently needed but even when some modified A-0s became available at the end of the year, icy conditions meant they could not be flown.

P 94, P 110, P 111 AND P 112

At the beginning of 1940, with the overweight BV 138 A all but useless for offensive operations, Blohm & Voss began further project work to see whether the type could be improved by giving it another change of engine or by shifting its main component parts around. This began with a BV 138 powered by a trio of Jumo 207 As – the P 94. Unfortunately, this was even heavier than the 14.5-ton BV 138 A at 15.2 tons. Oddly, the drawing of the type included in the E-Stelle report cites

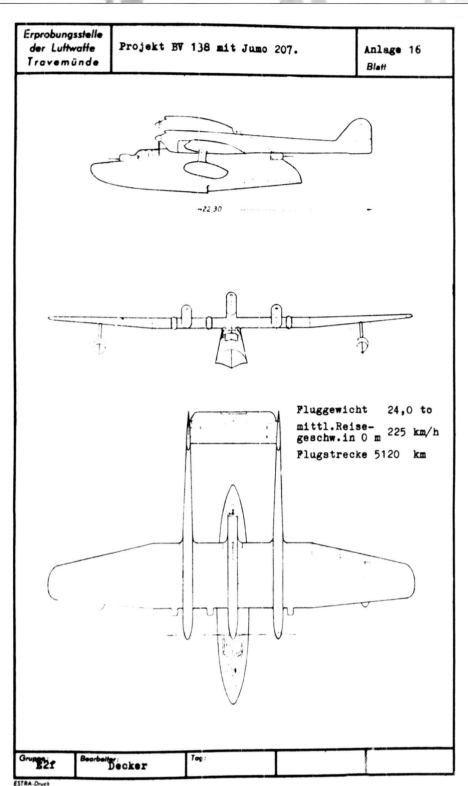

Erprobungsstelle der Luftwaffe Travemünde	Projekt BV 138 mit Jumo 207.	Anlage 16 Blatt

~22,30

Fluggewicht   24,0 to
mittl.Reise-
geschw.in 0 m   225 km/h
Flugstrecke 5120 km

Gruppe: E2f	Bearbeiter: Decker	Tag:		

ESTRA-Druck

ABOVE: When it became clear that the early model Jumo 205 was insufficiently powerful for the increasingly heavy BV 138, Blohm & Voss looked at fitting a Jumo 207 instead. The result was the design shown here, the P 94.

its weight as an over-the-top 24 tons.

Also studied were a trio of asymmetrical BV 138s under the project numbers P 110, P 111 and P 112. Unfortunately, only two of these were included with the report and neither is labelled with its project number so it is impossible to tell which is which. All had a wingspan of 29m, different lengths and a range of 5000km. They were rejected however because by this point "the development of the short boat had proved to be inappropriate". In addition, "the BV 138 A, which had lost its practical value as a result of the additional weight, was initially regarded as a trainee

aircraft and was later to be converted into sea rescue aircraft after being replaced by the B series with Jumo 205 D engines. But even the idea of the sea rescue aircraft had to be abandoned because the boat strength and the low engine power for this use was certainly not sufficient. In addition, the boat shape was impractical for distress use".

In April 1940, the Germans invaded Norway and supplies were urgently needed by the invasion force. Therefore, the handful of BV 138 As that had been delivered plus the two existing German Do 24s were pressed into service as makeshift ▶

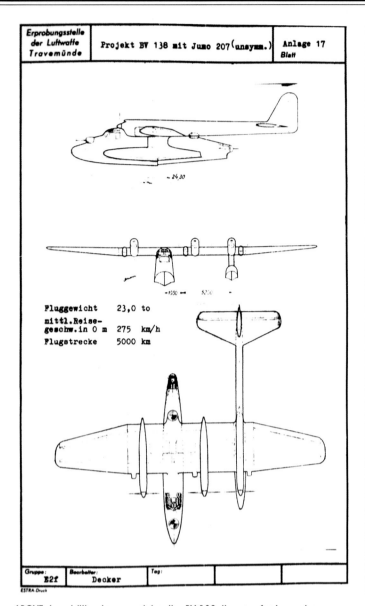

Erprobungsstelle der Luftwaffe Travemünde	Projekt BV 138 mit Jumo 207 (unsymm.)	Anlage 17 Blatt

Fluggewicht   23,0 to
mittl.Reise-
geschw.in 0 m   275 km/h
Flugstrecke   5000 km

| Gruppe: E2f | Bearbeiter: Decker | Tag: | | | |

Erprobungsstelle der Luftwaffe Travemünde	Projekt B&V mit Jumo 207 (unsymm.)	Anlage 18 Blatt

Fluggewicht   23,0 to
mittl.Reisegeschw.
           in 0 m   275 km/t
Flugstrecke   5000 km

| Gruppe: E2f | Bearbeiter: Decker | Tag: | | | |

ABOVE: In addition to re-engining the BV 138, its manufacturer also looked at altering the aircraft's fundamental layout. The result was a series of odd-looking asymmetrical versions.

ABOVE: The second of three asymmetrical BV 138s. If it still exists, the third design has yet to be discovered.

transporters. Since the Luftwaffe had not yet received any examples and had no pilots trained to fly it, the mission had to be flown by E-Stelle Travemünde personnel. Apparently the repurposed Seefernaufklärers "broke through the flak of the operating English fleet in front of Narvik several times and landed there at the German bridgehead with ammunition and explosives. In these operations, the Do 24 was superior in terms of take-off and landing as well as in the suitability as makeshift transporter compared to the BV 138".

Luftwaffe pilots finally began receiving BV 138 A training machines in May 1940 and found them very difficult to take off in and land – though they found the armament much better than that offered by the Do 18. After this rocky start, the Luftwaffe's opinion of the BV 138 dipped still further when it was discovered that the electrical system corroded easily and quickly became dangerous. The aircraft's flaps suffered constant damage from impacting the water's surface and the engines were difficult to maintain due to the routing of their associated cables.

All hopes now lay with the B-series. In addition to its improved engines, this had

its stern extended by 1m to improve take-off and landing, and the entire aircraft was reinforced – taking the flight weight to 17.1 tons. But according to the E-Stelle report: "Unfortunately, there was also an unfavourable star over this pattern. The delivery of the two planned 0-series aircraft as a test sample with Jumo 205 D engines was delayed from month to month due to exhaust and various other engine difficulties". Testing could not be carried out and production could not begin.

P 144, P 145 AND DORNIER P 173
During the summer of 1940, Blohm & Voss, Dornier and Heinkel were invited to prepare projects to meet another new requirement, this time for a flying boat which could handle both long-range reconnaissance and transport duties – a direct response to the Norwegian campaign. The E-Stelle believed that this was a poor idea however since "it must be said from the outset that in such a combined solution the long-range reconnaissance aircraft performs the least favourably, since the size of the fuselage required for the transporter means only dead space for the reconnaissance vehicle and therefore could be smaller".

At the same time, the station received its first BV 138 B to test – only to quickly discover that it suffered from terrible exhaust manifold problems. After a few hours in flight, vibrations from the Jumo 205 D engines caused their cowlings to crack. Nevertheless, the BV 138 was now badly needed for the Luftwaffe so Blohm & Voss pressed ahead with the B-series anyway.

Its projects to meet the reconnaissance transporter requirement were submitted in the autumn of 1940. First up was the P 144 – a flying boat powered by four Jumo 223 engines which somewhat resembled the BV 222 despite being a bit larger. It was 40m long with a wingspan of 53m and while the E-Stelle gave its weight as 73 tons, Blohm & Voss gave it as 52.8 tons. Its range was 12,400km and it fairly bristled with weaponry – a tail turret, a turret under the rear fuselage, a centre upper turret, a forward upper turret and gunnery positions on either side of the fuselage.

The P 145 was a floatplane, also with four Jumo 223s, which the E-Stelle said weighed 93.3 tonnes compared to a B&V figure of 59.1 tons. It had a range of 10,200km, a length of 39m and a 43m wingspan – making it slightly longer than a BV 222 but with slightly

Erprobungsstelle der Luftwaffe Travemünde	BV 222 Seefernaufklärer.	Anlage 19 Blatt

Fluggewicht		47,5 to
mittl.Reisegeschw. in 0 m		250 km/h
" "	in 3 km	282 km/h
Reichweite	in 0 m	5870 km
"	in 3 km	6530 km

Gruppe E21	Bearbeiter Decker	Tag			

ESTRA Druck

ABOVE: The BV 222 fitted out for long-range reconnaissance duties. Only around a dozen BV 222s were ever built.

shorter wings. There were turrets in the tail, lower rear fuselage, upper mid-fuselage and chin with two side positions as well.

Dornier's submission was the P 173 – a flying boat with four Jumo 223s, a 62-ton overload weight and 9200km range. This had a tail turret, rear dorsal turret, forward dorsal turret, nose turret and side positions. No details are given of the Heinkel entry, if one was tendered, but in any case no decision was made on any of the projects at this time. Then the original requirements were altered and none of the projects were quite able to meet them. The E-Stelle suggested – the report says "demanded" – that the BV 222 be

converted to perform the function of armed transporter "but even this demand was not granted, and the aircraft was prepared only as makeshift unarmed transporter. The testing of the BV 138 B, which was repeatedly interrupted by sheet metal damage and severely shortened by cracks in the housing cover of the middle engine, which occurred as a result of vibrations, suffered greatly from the sudden, severe winter. The flight operation could not be performed.

"Regardless, at Blohm & Voss series production continued, albeit initially only in small numbers. The known deficiencies were partially incorporated into the aircraft to be

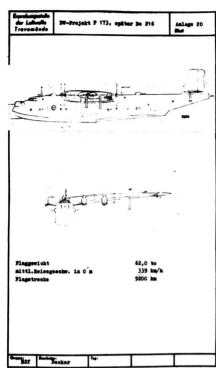

	DV-Projekt P 173, später Do 216	Anlage 20 Blatt

Fluggewicht	62,0 to
mittl.Reisegeschw. in 0 m	339 km/h
Flugstrecke	9200 km

	Bearbeiter Decker	Tag		

ABOVE: The P 173, later re-designated Do 216, was Dornier's competitor for what would later become the BV 238.

delivered. However, it was not possible to say whether the measures taken were sufficient to carry out a correct mission flight." Crews were told to simply identify the cracks if they occurred and turn off the centre engine.

P 144 BECOMES BV 238

By early 1941 it was thought that the cracking problem could be resolved with the introduction of a four-bladed propeller for the central engine and during the spring Blohm & Voss had delivered a substantial number of BV 138 Bs to front line units. But problems persisted. Take-off was still tricky and a number of BV 138 Bs were lost to British flying boats during training missions – which caused the confidence of pilots in the type to "sink considerably". And new technical problems arose – the engines' piston rings frequently disintegrated, lubricant consumption was excessive, fuel filters quickly became contaminated, the propellers frequently suffered damage striking the water, the hull often suffered stress damage and there were very common problems with the radiator valve system.

Working together, the test station, Blohm & Voss and Junkers tried to come up with a fix for each of these issues. By the autumn of 1941 there were 70 BV 138 Bs in service and when the fixes were introduced on the production line a new model, the BV 138 C, was created. However, the crews' opinion of the type was at rock bottom. According to the report: "At that time, the crew looked sadly at the assigned aircraft. The E-Stelle, together with B&V and Junkers, could only do their utmost to technically bring this aircraft, which was now solely a long-range reconnaissance aircraft, in order as far as was possible."

In November 1941, Blohm & Voss was awarded a construction contract for the P 144 under the designation BV 238. It was

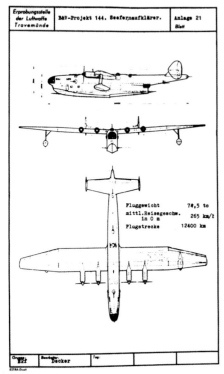

Erprobungsstelle der Luftwaffe Travemünde	B&V-Projekt 144. Seefernaufklärer.	Anlage 21 Blatt

Fluggewicht 74,5 to
mittl.Reisegeschw. in 0 m 265 km/t
Flugstrecke 12400 km

| Gruppe E2f | Bearbeiter Decker | Tag: |

ABOVE: Despite its unusual cockpit glazing and twin tail, both features that would later be dropped, the heavily armed four-engined P 144 design attracted a development and construction contract from the RLM and evolved into the six-engined BV 238.

to be a maritime patrol aircraft, long-range combat aircraft, armed transporter, unarmed transporter and airliner. Dornier's P 173 was also given a designation, Do 216, but no construction contract was forthcoming.

Instead, Dornier was commissioned to turn its existing Do 24 Holland – all examples of which had now been confiscated from Holland – into an emergency sea rescue aircraft. Evidently "the stubby boat was ideal for the execution of distress manoeuvres, but the danger of splashing water was too large. For this reason, a further development was needed. The boat got larger stubs and a larger foredeck and ran under the name Do 318".

During the winter of 1941-1942, Blohm & Voss made 43 separate changes to each of the existing 70 BV 138 Bs to bring them up to C standard. But when operations resumed in 1942 new concerns and problems were reported. The cooling air duct lacked proper sealing and continually suffered damage, the engine coolant system needed a new pressure relief valve, and an MG 131 was needed rather than an MG 15 in the gondola position at the rear of the aircraft.

According to Decker: "The changes were made over the summer in the now existing 120 aircraft. But even after these changes had been made, the great flood of complaints was not yet contained. Again new worries came. The sheet metal damage especially on the cooling air ducts and the engine cowlings occurred again and again".

The Jumo 205 Ds were the source of many of these concerns, but increasing weight continued to be a problem. The maximum loaded weight limit was 18.2 tons and at this the engines could barely cope while "the flight characteristics would deteriorate

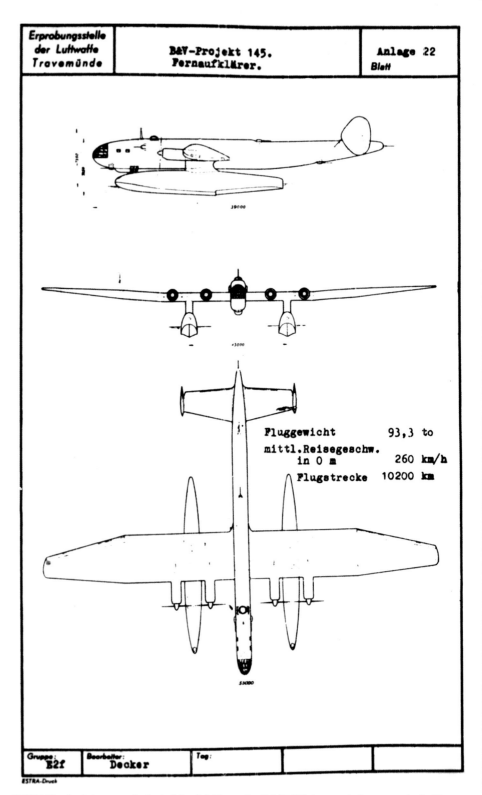

Erprobungsstelle der Luftwaffe Travemünde	B&V-Projekt 145. Fernaufklärer.	Anlage 22 Blatt

Fluggewicht 93,3 to
mittl.Reisegeschw. in 0 m 260 km/h
Flugstrecke 10200 km

| Gruppe E2f | Bearbeiter: Decker | Tag: | | |

ABOVE: The floatplane equivalent of the P 144 was the P 145. This heavy design was rejected in favour of its sibling.

significantly". The crews' dislike of the BV 138 continued to grow as well: "Of course, due to all the shortcomings and their consequences, the crews' confidence in their aircraft sank again and again. The difficult power setting of the engines in the flight is among the other deficiencies. Flight on two engines was criticised and added to this were new demands for a heating and de-icing system for winter use."

The report ends in 1943, with the sheet metal damage suffered by both the BV 138 B and C being remedied with the introduction of new intake fairings and new cooling air

shafts. But yet another problem had just occurred, with material and manufacturing defects being blamed for cracks being discovered in the wing spars of eight aircraft. Crews were apparently now flying their BV 138s only "reluctantly" and hoping for a new Seefernaufklärer, though none would be available in the near future, for which "the continued deferral in development is solely to blame. The compromise solution of the large aircraft as long-range reconnaissance aircraft, large-capacity transporter and combat aircraft had been considered in 1941. But one can rightly say

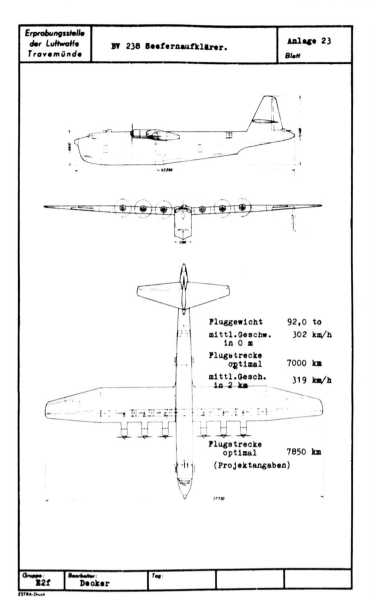

Erprobungsstelle der Luftwaffe Travemünde	BV 238 Seefernaufklärer.	Anlage 23 Blatt

Fluggewicht 92,0 to
mittl.Geschw. in 0 m 302 km/h
Flugstrecke optimal 7000 km
mittl.Gesch. in 2 km 319 km/h
Flugstrecke optimal 7850 km
(Projektangaben)

Gruppe: E2f	Bearbeiter: Decker	Tag:		

ESTRA-Druck

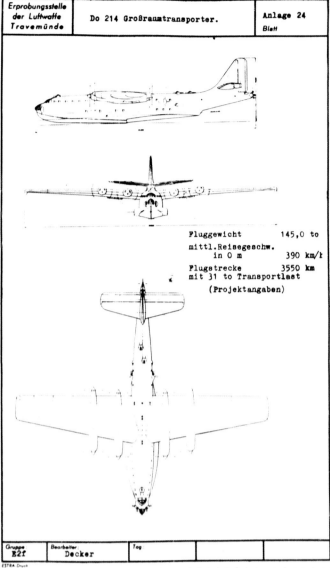

Erprobungsstelle der Luftwaffe Travemünde	Do 214 Großraumtransporter.	Anlage 24 Blatt

Fluggewicht 145,0 to
mittl.Reisegeschw. in 0 m 390 km/h
Flugstrecke 3550 km
mit 31 to Transportlast
(Projektangaben)

Gruppe: E2f	Bearbeiter: Decker	Tag:		

ESTRA-Druck

ABOVE: Almost unrecognisable from its project form, the BV 238 was intended as a multirole successor to the BV 138 – hence the numerical change of the '1' to a '2'. But only one complete example was ever built.

ABOVE: Dornier's eight-engined Do 214 was another competitor for Blohm & Voss's BV 238 but despite a mock-up apparently being constructed no prototype was ever made.

that this development step is wrong. The BV 222 as makeshift transporter and remote reconnaissance, the latter purpose of which is now converted, is a prime example of this".

As a parting shot, the report further rubbishes the idea of a 90-ton reconnaissance aircraft, arguing that a maximum of 35 tons is enough, and states that Dornier's Do 318 is overweight, short on range and lacking in any sort of fallback position should the project fail.

As for the BV 138: "Despite the fact that it was so much criticised for its appearance and its flaws, it should not be forgotten that the look of the aircraft itself benefited from excellent weapon design and the shortcomings were due to the fact that it was the first aircraft model to go into production at B&V. In a sharp competitive development, this pattern might never have been built.

"Despite being rejected by the crews as a result of its inherent limitations, the BV 138 is used time and time again and has been instrumental in fighting convoys in the North Sea and defending submarines in the Black Sea and is one of the most dependable due to its operating hours template." ●

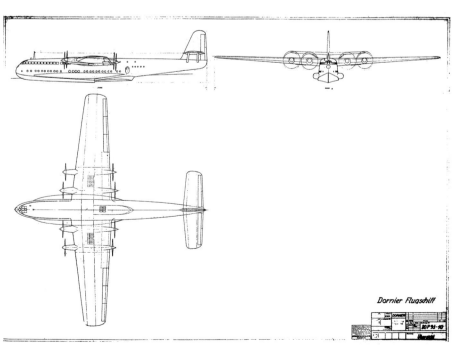

Dornier Flugschiff

ABOVE: The original civilian version of the Do 214 was Dornier's P 93.

Blohm & Voss

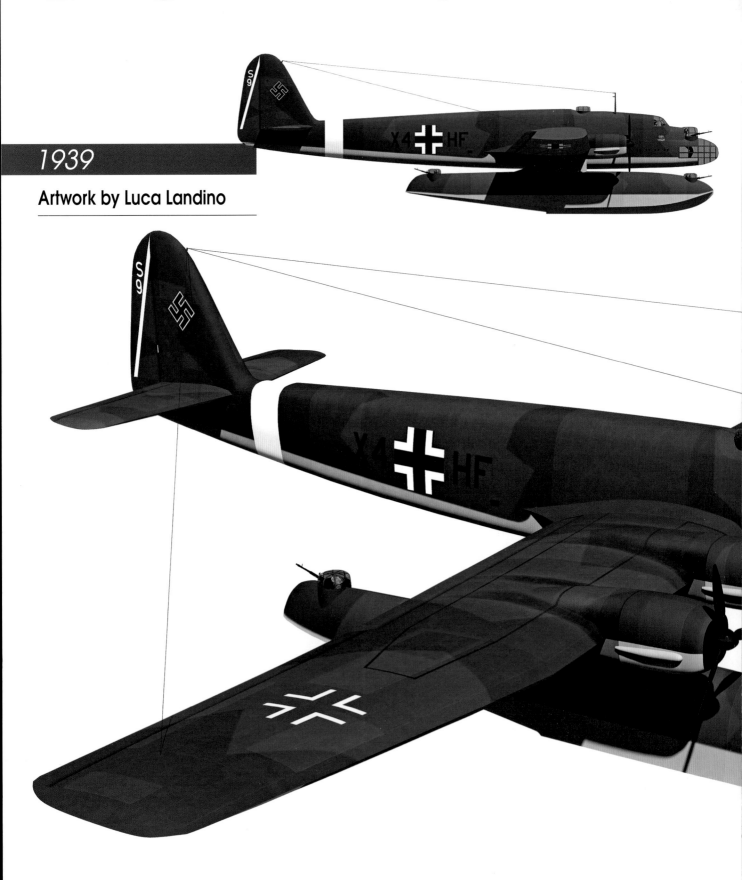

Artwork by Luca Landino

P 81

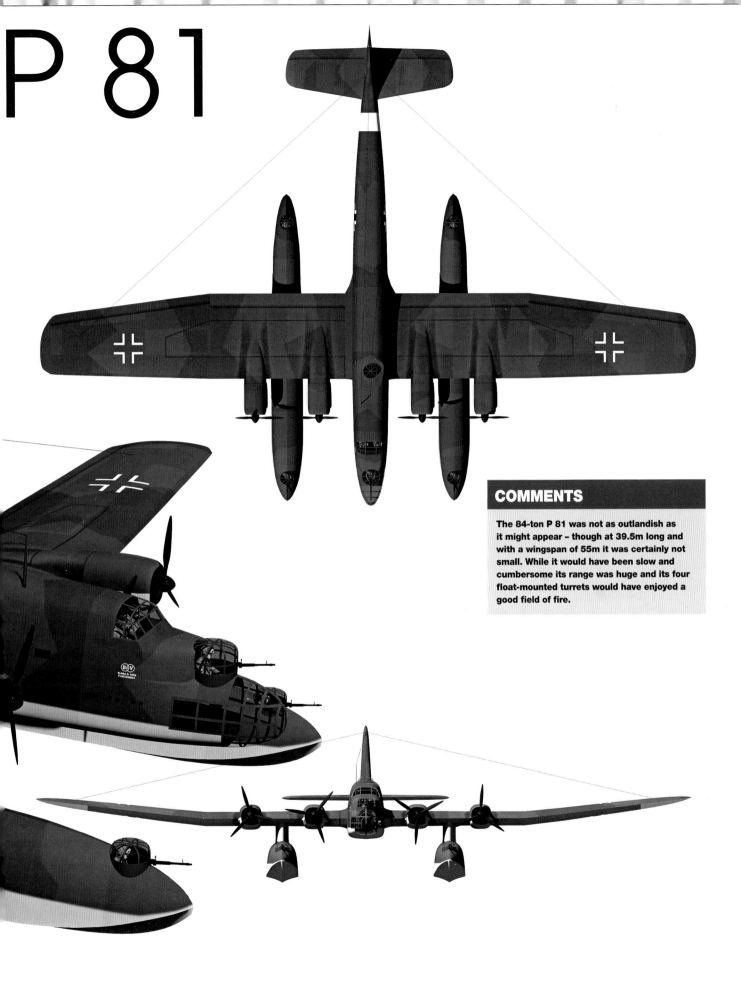

COMMENTS

The 84-ton P 81 was not as outlandish as it might appear – though at 39.5m long and with a wingspan of 55m it was certainly not small. While it would have been slow and cumbersome its range was huge and its four float-mounted turrets would have enjoyed a good field of fire.

Pushers a

Dornier fighters

Famous primarily for its bombers, Dornier was keen to enjoy similar success in the field of fighter design and manufacture. The company's experience with push-pull flying boat engines would result in some unusual designs.

The project work carried out during the war by Dornier is for the most part little known and poorly understood. But unlike other obscure firms such as Siebel, Heinkel and Henschel, most of Dornier's facilities were captured by the western Allies – including those around Friedrichshafen on the southernmost border of Germany where the Do 335 push-pull twin-engine fighter was developed and built.

For the most part, research and projects documentation captured by British, American and French forces was pooled and shared equally. However, it appears as though sheer logistics played a role in preventing absolutely all documents being duplicated and copies sent to each of the allies.

In particular, while the French gave up many of the German documents that had been in their possession when the British and Americans arrived as liberators during the late summer of 1944, some materials captured during the French advance into Germany during 1945 do not appear in modern day British or American archives. How this has come to be the case is unclear but certainly French leader Charles de Gaulle was instrumental in adding a note of reticence to the initial wave of French enthusiasm for helping and cooperating with their allies. By 1945, the French were keeping the British and Americans out of the French aviation industry and looking more and more to their own interests.

Whatever the reason, it would seem that French archives alone now hold much of what remains of Dornier's advanced projects work.

By the time of the Second World War, Dornier was one of Germany's oldest aircraft manufacturers and had become organisationally one of its most complex.

FIG.5

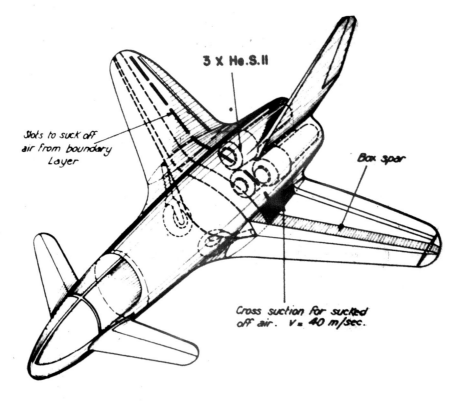

ABOVE: Claude Dornier and his son Peter were eager to tell American investigator Alfred V Verville about their company's most advanced designs, including this three-jet fighter.

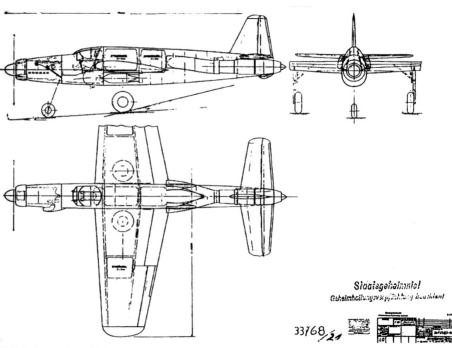

ABOVE: Dornier's P 232/2 had a piston engine in its nose and a jet in its tail, with side intakes.

The section of Dornier in the northern part of Germany, Norddeutsche Dornier-Werke, was based at Wismar and was almost entirely destroyed in bombing raids during April 1945 before what remained was captured and stripped by the Soviets.

In the south, the spiritual heartland of Dornier on the shores of Lake Constance, the company was based at Manzell in the Friedrichshafen area – with numerous additional facilities including those at Neuaubing and Oberpfaffenhofen near Munich.

The French First Army had existed before the capitulation of France in 1940 and was reconstituted during the summer of 1944 to fight alongside the British and Americans as they drove out the German occupation forces following the D-Day landings. During 1945, it was positioned on the right flank of the Allied advance, effectively driving across the southern part of Germany – including Friedrichshafen. Having taken Dornier's headquarters without a struggle, the French proceeded to strip out anything of value and send it back to France.

A team of British intelligence officers were sent to Friedrichshafen in July 1945 to assess Dornier's productive capacity and methods at facilities in Manzell, Constance, Immenstaad and an underground factory at Uberlingen, and their findings are detailed in BIOS Final Report No. 37 – German Aircraft Industry, Dornier-Werke, Friedrichshafen Area.

In a section headed 'production notes', the report states: "All the larger factories were inspected and the remainder were reported upon by French Air Ministry technical officers. In all the factories it was observed that the machine tools and most of the equipment and records had been, or were in the process of being, removed by the French Occupation Force. Sufficient information, however, was available to ascertain the production methods employed throughout the Dornier organisation."

It would appear that a good quantity of paper records survived at Manzell, despite the complete destruction of the factory itself. The report notes: "The main factory at Manzell had extremely well laid-out shelters under most of the factory which could house over 4000 people. Cross corridors had light services installed and work on instruments, equipment and small assemblies could have been carried out.

"The firm said, however, that no productive work was carried out in these corridors but they were used for storage of material and records. Although the factory was totally destroyed as a productive unit the shelters suffered no damage and it is interesting to remark that the

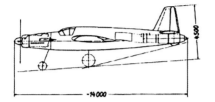

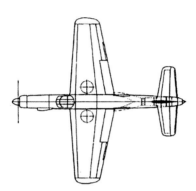
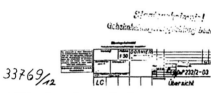

ABOVE: This drawing shows Dornier P 232/2-03, with straight leading edges on its wings.

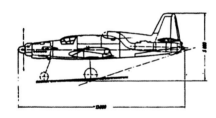

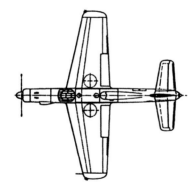
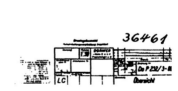

ABOVE: Another option for the P 232's jet intake is shown as P 232/3-01, with a dorsal arrangement. The wings have swept leading edges.

firm report that only one employee was killed as a result of the bombing."

The report ends by stating: "It is considered that no useful purpose will be served by any further investigation into the production methods of the Dornier Organisation. We would mark our appreciation of the courtesy and valued assistance given by the French Air Ministry Technical and Intelligence Staff at Headquarters, Kressbronn."

Exactly how much fighter projects material the French found at Manzell is uncertain but there was sufficient interest in it, and a sufficient lack of cooperation from the French ▶

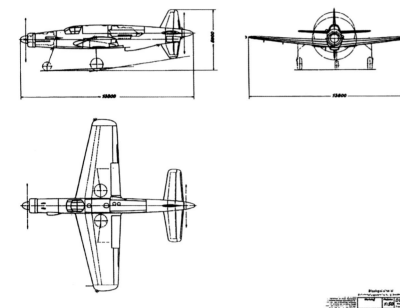

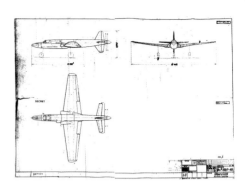

ABOVE: One of Dornier's last efforts of the Second World War was a series of three twin-engined contra-rotating prop pusher designs. This is the first – the P 252/1, with straight wings.

ABOVE: Now looking much more recognisable as the Do 335 – the P 238/1.

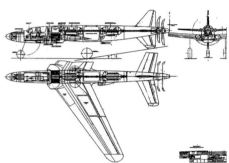

ABOVE: The Dornier P 252/2 had sharply swept wings and a consequently narrower track undercarriage but was otherwise similar to the P 252/1.

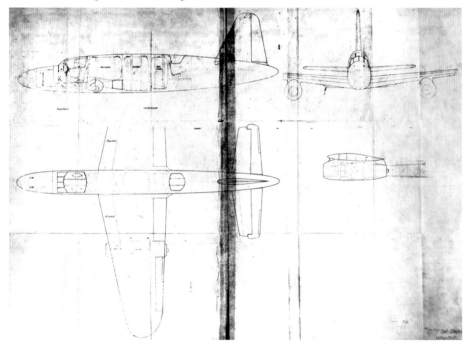

ABOVE: Dornier's last known fighter project – the twin-jet night fighter P 256/1-01. This design, rather than Dornier's radical triple jet, seems most likely to have been given the designation Do 350.

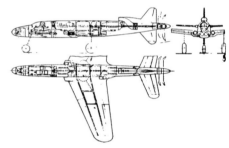

ABOVE: A middle ground between the /1 and /2 was the P 252/3, with mildly swept wings.

in supplying documentation, for the Americans to have a specialist interrogate company owner Claude Dornier and his son Peter about it.

ADVANCED DESIGNS

The result was an insightful though rather brief document: US Naval Technical Mission in Europe Technical Report No. 524-45 – Report on Dornier Pursuit Plane Development Program of October 13, 1945, by technician Alfred V Verville. This purports to represent "a brief illustrated digest of current Dornier pursuit plane developments and design studies". Verville was himself an aviation pioneer and aircraft designer who worked for Curtiss, Aeromarine, the Thomas-Morse Airplane Company, the General Aeroplane Company and the Fisher Body Corporation, before joining the army as a civilian specialist

then starting his own aircraft company. Between 1939 and 1945 he worked as a consultant to companies including Douglas and Curtiss-Wright and was 55 years old in 1945 – only six years Claude Dornier's junior.

The US Naval Technical Mission was established and given top priority to assess captured material which might be of use when it came to fighting the Japanese in the Pacific and as such it was looking primarily for cutting edge technology.

Verville's report begins: "This report was derived by interrogation and interview with Dr Claude Dornier and his son Peter Dornier while they were in French protective custody in Paris. They were asked to outline the pertinent features and advantages of the Do 335 design and to give a general review of current and projected

pursuit plane designs, for the future.

"This information was given without supporting engineering data or original drawings inasmuch as they had claimed the French had received practically all of the data that had not been destroyed through bombing. Dr Dornier invited the writer to Friedrichshafen in order to review more thoroughly their activities by interrogation of their technical specialists there, and to give blueprints and technical data to the writer.

"Also interned with Dornier for interrogation were Dipl. Ing. Jager and Dr Kohler who had to do with aerodynamic research and experimental development, respectively. Dornier's claims of advantages for his designs are outlined in the succeeding text. The design studies and wind tunnel tests on Dornier miscellaneous pursuit plane designs were partly lost and/or evacuated by French authorities."

The first part of what follows discusses the Do 335 push-pull twin-engine fighter, which Dornier says was presented to the RLM in 1937 and first flew in 1943 (see p108-115 for more on this). Only around 35 of these aircraft were built before the end

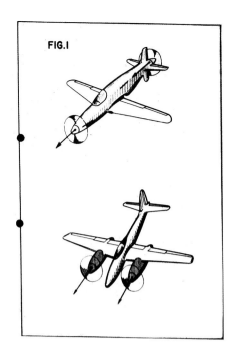

ABOVE: Illustration from Verville's report, presumably supplied from memory by Dornier, showing the reduction in drag resulting from placing one engine in front of the other.

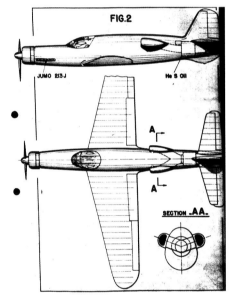

ABOVE: Another image from the Verville report, showing something similar to the Dornier P 232/2. Is this the P 254 or Do 435?

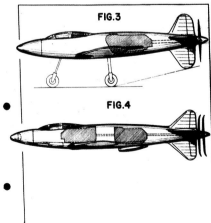

ABOVE: Verville report illustration showing how the P 252-style pusher prop arrangement would work.

of the war, the report says, and a long list of 'advantages' is given – particularly the streamlining effect of having a twin-engine aircraft with aerodynamic drag not much greater than that of a single-engine aircraft.

Next up is a section on the "Do 435 Pursuit Plane with Tandem (Reciprocating and Jet Power Plant Combination). This all-purpose pursuit plane is essentially the same as the Do 335 using either the large or small wings (38.5sqm or 41.5sqm) and either the Daimler-Benz or Junkers engines (DB 603 LA or Jumo 213 Ju) as tractor engines with or without VDM contra-rotating propellers and a Heinkel Hirth (He 011) jet engine in rear of fuselage. This combination would give an estimated speed increase of 60 to 70km/h at sea level. This combination was favoured in view of Dornier's reluctance to gamble on the limited operational endurance of pure jet aircraft.

"He advocates this compromise jet and reciprocating engine combination on the basis of the following claimed advantages: shorter take-off and landing run, improved tactical deceleration in flight, increase flight endurance as obtained by flying with tractor reciprocating engine along for cruising (eight hours at cruising speed) at 420km/h or 260mph equivalent to a range of 2100 miles which would be of advantage on long patrol flights and in bad weather.

"Saving of jet propulsion for the increased performance necessary in combat and utilising full force of both power plants. Increased cruising speed with tractor engine only about 10% greater than Do 335 operating with tractor engine only."

Verville, in his 'remarks' on the Do 435, says: "This design has merit and warrants conservative evaluation as to concept."

The third section is on "Miscellaneous Dornier Pursuit Plane Design Studies" and states: "As a result of the experience with the Do 335 tandem engine pursuit development dating from 1937, other German aircraft firms, Focke-Wulf and Heinkel, were likewise interested and were designing new models with tandem power plant arrangement, according to Dornier. The following interesting Dornier design studies were carried out embodying various qualifications and features for serious evaluation. The contra-rotating propeller, however, had not been developed to the high standard realised in the United States.

"(1) Single Seater Pursuit with Single Rear Pusher Engine/Prop Combination. This type was designed with a view of deriving the advantages (over a single tractor engine/prop combination) of higher propulsive efficiency of pusher type, and likewise, improved pilot location, improved armament and radar installation, improved visibility, increased speed climb and range, and better adaptability as a fighter bomber at low altitudes. Estimated maximum speed at sea level with Jumo 213 J is approximately 520mph.

"Dornier further claimed the advantage of facilitating good armouring protection for pilot, engines, cooling unit and fuel tanks from head-on and tail shots.

"(2) Twin Tandem Engine/Prop Pusher All Purpose Pursuit Plane. Dornier claims this to be the optimum design for a twin motor as a pusher dual propeller type. This type was studied for long-range operations

(night and bad weather fighters). The estimated maximum speed with two Jumo 213 J engines without SB [swept-back] wings or SB propeller blades was 900km/h or 560mph. With SB wings and SB propeller blades the estimated maximum speed was 950km/h or 590mph. The same claimed advantages of visibility, disposition of power plant and location of power plant, armament, etc. held as for the single engine pusher described in an earlier paragraph.

"(3) Multiple Jet Pursuit Plane. This design study was carried out by Dornier with a view of developing a high performing jet fighter of a concept opposite to that of the tailless type. It is of the so-called canard tail-first type using both SB wings and SB tail surfaces.

"The three Heinkel-Hirth 011 jet engines are arranged in clover leaf fashion. The combustion air is taken in through fuselage and from wing boundary layer suction slots. The pilot is situated in the fuselage nose. Dornier claims it is possible to increase range by stopping two engines for cruising and without having additional flow drag increase."

Summing up, Verville adds a note of caution to the evidence he has just presented: "This information, apart from the Do 335, is without available supporting test data with which to bolster flight performance convictions although research data had been made. However, in view of Dornier's wide experience and interesting designs, it is believed that his claims merit serious reviewing for evaluation in the field of pursuit plane development. Recommendations: In view of the lack of service experience in the United States with pursuit planes similar to the Do 335, etc., an extensive service test should be given this plane in order to learn at first hand the properties of tandem power plant aircraft as a type."

THE DO 435 MYSTERY

While Verville seems clear, from his conversation with Claude and Peter Dornier, that the Do 435 is a version of the Do 335 equipped with a jet engine to the rear, British intelligence report German Aircraft: New and Projected Types describes the Dornier P 254/1 night and bad weather fighter as "a two-seat fighter with a DB 603 LA or Jumo 213 J engine and a HeS 011 turbojet mounted in the tail", while in a separate listing for the Do 435 it states: "This Dornier project, intended as a night fighter, is a modified version of the Do 335. The main revisions involve a wider cockpit to accommodate a crew of two seated side-by-side; a pressure cabin; radar equipment; and long-span wooden outer wing panels. Jumo 222 engines were intended. The flying weight was nearly 26,000lb" – so something like a regular Do 335 but with longer wings and the crew sitting next to one another.

The idea of a Do 335-like aircraft fitted with a piston engine in front and a jet to the rear dates back as far as the Dornier P 232/2 of 1943. It has even been suggested that the P 231, the basis for the Do 335, was also offered with a jet engine to the rear. The P 254/1 was using this earlier engine arrangement idea as the basis of a night fighter. But was the Do 435 a jet/piston engine fighter or a long-winged purely piston engine fighter?

The minutes of a meeting of the chief

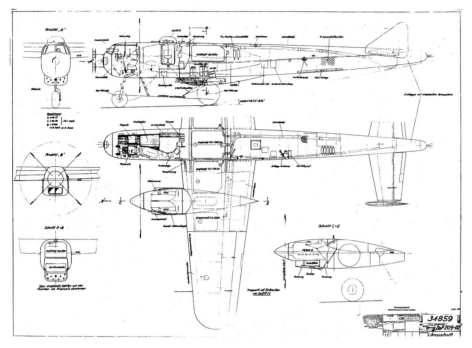

ABOVE: With an underslung weapons pack crammed with nine guns, the Dornier P 209 would have made a formidable night fighter and may have been a competitor for the Heinkel He 219.

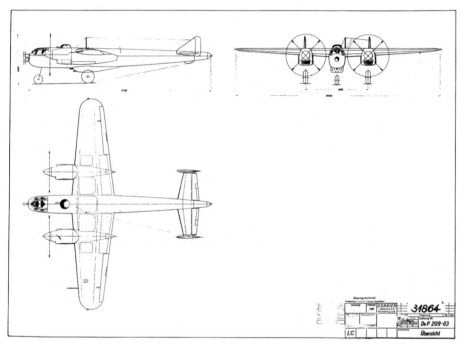

ABOVE: This three-view clearly demonstrates the P 209's origins as an offshoot of the Do 217 series.

commission for aircraft development, the Entwicklungshauptkommission, on November 21-22, 1944, only add to the mystery, stating: "The Do 335 was to be further developed as a 'bombing leader' aircraft, but cancellation of the development of the Do 435 was recommended since a suitable makeshift two-seat version of the 335 was available and the Do 435 represented practically a new aircraft." This description could probably be applied to either version of what the Do 435 might have been – since one would require an entirely new rear fuselage complete with jet intakes, mountings for the engine etc. and the other would require a new forward fuselage with a new cockpit, plus new wings.

It could be argued that the reference to a two-seater in the Entwicklungshauptkommission minutes makes the pure piston engine design a more likely candidate, but it seems odd that Verville would use 'Do 435' based on a conversation with the Dorniers themselves, when he doesn't use and probably doesn't know any of the other project numbers or designations. As part of the second set of minutes from an Entwicklungshauptkommission meeting included in German Aircraft: New and Projected Types, "Kurt Tank said it was agreed that the operational qualities of contemporary German bad weather fighters were not satisfactory; moreover the problem of designing aircraft for day fighting 'without optical vision' had not been solved. German night fighters in current use and proposed for the near future were far from adequate for dealing with the Mosquito. Night fighter developments of the Ar 234 and Do 335 were

only makeshift solutions and did not satisfy the operational demands of longer endurance and adequate facilities for navigation.

"He concluded that it was necessary to develop as a matter of the greatest urgency a 'superlative' fighter with an endurance of five to eight hours, a crew of three, and satisfactory provision for navigation. Tank mentioned a development of the Do 335 employing a turbojet."

This would appear to be a definite reference to the type described by Verville, yet Tank does not refer to it as the Do 435. There is clearly a mismatch between the two versions of the Do 335 and until further evidence emerges it does not seem possible, even more than seven decades on, to firmly pin down exactly what the Do 435 was.

TANDEM PUSHERS

Beginning in the summer of 1944, several firms began working on designs for a next-generation piston engine fighter in a pusher configuration, with the prop to the rear, under the designation Hochleistungsjäger, simply 'High-performance fighter'. Initial entrants to the competition were Focke-Wulf, Dornier and Blohm & Voss and the engine specified was the Jumo 222. But the Hochleistungsjäger specification appears to have changed either towards the end of 1944 or the beginning of 1945, with two other powerplants also being considered – the Argus As 413 and DB 603 N. There even appears to have been the option to include supplemental BMW 003 turbojets.

At this point, the Hochleistungsjäger competitors seem to have been re-tasked to become dedicated night and bad weather fighters. Blohm & Voss, which had initially tendered its P 207 design, seems to have dropped out early on to be replaced by Heinkel (whose involvement in Hochleistungsjäger is detailed later on in this publication) prior to the switch to night fighters. Dornier, which had been a proponent of the pusher prop for years, initially fielded a design which is unknown today but which later appears to have switched to the P 252, which fits Verville's description of a "Twin Tandem Engine/Prop Pusher All Purpose Pursuit Plane" reasonably well. Focke-Wulf was certainly working on similar designs. Both the Dornier and Focke-Wulf pusher fighter designs got larger and larger as time went on, presumably as revisions were made to the original requirement and the originally tendered projects fell further and further away from meeting the necessary spec.

Dornier's P 252/1 – a "heavy fighter for day and night operations with tandem engines 2 x DB 603 LA or 2 x Jumo 213 J" is described in the company's Baubeschreibung Nr. 1608 of January 1945. This begins: "This draft is a logical further development of the rear-engine drive used for the first time in the Do 335 series, with the elimination of the bow propeller and the use of contra-rotating propellers yielding a series of advantages that primarily affect the speed.

"These advantages can be summarized in the following points: best efficiency of the propellers, flawless airflow over the fuselage due to elimination of the bow propeller, whereby the disturbance of the flow path at the fuselage caused by the propeller is eliminated, omission of the annular radiator at

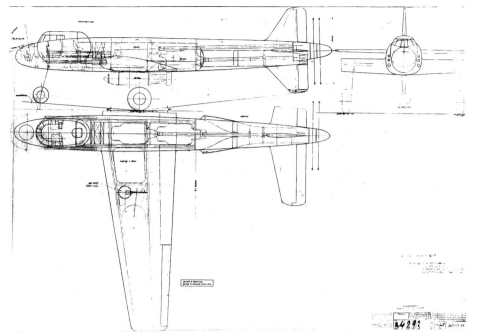

ABOVE: Perhaps Dornier's oddest design of the war, the P 215 was a high altitude fighter-bomber with highly unorthodox features – a tilted nose turret, wing turrets and a double pusher-prop.

the front of the aircraft and instead favourable arrangement of the radiators at the wing roots.

"As a result, a maximum of aerodynamic quality is achieved. The maximum speed of 900km/h, which seems barely believable for aircraft with gasoline engines, is substantiated by exact arithmetical documentation. In addition, the absolute aerodynamic optimum would be achieved by backward sweeping of the wing (35-degrees) and the tail, as well as with swept propeller blades, the maximum speed would be 950km/h.

"Due to the tandem arrangement of the engines also room-wise special advantages arise: best visibility for the crew, especially for the pilot; replaceable weapon at the nose tip, also suitable for the installation of the night fighter equipment; best protection of radiator blocks against fire. The equipment of this specification is intended for use as a fair weather heavy fighter. The prototype with its 2-man crew is also ideal as night fighter or bad weather heavy fighter."

There are three known versions of the P 252 – the P 252/1 with straight wings, the P 252/2-01 with sharply swept wings and the P 252/3-01, with only moderately swept wings. Given the contents of the report above, it may be presumed that all three were designed at roughly the same time. But none of them seem to have been seen as viable prospects for further development beyond January 1945 as attention became increasingly focused on purely jet-propelled projects.

TRUE UNKNOWNS

The Dornier canard triple jet fighter discussed by Claude and Peter Dornier with Alfred V Verville is otherwise completely unknown. It does not seem to be referred to in any other known document and there are no other known drawings of it except for the astonishing example featured in Verville's report. Elsewhere it has been suggested that this design might even have been given an official RLM designation as the Do 350 but no evidence was put forward to support this. The only known mention of the Do 350 comes from the March 16, 1945, to April 4, 1945, section of the war diary of the Chef der Technische Luftrüstung or 'Head of Technical Air Force Armament', essentially the office of General Ulrich Diesing. Under a bullet point labelled 'Nachtjägerprojekt' or 'night fighter project' it says: "Discussion with company DW [Dornier-Werke] about new night fighter project and issuing a preliminary ruling. The pattern is named Do 350."

Rather than being the radical triple jet canard fighter, this sounds much more like Dornier's very conservative 'safe' night fighter design pitched at the Schlectwetter und Nachtjäger competition (also evidently known as 2-TL-Jäger) meeting held at Focke-Wulf's Bad Eilsen design headquarters on March 20-21 – the P 256/1-01. The timing fits well and a conservative buildable design, as opposed to the host of radical designs competing against the P 256/1-01, would

certainly have suited the thinking of the time.

As for Dornier's triple-jet canard design, unless further evidence emerges to provide more background it must remain one of the war's more mysterious designs.

Another Dornier design about which little is known is the very blunt-nosed P 209, dating from November 1941. This tricycle-undercarriage night fighter, which was loosely based on the structural layout of the Do 217 N, was to be powered by a pair of DB 603 Gs. Its two crew would sit side by side in the cockpit and its offensive weaponry was a ventral pack containing a total of nine fixed forward-firing guns – four MG 17s, four MG 151s and a single MK 101. For defence there was a remote-controlled HD 131/1 dorsal turret. In terms of size, it was 17.1m long and had a wingspan of 19.8m.

Given the role, date, undercarriage arrangement, overall size and engine type of the P 209, it seems at least possible that the type was intended as a competitor for what became the Heinkel He 219 – a night fighter designed during the same period, with a tricycle undercarriage, which was 15.5m long and with a wingspan of 18.5m, and which was intended to have DB 603 G engines. There is no firm evidence for this, however, since the He 219's known competitors were versions of the Me 410, Me 110, Ju 188 and latterly the Ta 211/154.

Finally, there is the Dornier P 215. The drawing shows a pusher aircraft powered by a pair of fuselage-mounted DB 623 engines driving contra-rotating props to the rear. At the front is a pressure cabin for the three crew – the back seater operating the aircraft's defensive armament of two rear-facing turrets mounted on the wings. On either side of the cockpit is a row of three fixed forward-firing long-barrelled guns, presumably the upper two being machine guns and the larger one at the bottom being a cannon.

Then on the aircraft's nose, ahead of the cockpit window, is another turret with a 180-degree field of fire. Seated on the runway, the P 215 would have had a rather nose-down attitude, further adding to its already aggressive look and stance. A date for the P 215 is lacking but it seems not unreasonable to place it somewhere towards the middle of 1942, given that the P 231 appeared in late 1942.

There may well be further Dornier designs yet to be discovered within French archives – or perhaps even in German ones if the company's documents were ever repatriated. But while Dornier wanted to make fighters, its main business was in bombers... ●

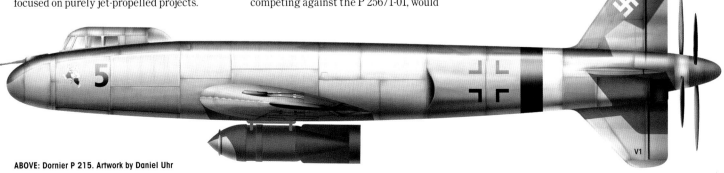

ABOVE: Dornier P 215. Artwork by Daniel Uhr

Line of succ

Dornier bombers

While it may have wanted to diversify into fighters, Dornier's core business was in flying boats and bombers. The latter proved highly profitable as war loomed at the end of the 1930s and huge effort was expended on new designs...

ABOVE: Contemporary artist's impression of an early Dornier Do 317 design.

Although it had occasionally tried its hand at fighter design with types such as the Do H and Do 10, the Dornier company made its name as a manufacturer of large multi-engine aircraft – both maritime designs and bombers.

During the secret rearmament of Germany, Dornier had specialised particularly in bombers and was responsible for the Do 11 and Do 23 which entered service in 1932 and 1934 respectively and of which collectively some 650 examples were built.

In 1936 the company designed and built the large four-engined Do 19 bomber design, then the following year the first examples of the Do 17 fast bomber entered service, beginning a dynasty of aircraft that would continue through the Do 215 and the Do 217. The latter was a larger and more refined design which built on experience of the Do 17.

In July 1939, a new medium bomber specification was issued to replace the Heinkel He 111, the Do 17 and even the new Junkers Ju 88. It would need to be capable of carrying a 2000kg bomb load 3600km and had to have a top speed of 600km/h. It also had to be capable of dive-bombing and was expected to be powered by either Daimler-Benz DB 604 or Jumo 222 engines. A crew of three in a pressure cabin was also stipulated.

The DB 604 had an anticipated power output of 2500hp, while the Jumo 222 was expected to have an output of 2465hp. It was the potential of these engines that made the programme, known as Bomber B, worthwhile, certainly in comparison to the Junkers Ju 88, powered by two Jumo 211s at 1400hp each, and Dornier Do 217 with its BMW 801s producing 1540hp each.

In 1939 documents, the new specification is referred to as "Kampfflugzeug B", but by 1941 it had become "Bomber

ession

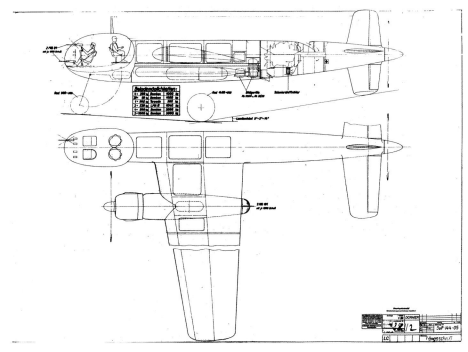

ABOVE: The unusual Dornier P 144-05 design had a tricycle undercarriage, three engines and remote control gun turrets on its engine nacelles.

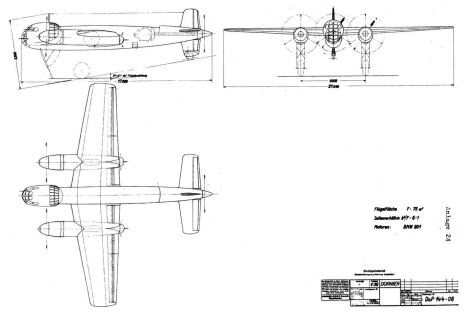

ABOVE: This three-view drawing, dated October 4, 1939, shows cockpit glazing detail of the P 144-08, which had a tail-sitter undercarriage and faired-in BMW 801 engines.

B" and five companies were invited to tender designs for it: Arado, Focke-Wulf, Junkers, Heinkel and Dornier.

With dozens of Do 17s rolling off production lines and early examples of the Do 217 undergoing testing, between October and December 1939 Dornier's designers worked their way through a series of projects, from P 144 to P 155, for a radical reconnaissance/bomber aircraft.

These designs seem to have been interwoven with work on developing the Do 217 as well as laying the groundwork for the multitude of different designs which would be produced the following year for Dornier's Bomber B entry – the Do 317.

The design featured in P 144-05 shows a tricycle undercarriage, a tractor prop engine in each wing and a third engine buried in the rear fuselage, driving a pusher prop. Options are given for different bomb or torpedo loads and cameras are shown fitted into the fuselage at the rear of the bomb bay. For defence, a rear observer has control over a pair of MG 131 machine guns, one mounted in the rear of each wing-mounted engine nacelle for a clear field of fire. Two forward-firing MG 81s are mounted in the front of the cockpit.

P 144-08 fills in the detail of the design's extensive cockpit glazing, but switches the configuration from tricycle undercarriage to tail-sitter. Here the engines are given as BMW 801s. The next drawing, P 144-09, is different again in having the crew cabin mounted lower down in the fuselage. And for P 144-11, drawn on November 1, 1939, the cabin has gone all the way down to sit flush with the base of the fuselage. Now the engines are to be a pair of Jumo 213s and the cockpit glazing structure has changed.

In P 144-13, the engines are back to BMW 801s and the cockpit has undergone a radical overhaul, with a much simpler glazing design. P 144-14 shows the internal structure of P 144-13, with the cockpit MG 81s replaced by a single MG 131.

Still drawn in 1939, though the remainder of the date is unclear, the P 149-01 appears to show a substantial simplification of the P 144 series, with a slightly more practical cockpit glazing arrangement, and just two tractor prop engines with a conventional tail to the rear. The reconnaissance cameras are now positioned within the cockpit, presumably to allow the crew easier access to them in flight, and the defensive weaponry is switched to a pair of fuselage-mounted MG 131 turrets, reducing the complexity of the P 144's nacelle arrangement.

Still further changes to essentially the same design are embodied in the P 150-02, which sees the fuselage side turrets replaced with even more conventional mid-upper and rear lower gun positions, though they are still remote controlled. Oddly, the cockpit has become more bulbous and in the rear fuselage above the rear turret is a rotating magazine for the gun. P 150-06 shows a significantly lengthened version of the same design and with a twin-fin tail replacing the earlier design's single fin.

With the P 151-02 there was yet another significant revision, with the crew cabin being squashed up to make more room for the bomb bay being slid forwards and underneath it. The twin fin tail was retained but now the wing-mounted engines were both pusher props.

The P 153-02 was almost a return to the P 149 with its side-fuselage turrets and tractor prop engines, but the P 155-01 radically altered the form of the aircraft, giving it a tricycle undercarriage once again, installing Jumo 222 engines in the wings and deepening the fuselage dramatically. This appears to have been the last in the reconnaissance/bomber series.

DORNER DO 317

Perhaps because of its ongoing work with the Do 217 or the multitude of different designs it was considering, Dornier seems to have been slow in

▶

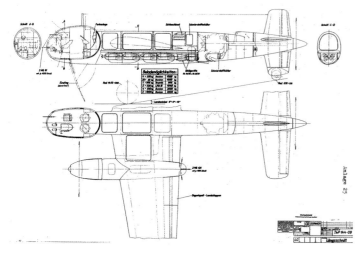

ABOVE: A detailed view of the tail-sitter version of the P 144 is shown in drawing P 144-09.

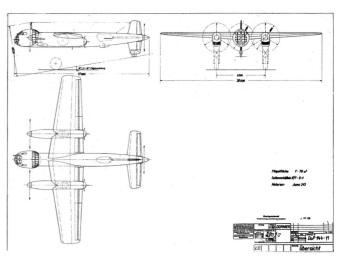

ABOVE: The P 144-11 features different cockpit glazing, a shorter wingspan and overall length, plus Jumo 213 engines.

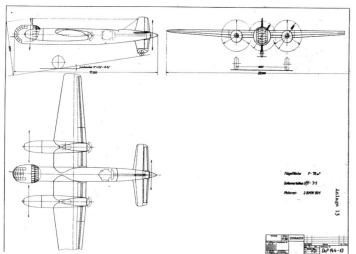

ABOVE: Another different cockpit is shown in P 144-13, along with a return to BMW 801 engines.

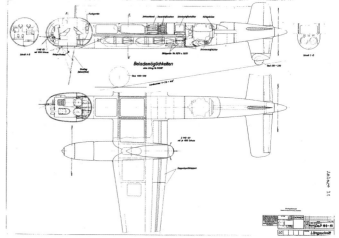

ABOVE: Detail view of the P 144-13 design. The nose would have been so high in the air, it would have required a lengthy ladder to climb aboard.

pressing ahead with the Do 317.

Despite being involved from an early stage, its first draft for the Do 317 was not presented to the RLM until February 1940. Nevertheless, the RLM quickly ordered six prototypes.

Another possible reason for Dornier's tardiness may have been some awareness of the slow progress being made on the Jumo 222 and DB 604. If neither engine was going to be available, and there were no performance gains to be made over the Do 217, there was little point in building a replacement for it.

Dornier made plans to fit the Do 317 with DB 606 engines to offer a performance edge over the Do 217 without the DB 604 or Jumo 222 but by June 1940, however, the company had been forced to specify BMW 801s for the Do 317 prototypes.

Mock-ups were inspected by the RLM, personnel from the Rechlin test centre and a group of sub-contractors on Thursday, October 17, and Friday, October 18, 1940. The result was a requirement to improve the type's turret armament and an order to speed up work on the aircraft's sighting devices and forward armament positioning. The mock-up seems to have been in a poor state of readiness for the visit, since the bomb bay was incomplete and armour

positioning had not been indicated.

Complaints about this seem to have stung Dornier into action and a second inspection was scheduled for the following Tuesday and Wednesday – presumably giving the works team three days to make the mock-up ready. Three days later, an even larger group of 29 inspectors turned up to look it over.

Despite all the design work carried out towards the end of 1939, or perhaps due to its overlapping nature, the inspectors remarked that the Do 317 mock-ups bore a distinct similarity to the Do 217 E-2 – which was being worked on in parallel.

By this stage, a remarkable number of different Do 317 designs had been drawn up, featuring a variety of different engines and layouts.

In January 1941 the RLM found that the Do 317 did not meet the basic landing speed requirement but Dornier countered by stating that it had already solved the problem during the development of the Do 217 by using double-slot flaps.

Without the DB 604 or the Jumo 222, the Do 317 project was effectively stalled. It had been proposed that the first prototype should fly in January 1942 but the whole year passed without it becoming airborne. The Do 317 V1 did eventually fly on

September 8, 1943, at Friedrichshafen but by now the whole Bomber B programme had been cancelled and the aircraft was scrapped before the end of the year.

DORNIER'S STUKA

Late in 1942 Dornier began work on the P 222, a new single-engined dive bomber which would seem to have been a competitor for the Junkers Ju 187 as a potential replacement for the Ju 87, which by now was ageing very badly. P 222 appears to have been a very lengthy design series but only a few examples of it are known.

The best drawing from the series is probably P 222/9-09. This shows a rather bizarre aircraft which embodies many of the same features as the Ju 187 – though not the rotating tail – but wraps them up in a decidedly unusual package. Rather than seating the crew in tandem or even back to back in the fuselage behind the engine, they sit back to back in their cockpit on the port side of the forward fuselage while directly to starboard is the type's single DB 603 engine. This arrangement would certainly have improved visibility for the pilot when attacking ground targets.

Positioning the engine right beside the cockpit had another benefit – it meant that in addition to the pair of fixed

ABOVE: This piece of contemporary Dornier art shows a P 144 push/pull bomber diving through a storm.

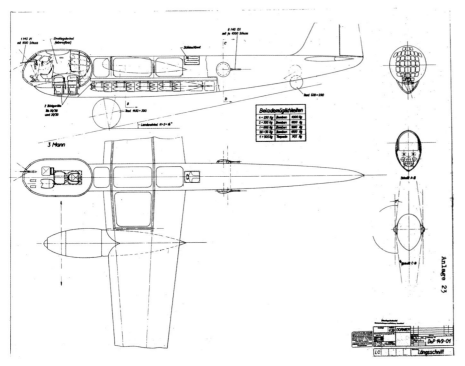

ABOVE: The P 149-01 had just two engines and fuselage-side turrets but once again its cockpit glazing, shown in the top right corner, was incredibly elaborate.

forward-firing 20mm MG 151 cannon in the wingroots, the DB 603 could be fitted with a 30mm MK 103 motorkanone firing through the propeller hub. This combination of heavy weapons would potentially have made the P 222 an effective tank-destroyer.

This was not the end of the P 222's arsenal however. The second crewman is pictured operating the aircraft's remote-controlled defensive turret and the aircraft was capable of carrying a substantial bomb load on four external hard points. There was even an internal bomb bay just behind the turret for smaller munitions.

In terms of general structure, the P 222 had a fixed undercarriage, which would have made it slow, and a large dive brake mounted at the end of its tail. It was 15.35m long with a wingspan of 16.5m. Drawing P 222/9-12 shows essentially the same aircraft but the turret is moved back to sit parallel with the undercarriage legs and the overall length is reduced to 15.25m.

While the P 222 seems to have been a failure, the same basic design was reused shortly thereafter as the basis of a new bomber design – the P 223. This took the basic premise of positioning the single engine next to the cockpit

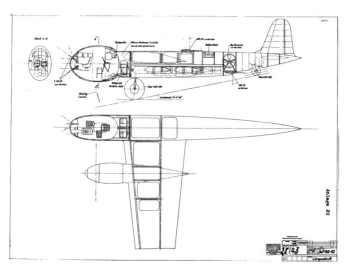

ABOVE: Evidently from the same line of development as the P 144, the P 150-02 had a very bulbous cockpit and short undercarriage with very large wheels.

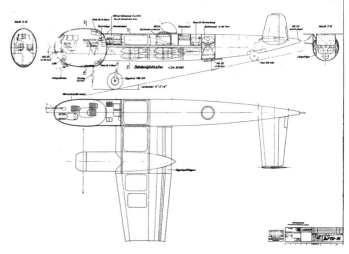

ABOVE: P 150-04 appears superficially similar to P 150-02 but had a twin fin tail, small wheels with longer undercarriage legs, and a longer fuselage despite no room being made for a camera.

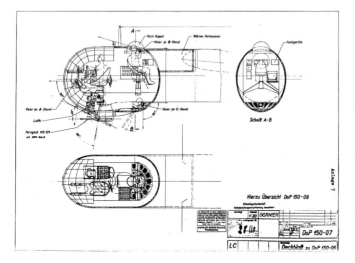

ABOVE: One of several Dornier P 150 cockpit arrangements, showing suspended seating arrangements and a chin turret.

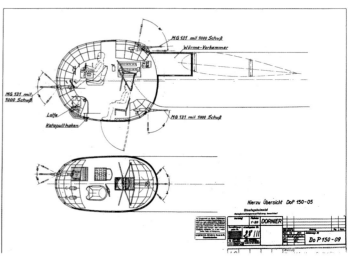

ABOVE: Another P 150 cockpit arrangement with extensive glazing both to the front and the rear.

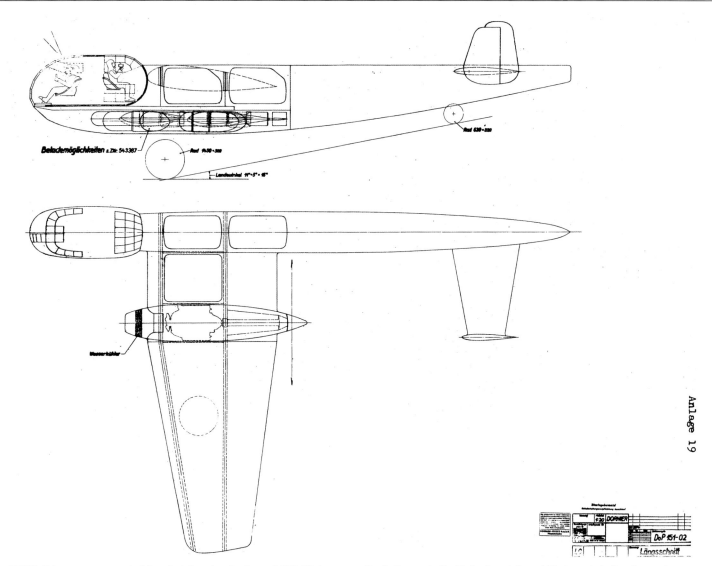

ABOVE: This rearrangement of Dornier's bomber features, P 151-02, has a smaller flatter cockpit with the bomb bay shifted much further forward. The twin engines were both pushers in this layout.

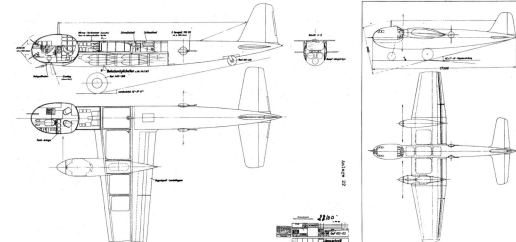

ABOVE: Dornier's P 153-02 looks like an amalgamation of elements from several earlier designs.

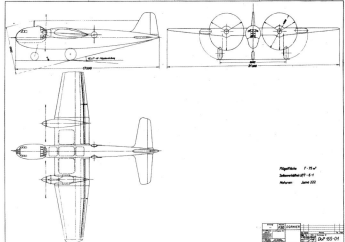

ABOVE: The last known design in the pre-Do 317 series, the Jumo 222-powered P 155-01 marked a return to a tricycle undercarriage but also features the flat cockpit of the P 151. Perhaps its most striking feature is its very deep fuselage.

and added a thicker fuselage, a bomb aimer position in the cockpit, a prone tail gunner position and perhaps most importantly – a retractable undercarriage.

DORNIER DO 417
Relatively little is known about the Dornier Do 417, although multiple designs certainly existed under that

designation. Elsewhere it has been stated that the design was a response to a new requirement issued on July 23, 1942, for a multirole aircraft under the title of Arbeitsflugzeug or 'workhorse aircraft'. As with the ill-fated Bomber B, the goal was evidently to replace all the various different medium bombers then employed by the Luftwaffe with a single type –

thereby eliminating the need for multiple overlapping supply lines and the need to maintain several different sets of spares.

With minimal modifications between roles, the Arbeitsflugzeug was to be capable of operations as a level bomber, a dive-bomber, a reconnaissance aircraft, a torpedo carrier or a carrier for guided missiles. It would have a crew of three, a

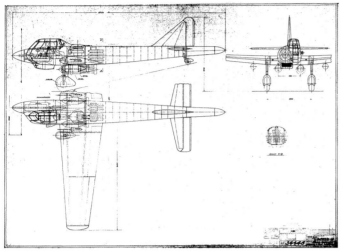

ABOVE: Dornier's Stuka was the P 222, this version being the P 222/9-09. It had a fixed undercarriage and rear-facing turret for defence, plus forward firing MK 103 and MG 151s for ground-attack. The engine arrangement is highly unusual.

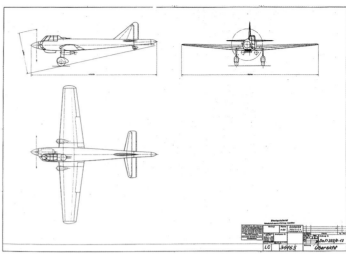

ABOVE: A slightly different version of the P 222 with the turret moved closer to the cockpit.

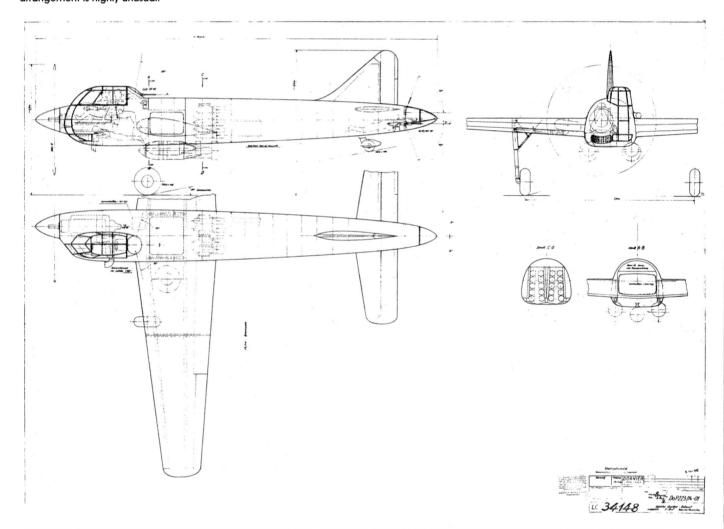

ABOVE: The distinctive P 222 layout was recycled for P 223/14-01 – a somewhat more conventional bomber with a retractable undercarriage.

take-off weight of 17,000kg to ensure a top speed of 600km/h, and only engines that were already available – the BMW 801, DB 603 or Jumo 213. Range would be 2500km with a bomb load of 2000kg.

It has been suggested that the Arbeitsflugzeug competitors were Blohm & Voss's P 163 – certainly possible because the brochure outlining it was dated August 29, 1942, and was entitled 'Arbeitsflugzeug BV-P 163', Heinkel's P 1065 which is

described as 'Arbeitsflugzeug (3 Mann)' in the postwar list of projects compiled for the Americans by Heinkel staff, the Junkers Ju 188 and Dornier's Do 417.

Three Dornier drawings appear to show the Do 417, although one of them is actually labelled '8-217.000-1811' despite showing something that clearly is not a Do 217, and the title of another is illegible. Although these designs did bear a strong familial resemblance to other

Dornier medium bomber designs, the Do 417 differed primarily in having a large manned tail turret. Two drawings show the turret positioned beneath a single tall tail fin while the third shows the turret as a humped bulge sitting between twin fins.

Supposedly the Do 417 was one of the two finalists in the competition alongside the Ju 188, but clearly the latter won and Dornier's last attempt to revive its flagging series of bombers was extinguished. ●

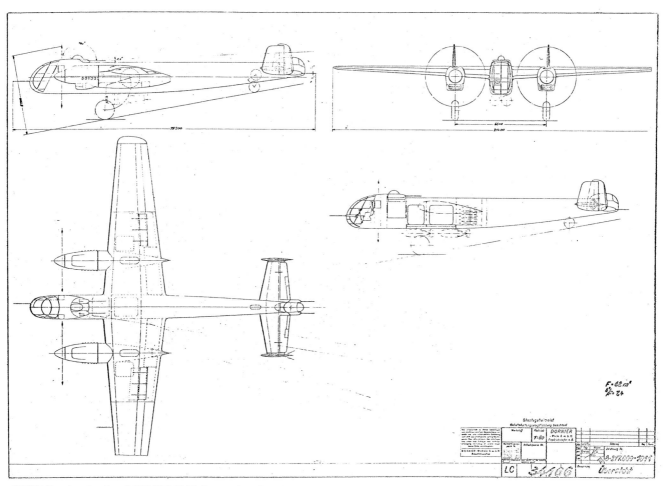

ABOVE: Dornier drawing 8-217.000-1811 shows a bomber design that appears to have been the basis for the Do 417 – a competitor for the Ju 188. It features comparatively straightforward glazing and an unusual manned rear turret.

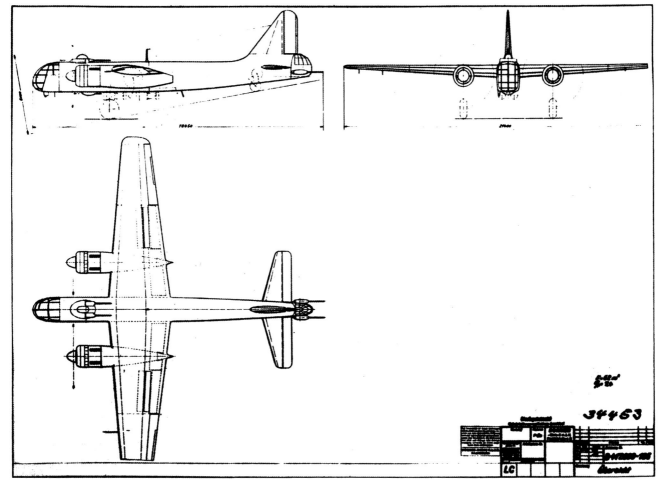

ABOVE: This Dornier Do 417 design replaced the DB 603 engines and twin fin arrangement seen in drawing 8-217.000-1811 with BMW 801s and a single tail fin.

Dornier P 223

November 1942

Artwork by Luca Landino

COMMENTS

Though it is not immediately obvious externally, the asymmetrical P 223 actually had a three-man crew. The tail gunner lay prone at the very end of the fuselage. The aircraft was 14m long with a wingspan of 16.5m.

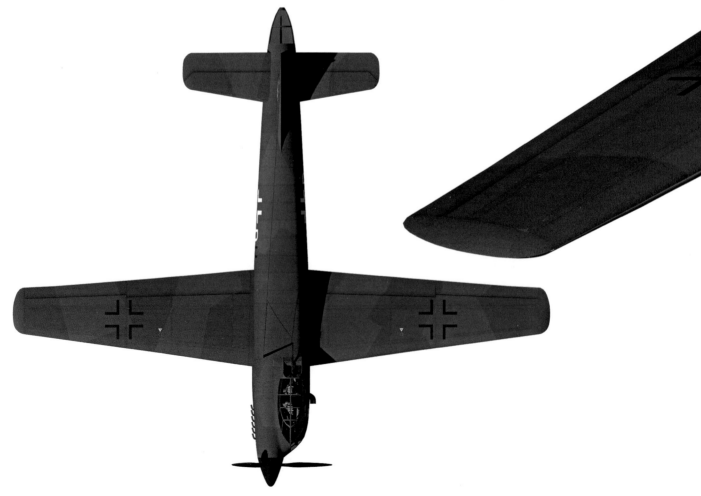

Prone pioneer

DVL jet fighter

Sketches suggest that some of Nazi Germany's most ambitious late-war jet fighter projects may have been the direct result of ideas jotted down by a scientist working for the DVL.

One of the many mysteries concerning German jet fighter development is where some of the more radical ideas put forward actually came from – such as Blohm & Voss's tailless designs.

Specifically, who came up with the idea of trading the entire rear fuselage and tail of an aircraft for wingtip booms and fins? This layout was used for the pusher-prop P 208 fighter in the autumn of 1944, the first iteration of the P 209 jet fighter, the P 210 Volksjäger competitor, the P 212 1-TL-Jäger competitor and the P 215 twin-jet night fighter competitor right at the end of the war in 1945.

The five most obvious candidates would be Blohm & Voss's chief designer Richard Vogt; the head of the firm's projects department Hans H Amtmann; their colleague Hermann Pohlmann, who had been heavily involved in designing the Junkers Ju 87 dive-bomber before joining Blohm & Voss, head of aerodynamics Richard Schubert or George Haag, who is variously described in Allied reports as the company's 'wing design chief', 'wing group chief' or 'chief of wing design branch' – he had evidently worked with the Berliner-Joyce Aircraft Company and the Fairchild Airplane & Engine Company from 1932 to 1934 when he returned to Germany and joined B&V.

Alongside work on the BV 155, the aerodynamics of these tailless types – particularly the P 212 and P 215 – occupied much of the designers' and engineers' time during the most critical period of the war, yet Vogt hardly mentions them in his brief autobiography Weltumspannende Memoiren eines Flugzeug-Konstrukteurs. An American report of August 3, 1945, entitled Blohm & Voss Production Types and Design Proposals by H E Weihmiller and H P Meiners, states under a heading of 'Blohm & Voss Design Proposals' that the "B&V design center" was "headed by Dr Vogt as both director and chief engineer" and "was very prolific in ideas and development". This may support Vogt as the man behind the tailless types.

Amtmann does not mention them at all in his own short memoir The

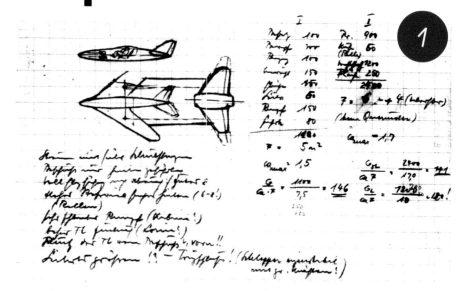

ABOVE: The first drawing in the sequence shows design for an engineless aircraft attached to a winged engine pod by two slender booms.

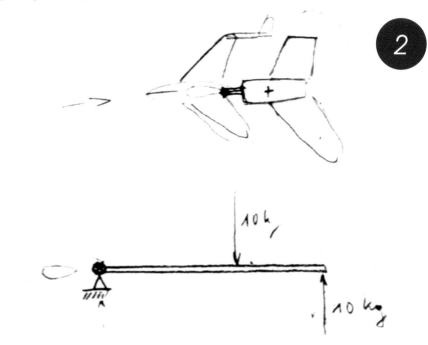

ABOVE: Next, the nameless designer revised the arrangement to feature a central attachment point for the engine pod and wingtip control surfaces instead of full booms.

Vanishing Paperclips, although Blohm & Voss documents show he definitely worked on them and Pohlmann resorts to quoting from the type brochure for the P 208 rather than giving any real background to the design and its origins.

Schubert's name does occasionally appear on some of the original calculation and pre-design papers associated with the tailless types, alongside Vogt himself, Amtmann and several others about whom little is known – Peters, Baccius, Thieme, Jans, Hagel and Schulze.

Haag is often cited as the source of the wingtip controls idea and the American report paints him as Vogt's right hand man: "[Vogt] speaks English very well, needing no interpreter. At other times, his Wing Group Chief, Mr Haag, assisted as interpreter, guide and source of information." Yet Haag appears to have been more of a manager than a designer, and in the report he seems to have been mostly concerned with leading on B&V types which had reached production – particularly the BV 155 B but also the BV 139 B, BV 141 B, BV 222, BV

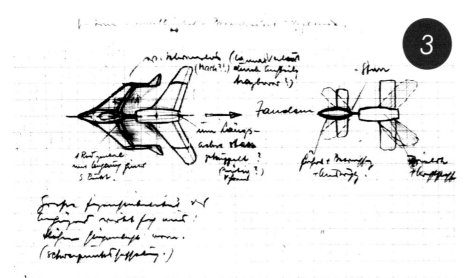

③

ABOVE: The third design shows the fighter now with full wingtip booms and a central attachment point for the engine pod.

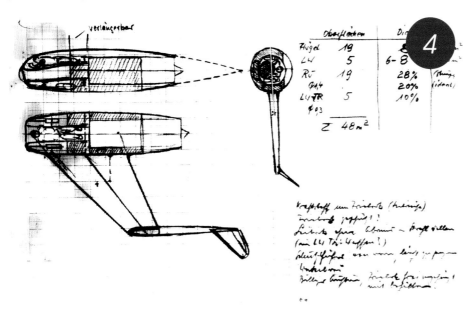

④

ABOVE: Finally, the aircraft and engine pod are merged to create a one-piece tailless fighter. The cockpit is reduced to a narrow space above the engine intake.

Me/Ge/DVL/527
     R   F
Deutsche Versuchsanstalt für Luftfahrtforschung E. V.
   Projected jet-powered aircraft (Hochgeschwindigkeitsmessungen)
Berlin-Adlershof, Deutsche Versuchsanstalt für Luftfahrt e.V.,
Jan.1944   Germ.Unclass.   5p of diagrs, 1p of folded graph
                ABSTRACT
   Surface, lift, and weight calculations for: (1) an aircraft
having 2 main parts, the pilot cabin with sweepback wings being
connected in tandem with jet engine nacelle by means of booms;
(2) an aircraft steered by pilot in probe position, with jet
engine directly aft in fuselage, the sweepback wings having
outrigger stub-wings. Graph showing thrust plotted against fuel
consumption for He S 109-011 jet engine.
(5)   (1) Jet propulsion   (2) He S 109-011   (3) Airplanes,
     Unorthodox I. T

Me 3367

AIR DOCUMENT INDEX (TECH)   (GERMAN)   T-2 Hq AMC USAAF

ABOVE: The Allied reference card describing and dating the unorthodox jet fighter designs.

238 and BV 155 C. No one at Blohm & Voss appears to take credit for the tailless idea.

Skodawerke, aka Skoda Kauba, is also associated with the wingtip control surfaces designs, but only appears to have got involved with them directly after being contracted to do so in the autumn of 1944 by Blohm & Voss.

So if not Vogt and his men, or Skoda, where did the idea come from? Shortly after the war, while documenting a set of high-speed measurement graphs found among papers taken from the Deutsche Versuchsanstalt für Luftfahrtforschung (DVL), the German institute for aviation

research, based in Berlin, US personnel discovered some handwritten notes on their reverse side alongside four sketches.

Three of the sketches show what appears to be a tandem arrangement of a tailless and engineless but highly aerodynamic fighter aircraft at the front attached to a winged pod containing the engine at the rear. Exactly what advantage this was intended to give is unclear, but it may have been an attempt to avoid having a long intake tube, or to provide the engine with air already 'smoothed out' by its passage over the aircraft shape in front.

In the first sketch, the pod is attached via two long narrow booms. In the second more tentative sketch, the pod is attached at a central point and one of the wingtips has sprouted a shorter boom with a little winglet on the end. In the third drawing, the central attachment point and wingtip booms have become better established, with the aircraft at the front shrinking somewhat and the pod growing in size.

In the fourth drawing, the aircraft section and engine pod have effectively been combined into a single structure. The cockpit, which previously had the pilot seated in a reclined position, has been shrunk to a tiny chamber above the gaping engine intake where the pilot is shown lying in a prone position. The aircraft's weapons, presumably a pair of MK 108s, are crammed into spaces within its chin. Exactly how the aircraft would have landed is unclear, but it would most likely have used a belly skid.

The place where the drawings originated, the DVL, was involved in aviation research across a vast range of topics, ranging from pure theory and physics to wind tunnel-testing the latest aerodynamic designs. It was also responsible for assessing the work of the aircraft manufacturers to a degree and applying the formidable weight of the huge body of data it had amassed to aviation problems. At its peak, it employed some 2000 personnel including some of Germany's foremost aeronautical engineers.

The evidence for a link between the DVL designs and the work of Blohm & Voss is purely circumstantial, however. The drawings themselves are undated but the sheets they were drawn on were from January 1944 – which is undoubtedly what led the US serviceman describing them to give them that date. But exactly when they were drawn is unknown. Furthermore, how would an idea sketched on the back of some graphs find its way to Blohm & Voss? Perhaps it is merely a coincidence and the unnamed DVL man and an unnamed designer at Blohm & Voss both had the same idea but separately.

Nevertheless, if the sketches were made in or not long after January 1944, they would appear to pre-date Blohm & Voss's use of the wingtip boom arrangement by around eight or nine months. And if the original idea did come from the DVL, this might explain the postwar reticence of Blohm & Voss personnel to claim credit for what was a bold reimagining of how an aircraft's key components should be arranged.

Further research may yet reveal the answers but for now the mystery of who conceived the idea used for Blohm & Voss's radical tailless fighters remains tantalisingly unsolved.. ●

DVL Jet fighter

January 1944 (see p52-53)

Artwork by Luca Landino

COMMENTS

The simple design of the DVL's unnamed jet fighter belies its clever use of space. The pilot lies prone directly above the turbojet's intake, while the engine itself fills most of the stubby fuselage. Just how well it would have flown with such small control surfaces is unclear, however.

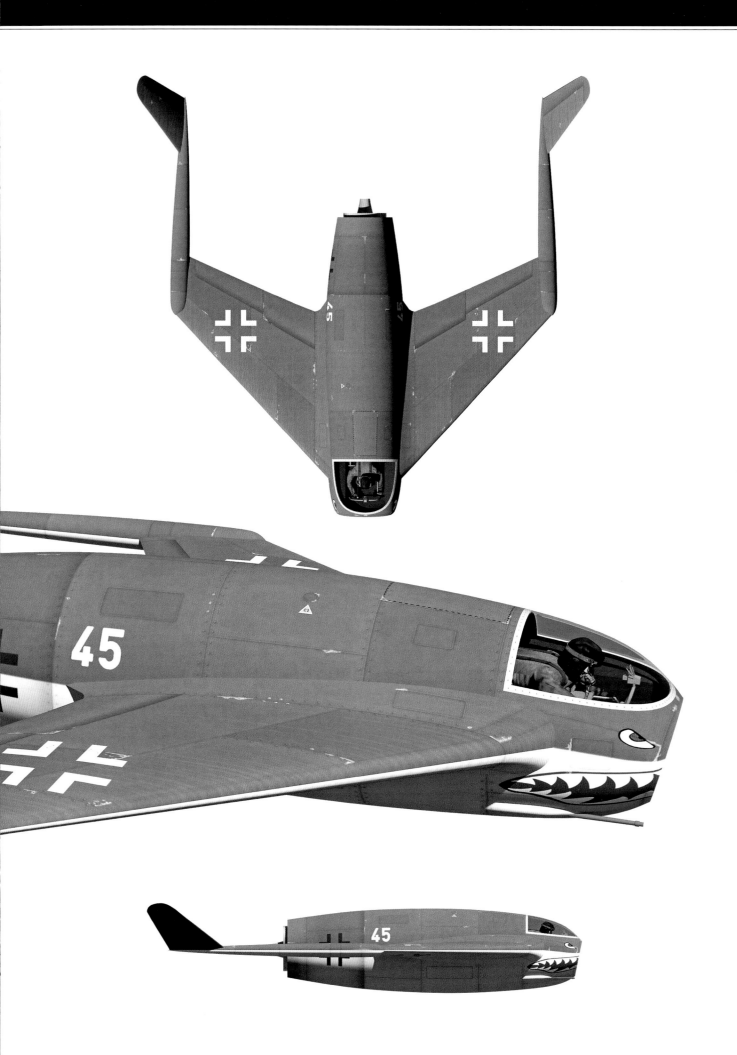

The heavy

Fw. Grt., Blatt 1

Großtransporter

ABOVE: The vast Focke-Wulf Grosstransporter of June 6, 1942.

Focke-Wulf Grosstransporter

Having enjoyed success with the relatively large Fw 200 Condor, Focke-Wulf confidently believed that it would go on to design yet more large aircraft – a belief that would find its ultimate expression in the ginormous Grosstransporter.

Focke-Wulf started work on two separate large aircraft projects in 1940 – neither of them particularly suitable for operations that involved carrying bulky cargo. The first was the Fernkampfflugzeug, a heavy bomber designed to meet the same requirement as the Messerschmitt P 1061, later to become the Messerschmitt Me 264, and the second was a scaled-up version of the Fw 200, the straightforwardly named Fw 300.

The Fw 300 was intended as a commercial airliner for Deutsche Luft Hansa. Where the Fw 200 was 23.45m long with a wingspan of 32.85m, the Fw 300 was over 31m long and with a wingspan of over 45m. Like its predecessor, it was a tail-sitter with narrow doorways in the sides of the fuselage through which the passengers could enter and exit.

In mid-1941, the Focke-Wulf Fernkampfflugzeug was rejected in favour

of the Me 264. However, before long it was realised that Messerschmitt's designers had got their sums wrong and the design competition had to be re-run – Focke-Wulf now had an opportunity to redesign its bomber and set to work on doing just that.

It would appear that this renewed focus on the Fernkampfflugzeug design resulted in the company handing the Fw 300 over to its French 'partner' – the Société nationale des constructions aéronautiques du sud-ouest

ifter

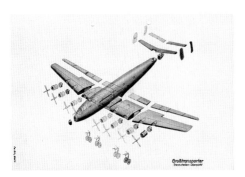

ABOVE: The Grosstransporter would not have been a quick or cheap aircraft to build.

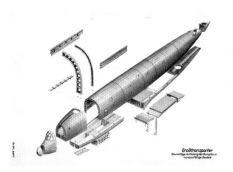

ABOVE: Internal structure of the Grosstransporter.

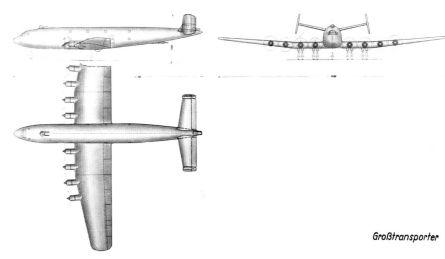

Großtransporter

ABOVE: From every angle, the eight-engined version of the Grosstransporter would have been an imposing looking aircraft.

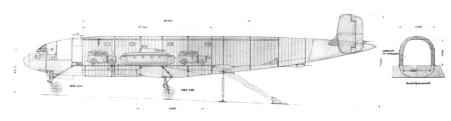

Großtransporter
Längsschnitt

ABOVE: Side view of the eight-engined Grosstransporter of Baubeschreibung Nr. 246, showing its capacity to carry a 20+ ton tank and more besides.

or SNCASO at Chatillon-sous-Bagneux in Paris. And this meant that by early 1942 Focke-Wulf's own designers had a little spare capacity to take on further work.

In January 1942, Blohm & Voss suggested to the RLM that its BV 238 seaplane design would make a good basis for a large land-based transporter/bomber. This seems to have been regarded as an idea worth pursuing since it received the designation BV 250 and was outlined in a brochure dated March 25, 1942. It had an all-up weight of 108 tons and, powered by six Daimler-Benz DB 603 engines, it was designed to carry a massive 40-ton payload up to 2000km.

The BV 250 boasted a feature borrowed from Messerschmitt's huge Me 321 cargo glider whereby a huge set of doors directly under its nose could be opened wide enough for motorised vehicles to drive up a ramp and right into the aircraft's cavernous cargo bay. However, in order to accomplish this, the aircraft had to be made to 'kneel' forward by retracting its nosewheel.

At around the same time, Junkers seems to have produced the first brochures for converting its Ju 290, which was slightly smaller than the projected Fw 300, into an even larger transport with the addition of a lengthened fuselage and two additional engines. This was to receive the designation Ju 390. The Ju 290 was a tail-sitter but had its own novel feature for loading

vehicular cargo – a long ramp extended from the aircraft's rear underside which, when it made contact with the ground, levered the whole tail up into the air.

It is unclear whether an actual requirement for a very large transport was issued by the RLM at this time, but with the German army having just fought and lost the Battle of Moscow between October 1, 1941, and January 10, 1942, it would certainly have made sense to produce an aircraft capable of rapidly transporting men and equipment to and from the Eastern Front. Moscow is some 1600km from Berlin by air, which matches reasonably well with the 2000km range Blohm & Voss had offered for the BV 250.

On April 1, 1942, Focke-Wulf leader Kurt Tank told the company's Flugmechanik 'L' department to begin work on a Grosstransporter – literally a 'big transporter'. He asked for an aircraft capable of carrying 40 tons for 1500km at an altitude of 2000m, or 6500ft. It also had to be able to take off fully loaded in under 1000m and be able to fly comfortably with a full load at 75% of maximum engine power. The head of Flugmechanik 'L', Oberingenieur Herbert Wolff, gave the job to one of his engineers – Voigtsberger.

At first, Voigtsberger began crunching numbers on how many engines the Grosstransporter would require and settled on six Jumo 222s. The aircraft, outlined in drawings 0310 215/269 015/14, was to

have a wing area of 435sqm, a wingspan of 57m, and an all-up weight of 100 tons.

By the beginning of the following month the engine options had increased, Voigtsberger having by now also run the numbers for eight BMW 801 Cs and eight Jumo 222s. For some reason Tank himself seems to have been particularly keen on using the BMW 801 C and in mid-May asked Voigtsberger in a memo how fast the Grosstransporter could be expected to fly using eight of them. Voigtsberger attempted to respond to him on May 18 saying that top speed at sea level would be 360km/h or 224mph – although Tank missed the message because he was in transit.

By the end of the month, four options were being considered – six Jumo 222s, six BMW 802s, eight BMW 801 Ds or six DB 603s. And by June 2, the beginnings of a report had been put together with outline details of what the Grosstransporter would look like with each of the four options. All four would have a wingspan of 58m and a wing area of 440sqm but where the BMW 802 design would weigh 107 tons and the Jumo 222 and BMW 801 D designs 106 tons, the DB 603 design weighed just 90 tons. However, on a concrete runway the DB 603 design would need 1100m to get airborne and the BMW 802 design would need 1050m. No figure is given for the BMW 801 D design but the Jumo 222 achieved the spec with a 1000m take-off run.

▶

Fw. Grt., Blatt 2

ABOVE: Powerful winches were included in the Grosstransporter design to help with heavy cargo – such as tanks.

Großtransporter

Einfahren eines 40 t Tanks

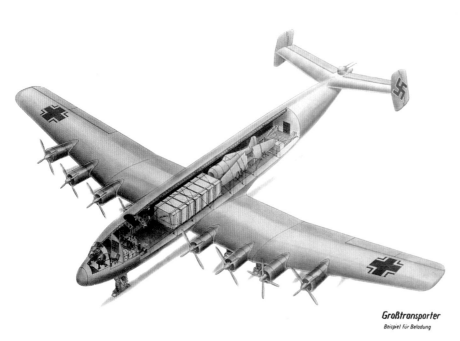

Großtransporter
Beispiel für Beladung

ABOVE: Various load options were offered for the design – here an Fw 190 fighter provides a sense of scale.

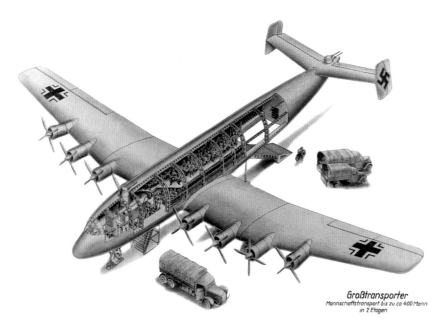

Großtransporter
Mannschaftstransport bis zu ca. 400 Mann in 2 Etagen

ABOVE: Up to 400 fully equipped soldiers could fit inside the Grosstransporter, though an internal floor was needed to create two levels.

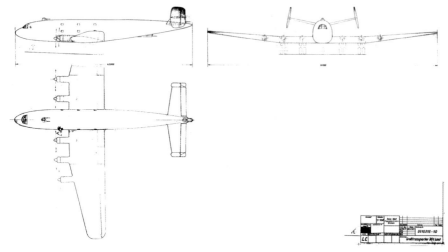

ABOVE: The smaller six-engined Grosstransporter of Baubeschreibung Nr. 249.

NR. 246 GROSSTRANSPORTER

Four days later, on June 6, 1942, the first full construction description of the type was issued: Baubeschreibung Nr. 246 Grosstransporter. Multiple drawings were produced showing a truly huge aircraft with four engines on each wing and a twin-fin tail. It measured 47m long with a wingspan of 58.2m. The nosewheel undercarriage arrangement meant that the aircraft could be loaded simply by lowering a ramp to the rear of the fuselage – no kneeling or tail lifting required.

Maximum permissible payload was 40 tons and the cargo bay was 26m long with a cross-section larger than the profile of the Reichsbahn – the German national railway. In other words, anything that could fit on a railway wagon could fit into the Grosstransporter. There would be an overhead pulley crane capable of lifting three tons stretching the length of the bay and there would be two winches at the far end, each with 10 tons of pulling power.

The drawings showed that the Grosstransporter was capable of carrying a single Panzer III or IV plus two other motorised vehicles besides. Other load options included 400 soldiers or a complete Focke-Wulf Fw 190 fighter with its wings removed plus seven large cargo crates.

Just two engine options were presented – eight DB 603s or eight Jumo 222s.

With the DB 603s, the Grosstransporter could manage a top speed of 435km/h (270mph) at an altitude of 5.7km (18,700ft). Its ceiling would be 6km (19,685ft) and after take-off its maximum rate of climb would be 0.9m per second. At altitude, this figure increased to 2.3m per second.

However, performance was significantly improved with the Jumo 222s – a top speed of 490km/h (304mph) at 5.7km and ceiling was 7.1km (23,294ft). Climb from take-off was 2.3m per second, or 4.7m per second in flight.

Either way, defensive weaponry was to consist of three turrets, each with a pair of MG 151s with 600 rounds apiece. Allowance was also made for a 'window gun' – one additional MG 131 pointing either forwards or downwards.

Voigtsberger gave serious consideration to how much of the Grosstransporter could be made out of steel, rather than the scarcer and more in-demand aluminium-zinc alloy commonly used in the construction of aircraft. He wrote: "An extensive use of steel is possible in addition to the basic introduction of aluminium-zinc alloy. However, the use of steel going beyond the normal range substantially reduces the load that can be transported while maintaining the maximum permissible flying weight."

He gave two examples – a 20% steel content and an aircraft made entirely out of steel. With 20%, the load capability was 40 tons. But with 100% "(i.e. machine built entirely in steel) the military payload is only 20 tons, so in this case twice the number of aircraft would have to be built to carry the same load but the transport of a 40-ton tank would be omitted.

"Of particular importance, however, are the consequent conclusions that an aircraft built with too much steel is fuel-inefficient."

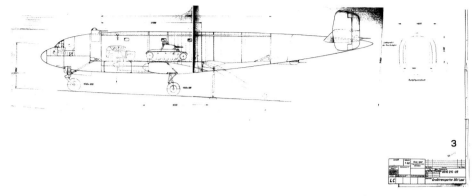

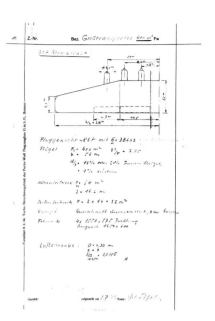

ABOVE: Even with only six engines and a maximum capacity of 30 tons, the Grosstransporter could still manage a tank.

He argued that the resources saved by using less light metal would be squandered in the form of greater fuel consumption to keep the heavy aircraft aloft.

NR. 249 GROSSTRANSPORTER

Just two days after the publication of Baubeschreibung Nr. 246, Voigtsberger produced another Grosstransporter description – Baubeschreibung Nr. 249. This was essentially a downgraded version of Nr. 246, again with two engine options: six DB 603s or six Jumo 222s. But rather than a 40-ton load, the Nr. 249 was designed to carry only 30 tons. As a result its flight performance was comparable with that of the 40-ton eight-engine design. Visually, the two were very similar with the latter simply having a shorter fuselage and wings – 43m long with a 56m span.

Four days after the publication of Baubeschreibung Nr. 249, on June 12, 1942, Voigtsberger produced yet another short and rather frank report on the Grosstransporter project – General Considerations on the Performance of the Grosstransporter. He began by listing the four performance requirements set down by Tank, then wrote: "These requirements are to be achieved with existing engines in order to avoid setbacks so practically only the DB 603 and BMW 801 engines are available to solve this task. Now the design of the Grosstransporter is determined primarily by the demand to carry a largest single load of 40,000kg. This condition necessarily results in a flying weight of more than 100 tons, taking into account the required range and arming."

He then mentions two further requirements apparently added since April 1 – a climbing speed of 1m per second at an altitude of 2km (6562ft) at maximum power and the necessity to be able to house the aircraft within a 60m hangar. He said that with these in mind "a draft was created in which, considering propeller diameters, the following engines could have been accommodated: 6 x Jumo A-oc, 6 x BMW 802, 8 x BMW 801 D, 6 x DB 603.

"The version with six DB 603s was intended only as a fallback solution. At least the possibility of carrying out a comprehensive flight test of this type would exist before the availability of a Jumo 222 or BMW 802 engine. The flight weight of this version was determined to be the same starting as in the design with

six Jumo 222s or BMW 802s, waiving the carrying of the entire load of 40 tons."

He said the six DB 603s would not meet any of the necessary requirements and even the six Jumo 222s would only meet one of them, the 1000m take-off distance. None of the other engine arrangements could meet the full set either – particularly the required climb rate at 2km.

He said most of the engines would only be able to meet it at 1km and at 2km "a drop in performance already occurs".

With regard to the requirement to flying on 75% of engine power at full load, he said: "Four-engine flight with six-motor design is impossible. Particularly critical at such high power loads, however, is the behaviour of the aircraft in the starting state! The limited span (accommodation in the 60m hangar) requires a small extension and thus a very high induced resistance at the start.

"This results in a very low power surplus immediately after taking off. This is further greatly worsened by the high chassis resistance (4 x dual wheels + nose wheel) and results in climb speeds of 0.6-0.8m/sec up to 20m altitude, instead of the rolling distance of 1000-1200m, a total of 2200m is needed (the start with 8 x BMW 801 D without additional boost is not possible at all, because when taking off no excess power exists!)."

He presented a table comparing different engine configurations of Grosstransporter against the known quantity of the Fw 200 C-3 and wrote: "The rolling distance of the Fw 200 is 850m, the rate of climb with climb performance on the ground at full flight weight is 4m/sec (flight condition: chassis + flaps 'on'). According to the predicted results, the solution of the task with six engines of the performance class Jumo 222 or BMW 802 is very unsatisfactory or with eight BMW 801 Ds impossible.

"The minimum requirements can only be achieved with an eight-motor version; because there is a bearable power load! To avoid setbacks, double engines of type DB 606, DB 610 and DB 613, because of their high unit weight and their operational deficiencies are not usable engines for the Grosstransporter."

The only possible solution with existing engines, he said, was eight single powerplants on the leading edge of the wing and with the wingspan restriction waived.

"The new design has therefore been

ABOVE: Design notes and sketch from July 8, 1942, as the Grosstransporter project was winding down.

carried out with 8 x DB 603. By increasing the wingspan to 62m it is possible to accommodate the engines at 4.20m diameter. From the point of view of fuselage construction, it seems absolutely necessary, especially for the solution of the demands made here, that the development of aircraft engines class Jumo 222 and BMW 802 be promoted by all means; because only then is the performance of the Grosstransporter satisfactory.

"The draft therefore provides that the DB 603 motors, if the Jumo 222 becomes available, can be replaced without modification. For the performance with 8 x DB 603, it should be noted that full load take-off performance is approximately equal to that with 6 x Jumo 222. The aircraft design is thus already at the permissible limit of the load.

"It is therefore proposed to start with additional thrusters when carrying the entire load of 40,000kg to improve launch performance. When taking a load of 30,000kg, existing engines give a satisfactory performance."

For the remainder of June and into July, Voigtsberger worked on updating Baubeschreibung Nr. 249 and carrying out more detail work on six- and eight-engine arrangements of the Jumo 222 and DB 603. The last evidence of the project appears to be a final project summary for six-engine designs able to carry up to 30 tons, produced by Voigtsberger on August 11, 1942.

His calculations evidently showed that a six-engine design with existing DB 603s could satisfactorily carry a 30-ton cargo but either 30 tons just wasn't enough or the whole concept of large vulnerable 'grosstransporters' was simply abandoned as impractical and, perhaps, a waste of resources that could be put to better use building fighters. Although Junkers would eventually build the Ju 390 and Blohm & Voss completed a single example of the BV 238, upon which the BV 250 was based, the age of the German giants simply never came about. ●

The fourth wing

Gotha P-60.007

The creator of the twin-jet Gotha P-60 fighter, Dr Rudolf Göthert, by his own admission, designed a version with its engines recessed next to one another on its underside. But until now no one knew what this looked like...

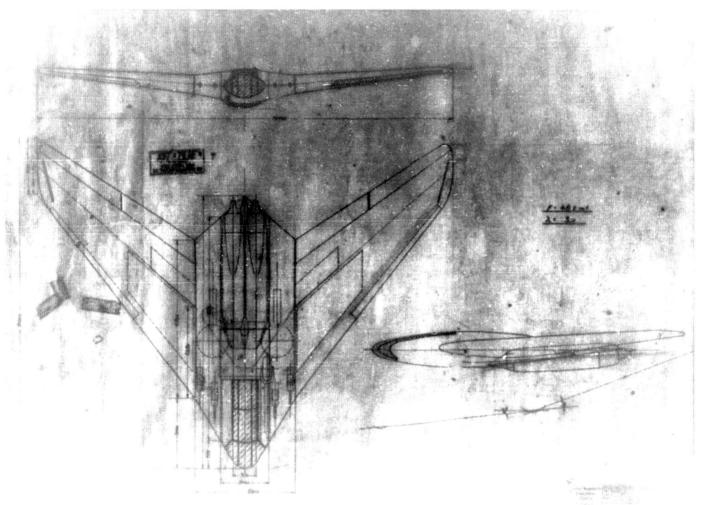

ABOVE: The previously unknown Gotha P-60.007.

The P-60 story begins with maverick aircraft designers the Horten brothers, Reimar and Walter, presenting their idea for a twin-jet flying wing bomber to Hermann Göring personally in late summer 1943 and receiving a development contract shortly thereafter.

The aircraft which they had called the H IX, and which the RLM designated 8-229, was to carry a 1000kg payload for 1000km at a speed of 1000km/h. But the Horten brothers had no appreciable production facilities with which to build and develop all the components and systems necessary for such a complex aircraft – they needed a subcontractor to take on the job.

Precisely when Gothaer Waggonfabrik, based at Gotha in Thuringia, central Germany, was chosen as that subcontractor is debatable

but not long after the arrangement had been agreed the company decided that it could design a better twin-jet flying wing than that proposed by the Hortens.

Gotha chief aerodynamicist Dr Rudolf Göthert set to work on this 8-229 alternative during the autumn of 1944 and it received the company designation P-60. On March 11, 1945, he published a report on his progress entitled Go P-60 Hochgeschwindigkeitflugzeug or 'High-speed aircraft'.

This gave the P-60's intended roles as heavy fighter, fighter-bomber, reconnaissance aircraft and night fighter. Three different two-seater designs had been drawn up: the P-60 A and P-60 B, in which the crew lay prone in the nose, and the P-60 C, which had conventional upright seating in tandem. The BMW 003-powered P-60

A was based on experience of working on the 8-229 and was a direct competitor for it. The P-60 B was an HeS 011-powered replacement for the P-60 A/8-229 and the P-60 C, also HeS 011-powered, was designed to compete against new jet night fighter designs already being worked on by other major aircraft manufacturers as 1944 drew to a close.

Göthert's report outlines each of the three versions in detail – the P-60 A and P-60 B had armoured and pressurised crew compartments with air conditioning, adjustable air-cushioned couches for the pilot and radio operator, and 'hanging' foot pedals. The P-60 C was also pressurised and the seated position of the crew allowed for the inclusion of ejection seats.

There were control surfaces towards the wingtips on the P-60 A and B which

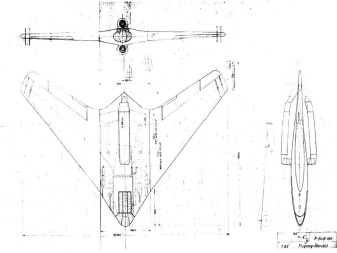

ABOVE: Gotha P-60 A with BMW 003 engines.

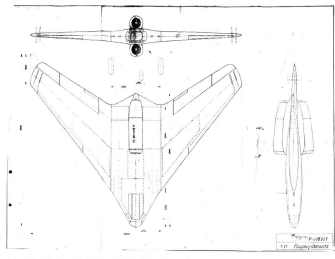

ABOVE: Gotha P-60 B with HeS 011 engines.

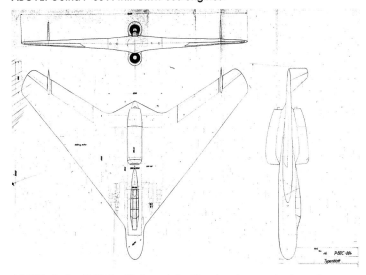

ABOVE: Gotha P-60 C with the original tandem two-seater layout.

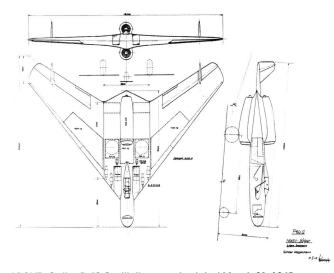

ABOVE: Gotha P-60 C with three seats, dated March 21, 1945.

extended downwards to act as fins. The P-60 C had a small fin of normal design on either wing. The tricycle undercarriage of all three was the same – a castering nosewheel and mainwheels lifted from a Junkers Ju 88 A-4 or A-7 – and all three had their engines positioned symmetrically to one another above and below the central wing.

However, at this point Göthert mentions a fourth P-60 but does not name it beyond calling it a 'variant'. He writes: "In a variant, a twin arrangement, in which the engine units are arranged below the central wing, recessed next to one another, is possible. Current wind tunnel tests will prove whether this type of installation is also suitable."

A FOURTH VERSION

The way Göthert writes, it would appear that the 'variant' was a work in progress as of March 11, 1945, and a newly discovered contemporary drawing labelled P-60.007 appears to show this design. At first glance it appears to have more in common with the P-60 A than the P-60 B, with an elongated upper canopy to the crew compartment, but closer inspection reveals that it is quite significantly different from any of the other P-60s.

The most obvious difference is the two turbojets being recessed deep within the rear of the wing centre section, with only a broad lip intake protruding below. In addition, compared against the P-60 A, the centre section protrudes

further rearwards and the point where it meets the wings is sharp and angular rather than the gentle curve shown in the other designs.

The outer sections of the wing have a pronounced dihedral– angling upwards compared to the other versions – and have different control surfaces at their tips.

In fact, even apart from the P-60.007, the Gotha report on the P-60 actually lists six potential versions of the design including two with additional rocket motors fitted at the rear of the centre section between the two turbojets – P-60 A mit BMW 003, P-60 A mit HeS 011, P-60 B mit HeS 011, P-60 B mit HeS 011 und R-Gerät, P-60 C mit HeS 011 and P-60 C mit HeS 011 und R-Gerät. There is no mention of a version of the P-60 A with 'R-Gerät' – rocket propulsion – however.

This made a total of seven versions of the P-60, but there was still one more to come. After the war, Göthert was interrogated by the Americans on June 5, June 30 and July 5, 1945, summarised in Technical Intelligence Report I-68, and he told them that "the P-60 C was entered in the night fighter competition which was opened by the RLM in December 1944. Seven aircraft including two other tailless aircraft were entered by the following firms: Arado, Blohm & Voss, Dornier, Focke-Wulf and Gotha. At the conference on night fighters, held in March of 1945, the P-60 C was shown to have the best performance of these aircraft, and Dr Göthert believed it would have won

had not the war disrupted the competition".

The first round of the night fighter or 'Schlechtwetter und Nachtjäger' competition took place on February 26, 1945, and featured five designs: the Blohm & Voss P 215.01, the Dornier P 252/1, the Dornier P 254/1 and night fighter versions of the Me 262 in two-seater and three-seater configurations.

Göthert's Go P-60 Hochgeschwindigkeitflugzeug was dated March 11, 1945, and the second round of the competition was scheduled to take place during a meeting of the Entwicklungshauptkommission at Bad Eilsen on March 20-24. Of the original five competitors, only one remained: the P 215. Dornier now fielded a new design, the P 256, Arado offered two designs, Focke-Wulf another two, and Gotha's P-60 C joined the fray.

But since February 26, the requirements had changed and a three-seater was now necessary. This resulted in a Gotha drawing dated March 21, showing the P-60 C with the main cockpit shrunk to accommodate a single occupant, the pilot. His radio and radar operators were to be accommodated either side of him under Perspex panels in the wings.

With the end of the war, all work on the P-60 came to a halt. It is believed that this is the first time drawings of all five major variants of the P-60 (not including the P-60 A mit HeS 011 or either of the rocket motor versions) have appeared together. ●

Gotha P-60.0

March 1945

Artwork by Luca Landino

COMMENTS

Gotha's P-60.007 differs significantly from the P-60 A, B and C in having its twin engines positioned side-by-side within its fuselage. Their narrow intakes are only really visible from the front – resulting in an exceptionally clean design. Also visible only from the front is the slight upwards angle of the aircraft's wings. Without a fin or the engines themselves providing a fin-like form, directional stability may well have been a problem.

One hit Wundes

Gotha oddities

Some of them are well known, others previously unknown, but what unites Gotha's string of 1943-1944 patents is their oddness.

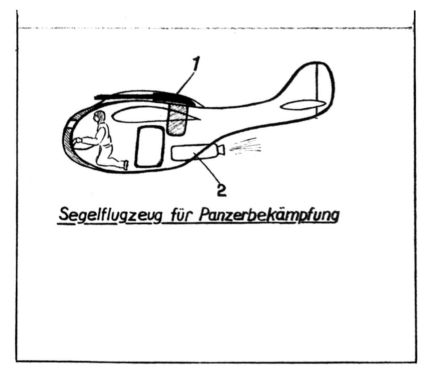

Above: Gotha Oberingenieur Walter Wundes' idea for a front-line rocket-propelled tank-busting aircraft.

Beginning in December 1943, Gotha Waggonfabrik seems to have filed a series of patents for highly unusual and innovative weapons systems – none of which appears to have been taken forward by the company itself or anyone else. In fact, it is unclear whether any of the patents was actually submitted for approval since they are all known from sketches and hand-typed documents captured from Gotha itself, rather than from official Reichspatentamt (state patent office) forms.

At least two of the seven presented here were certainly the work of Gotha Oberingenieur Walter Wundes and it is possible that all seven were his work, though almost nothing is known about the man himself.

With the exception of the V-1 based naval attack system, none of the patents mentions specific types of weaponry, or engines, or specific targets such as a B-24 Liberator. And none of them mention particular Gotha project numbers. It has been speculated that some of these designs may have been this or that Gotha project, e.g. P 54 or P 55, but there appears to be no evidence to support this. Similarly, later writers who have attributed particular engines or weapons for these designs appear to be speculating rather than relating source-based historical fact.

GLIDER FOR ANTI-TANK

The earliest of the seven presented here was drafted by Wundes on December 15, 1943, and was entitled Segelflugzeug für Panzerbekämpfung or 'Glider for anti-tank'. His sketch shows a bizarre-looking rocket-propelled aircraft with a bulbous nose and upswept rear fuselage. The pilot kneels rather than sits and peers out of a slit in a huge shield of armour covering the front of the aircraft. Housed in a hump on the aircraft's back is a long-barrelled cannon.

In the accompanying description, he writes: "With surprising attacks of enemy tanks, it is often not possible to pull together the armour-piercing weapons at this point. If aircraft are requested for the defence, then in most cases a longer time will pass until they have arrived on the spot, because the aircraft are not immediately ready to go and usually have to cover a longer flight distance to the mission target.

"To overcome all these disadvantages, and immediately to have everywhere an armour-piercing defence weapon available, it is proposed to equip a small

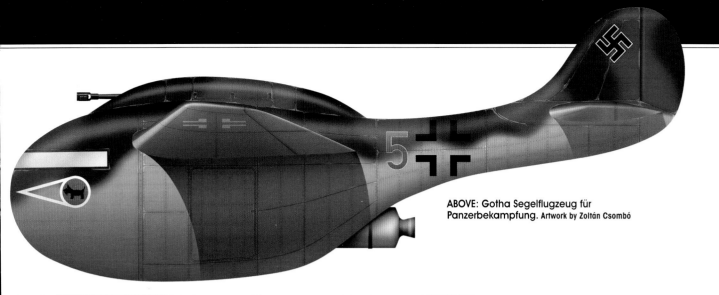

ABOVE: Gotha Segelflugzeug für Panzerbekämpfung. Artwork by Zoltán Csombó

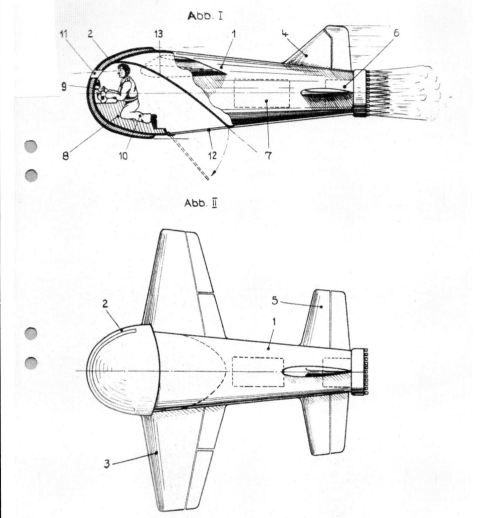

Abb. I

Abb. II

glider with a cannon (1) to combat enemy tanks. The drive is a booster rocket (2), which only needs to be sufficient for short periods of use.

"Since these aircraft with additional take-off rockets can also ascend and land from any small meadow or field, you can put them directly in the front line, so they are ready in no time. Since these aircraft can be very small, camouflaging them directly behind the front line by throwing camouflage nets etc. is easily possible."

With machine guns installed instead of a cannon, he notes, supply columns could also be attacked immediately.

Some time after the Segelflugzeug für Panzerbekämpfung was designed, Gotha appears to have used aspects of the design to create an unarmed rocket-propelled rammer aircraft. An undated patent drawing – it has the distinctive patent numbers but is, if anything, better drawn than the Segelflugzeug für Panzerbekämpfung – shows a similar aircraft but with a simple escape hatch in the lower fuselage. There is no known accompanying documentation but it seems likely that in this case the pilot's armoured shell was intended to punch through aerial targets.

GLIDER AS WEAPONS CARRIER

Gotha drew up a second patent in December 1943, this time for a Segelflugzeug als Waffenträger or 'glider as weapons carrier'. This essentially involved attaching an armed glider to

Above: Similar to Wundes' tank-buster was this heavily armoured rocket-propelled rammer, with underside escape hatch.

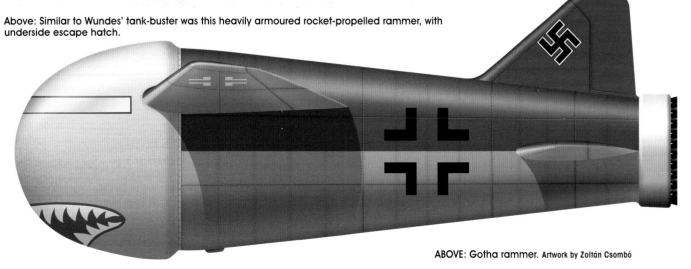

ABOVE: Gotha rammer. Artwork by Zoltán Csombó ▶

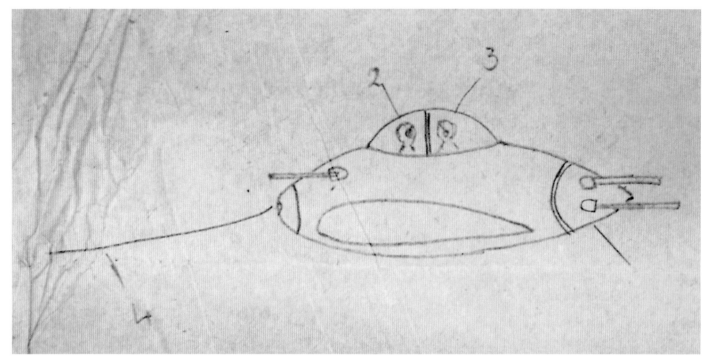

ABOVE: Sketch for a tailless Gotha weapons glider – designed to be towed by bombers for extra defensive firepower.

a large aircraft in order to defend it. If the large aircraft didn't need to carry its own defensive weapons, it was argued, it could carry more bombs or fuel or both.

The description states: "The interior space of a bomber aircraft is largely exploited by the bomb load, the equipment and the fuel tanks, so that the demand for a strong defensive armament cannot be met. This requirement is to be fulfilled according to the invention in that a glider is taken in tow, which is equipped with a strong defensive armament.

"It is advantageous to accommodate the defensive armament in a rotating tail-tip turret. The advantages that are drawn out are that the defensive power of a bomber can be significantly increased and adapted to the respective prevailing conditions. It is also possible to take heavy weapons with you. In addition, different types of defensive armament can be taken for different types of aircraft. Also, defensive armament can subsequently be changed

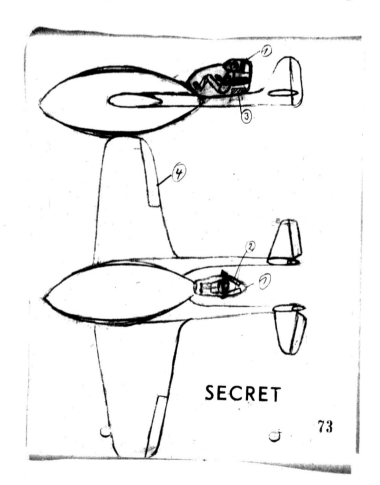
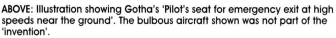

ABOVE: Illustration showing Gotha's 'Pilot's seat for emergency exit at high speeds near the ground'. The bulbous aircraft shown was not part of the 'invention'.

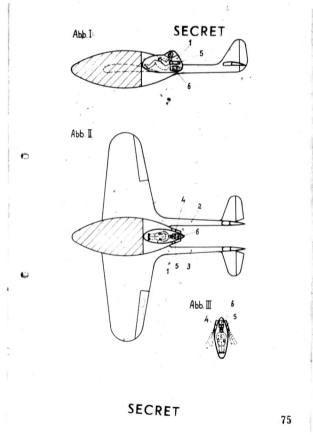

ABOVE: Refined version of Gotha's escape capsule design showing a pair of rocket motors intended for slowing the capsule's descent.

Fliegender Torpedo

Abb. 1

Fliegender Torpedo mit angeseiltem Gleitboot

Abb. 4

Abb. 2 Angriff auf Schiffe

Abb. 5 Angriff auf Brücken

Abb. 3 Talsperre u. Kaimauer

Abb. 6 Kaimauern und dahinter liegende Lagerschuppen

ABOVE: Gotha invention showing a V-1 intended for use against shipping and coastal targets, and a V-1 towing a speedboat hull.

without having to alter the bomber.

"The invention is illustrated in the drawing. The picture shows a towed glider in side view. The glider, which serves as an anchor to a bomber aircraft, is equipped with an up and down pivoting tail tip, which carries the defensive armament. As a crew, the pilot 2) and the operator 3) are provided for the weapons. The glider is connected by means of the tow rope 4) with the combat aircraft. The glider can perform lateral movements up to approximately 20-degrees compared to the aircraft."

The glider shown in the drawing was tailless, and the text mentions this, but no further detail on this point is provided.

PILOT'S SEAT FOR EMERGENCY EXIT
On March 24, 1944, Gotha drafted a proposal for an escape capsule – referred to simply as 'the driver's seat' in the patent – which would enable a pilot to survive after directing a flying bomb on to its target.

This system is described as "Pilot's seat for emergency exit at high speeds near the ground". The description says: "All-purpose bombing aircraft must be controlled to the last moment to ensure the target is hit with certainty. In order to give the pilot an opportunity at the last moment to jump out of the aircraft falling at high speed almost vertically onto the target, it is proposed to place the pilot in a driver's seat (1) covered on all sides, which is mounted separately from the actual bomb body or part of it.

"If the pilot wants to disconnect from the bomb carrier shortly before the target, he releases the coupling with which the driver's seat is connected to the aircraft. In order to reduce the excessive speed with

which the driver's seat would continue to fall, the rocket (2) attached to the driver's seat is triggered, which delays the driver's seat so much that the human body can barely sustain this delay. Subsequently, the parachute (3), which is located in the rear part of the driver's seat, releases the driver's seat down to the ground."

In other words, as the guided bomb was dropping on to the target, at the last minute, the pilot could unhitch his mini cockpit, fire one or more retro rockets, and activate a parachute which would allow his cockpit to float safely down to the ground.

The cockpit was to be designed so that "against bombardment from the ground, or against the explosion caused by the bomb carrier the front seat is armoured in front. These armour or other impact-receiving parts should simultaneously absorb the impact upon hitting the ground or water. The armour is also sealed or there are attached to the driver's seat floats so that it can float on the water".

The action of the seat was illustrated with a picture of "a split-wing aircraft (4) in which the disguised driver's seat (1) is housed between the tailplane supports, which can be released freely to the rear without damaging parts of the aircraft. It is also possible to use an aircraft with a so-called V-tail, whereby the space to the rear would also be free".

The "disembarkation" could be made completely automatic so that it would operate at a certain point even without the pilot's intervention because he "may be injured, or may have temporarily lost consciousness due to the various delays".

It is worth noting that the application was for the seat, not the aircraft it was shown attached to in the accompanying drawing. It seems unlikely that Gotha was proposing to actually create an aircraft looking like this – its shape was merely an analogue for any of the various sorts of explosives-carrying aircraft that the escape capsule could be attached to.

Attached to the patent description for the escape capsule was a single typed sheet headed 'Vorschlag' or 'proposal'. This states: "In the event of a very quick and urgent increase in the aggressive fighting power of our Air Force, the following proposal is made:

"It is well known that the development and manufacture of rocket-powered self-propelled bombs or of bomb-bearing unmanned remote-controlled missiles takes a very long time. The use itself can only be done with great effort on people and devices and with relatively small accuracy. In addition, the deployment sites are largely localised, apart from such controlled bombs or gliders, which are dropped from aircraft, and their size can therefore not be increased arbitrarily.

"The effective control of individual target points, e.g. of ship targets, requires in addition to great accuracy certain quantities of explosives. Both can be combined by the use of modern, single-seat fighter or combat aircraft, whose carrying capacity can be fully ▶

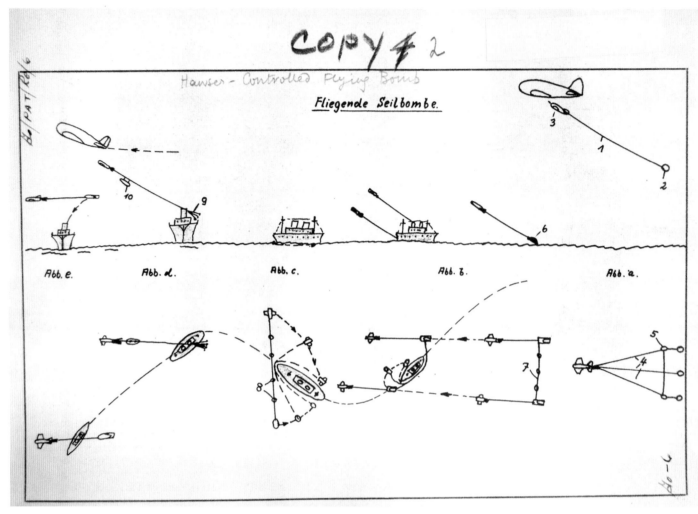

ABOVE: Five different possibilities produced by Gotha for anti-shipping weapons involving tow cables.

exploited for explosives or incendiary devices. These aircraft are controlled in direct use by the pilot on the target.

"Shortly before reaching the point of impact (100-200m), the pilot leaves his aircraft by means of a catapult seat and parachute or by a firing cab. In most of these attacks, the pilots become angry when they cannot be recovered by submarine or rescue aircraft.

"The proposal, however, is very similar to that used by the Japanese Air Force with such success. The effort to carry out this proposal is:

"1) In the human. It is necessary to find the men who are ready to sacrifice freedom and perhaps life for the fatherland. With their deed they acquire the honorary name 'Saviour of the Fatherland' and their relatives receive the special protection of the state. If the deployed men come from the ranks of the party structures, i.e. the SS, SA, NSFK, NSKK, then their heroism proves the strength of their new worldview and will light up new fires again and again with brilliant examples.

"The loss of valuable, well-educated people should be accepted in view of the achievable results, if a large, well-protected fleet, can be 100% destroyed in this way by about 200 aircraft and 200 crew.

"2) In the technical. Only existing and proven aircraft designs will be used.

The additional expenses are: a) Strong armour protection for the pilot (to be realised in the shortest possible time). b) Improvement of the catapult seat or design of a firing bullet cabin with gliding ability. c) Equipment of the aircraft with explosives or incendiary devices. d) Construction of simple wooden aircraft to test the point. e) In gliding flight at different speeds and for training. At the same time, a series of experiments could be started with the broader goal of returning the pilot to the port of operations."

Here, Gotha appears to have been advocating 'self-sacrifice' operations on a grand scale, where pilots would crash aircraft carrying explosives into high-value targets in the Japanese style. However, the Japanese only began kamikaze operations in October 1944, so it would appear that this 'proposal' was added to the rest of the Gotha patent at a later date.

FLYING TORPEDO

Five months after the escape capsule was drawn up, on August 11, 1944, Gotha had two more bright ideas – to turn the V-1 flying bomb into a flying torpedo for use against ships, bridges, dams, quay walls and dockyard warehouses or to attach the V-1 to a speedboat-like hull which it would tow on to its target.

In the first case, the flying torpedo

would be air-dropped and would "slowly sink to the surface of the water, where it is slammed at a high speed like a hydroplane on to the object to be attacked". In the second, the speedboat would be attached to the flying V-1 at its centre of gravity via a rope.

Explosives could be put only in the V-1 itself, only in the speedboat, or in both. This unusual combo would either be controlled remotely from a host ship or by a pilot actually sitting in the speedboat hull (rather than inside the V-1 as has been stated elsewhere), who would be expected to bail out at the last moment.

A second, undated, Gotha proposal for anti-shipping operations, entitled 'Fliegende Seilbombe' or 'Flying cable-bomb' appears to show five further flying bomb and tow rope systems. On its right hand side in 'Abb a', the drawing shows a large host aircraft dropping a smaller flying vehicle to which a web of ropes and circular objects is attached. Presumably, the small flyer would drag the roped objects – perhaps mines – on to the target.

'Abb b' shows a pair of flyers each dragging what looks like a speedboat hull with a rope linking them both together. As the link rope hits the target, it wraps around it, bringing both speed boats and the mines attached to their rope into contact with the target's hull.

'Abb c' appears to show a similar system but with the flyer also crashing on to the target. 'Abb d' seems to involve a towed rope with a sort of grapple on the end which would grab on to the target and 'Abb e' appears to show the small flyer towing another small flying weapon which is dropped down the target vessel's funnel.

RAMMFLUGZEUG

The last in this series of seven Gotha patents is the Rammflugzeug with detachable cockpit of October 10, 1944. The idea was for the rammer, either an unpowered glider or with its own rocket engine, to smash into the target aircraft, whereupon the pilot's cockpit would be shot forward like a bullet through the breach to fall away safely on the other side, leaving the rest of the rammer wedged in the target.

The drawing supplied showed two versions of the same aircraft – one with the armoured spike of a cockpit positioned right at the front of the fuselage, and one with it set above the fuselage.

The accompanying text says: "A ramming aircraft can only confidently kill an enemy aircraft if it impacts on the attacked aircraft. Here, both aircraft are entangled with each other and crash together. So that the pilot of the attacking aircraft can bring himself to safety, it is necessary for him to be released from the aircraft shortly before the collision, or afterwards. In the former case, it is already known how to separate the pilot's seat by special devices from the aircraft. However, it is not certain that the aircraft's pilot will be released from the aircraft after the collision, since the collision conditions are different.

"If the attack is from below, so the driver's seat must be separated downwards, and if the attack is made from above, only a separation of the driver's seat upwards will save the pilot.

"In order to eject the driver's cab from both aircraft in any case, it is proposed according to the invention that the pilot's cockpit forms the tip of the aircraft as an armoured vehicle. Such an aircraft will use the armoured form to negotiate the enemy aircraft smoothly on impact. The following fuselage hangs on the attacked aircraft, while the pilot's cockpit detaches itself like a projectile from the attacked aircraft.

"The pilot's cockpit can also be mounted outside the fuselage and the tip can be provided with an explosive device which ruptures a collision hole in the attacked aircraft for the following cockpit or can be exploded at will.

"To give the pilot a larger viewing angle during normal flight, it is expedient to form the backrest of the actual driver's seat pivotally. In order to protect the pilot against splintering effect at the moment of the ramming impact, a device can be provided on the thorn-shaped pilot's cockpit, which automatically pivots the backrest down on impact. It is expedient to provide the pilot's cockpit with a device for ejecting the pilot.

"Since according to the invention, the pilot's cockpit is located in the front part of the aircraft, it is possible to make the actual aircraft body as simple as possible; behind the aerodynamically encased cockpit, the hull and the wings are made of a cruciform frame. Such an aircraft is easy to produce and with little cost. The solid frame is a good way to cut the attacked aircraft."

With either of the two designs, the pilot would have the option either to release himself shortly before the collision, or to use his own armoured cockpit as the point of impact. The nose of the cockpit could either be fitted with an auto-release mechanism for the pilot's backrest, putting him into a reclined position at exactly the right time, or an explosive device which would blast an even bigger hole in the victim aircraft – allowing the detached cockpit to shoot cleanly through it and out into open air on the other side.

Although only seven Gotha patents from the December 1943 to October 1944 period are known, it is likely that others do exist and are simply waiting to be discovered. None of them had any effect on the Second World War, but they do nevertheless provide an interesting barometer of German aircraft designer thinking during this stage of the conflict. ●

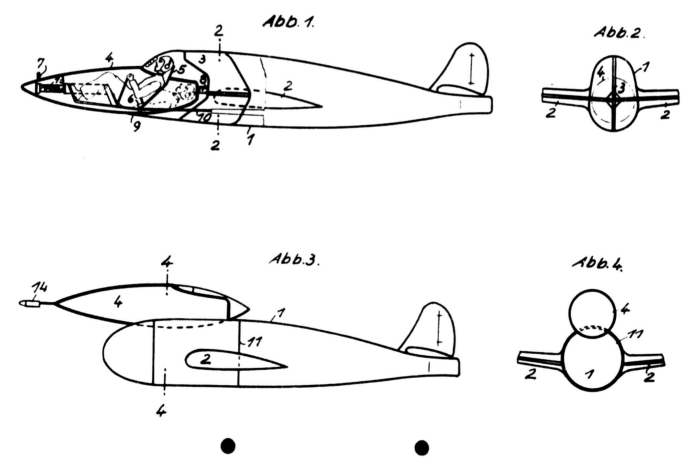

ABOVE: Two different options for Gotha's Rammflugzeug – one with a penetrating nose, above, and one designed to skip away from the point of impact, below.

Robots on the wing

German scientists and engineers worked on ever more technologically ambitious missiles, glide weapons and flying bombs throughout the war. Here are four examples of previously unknown projects dating from 1940, 1941, 1942 and 1944 to give some idea of this rapid progression.

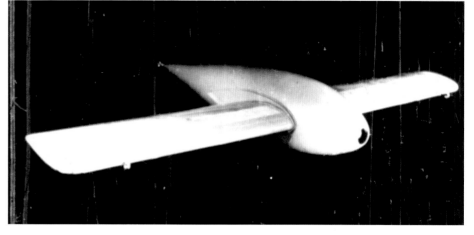

ABOVE: AEG's glide bomb, with its teardrop shape and cyclopean intake, has a slightly sinister look.

Today AEG specialises in making washing machines, ovens and fridge freezers – but on January 17, 1940, the company produced a report on a rocket-propelled remote-controlled glide bomb it had designed as a result of working on rotor blades for a helicopter.

The key focus of AEG's research at this time was ensuring that the Gleitbombe weapon could be held to a steady altitude without its human operator having to continually make small corrective movements with the control mechanism. The company came up with a system where air would be sucked through an intake in the bomb's nose and blown over its stubby wings, generating lift. When the required altitude was achieved, the system would shut off, reducing lift. When the bomb began to lose height, the system would reactivate to maintain a steady altitude.

A model of the bomb was made and tested at the Technical University of Berlin-Charlottenburg.

The report begins: "Following attempts to create a free-flying helicopter, we have been investigating inertia-free wing controls. The purpose of this work was to use rigid rotary wings and to achieve helicopter control through a lift pattern imposed on the rotating wing."

AEG had found that with the rotor blades it was working on, a steady amount of lift could not be applied using pitch changes, flap controls or other mechanical aids – instead "the path we took was to blow out air from the top of the wings to bring about the desired changes in lift, and the tests showed that with the blow-off, lift changes occur virtually simultaneously. In the problem of the rocket propelled glide bomb, similar demands are placed on the controller as described above.

"If there is a requirement that the glide bomb fly as low as possible and constant height of about 4-5m above the water surface, so the controller must watch the height regulator constantly. The normal control over the angle of attack of the wings by means of the usual height control is relatively unsuitable for this, since this requires the entire Gleitbombe to be moved about its transverse axis."

Small changes in altitude or flying at a constant height required rapid control input which "in the case of the normal controls causes rapid pulsating movements of the control flaps and rapid movements about the transverse axis. Similarly, the conditions with respect to the transverse stabilisation, to which higher demands are made here because of the short wings and the associated low drag compared to a normal aircraft.

"Therefore, in order to explore the possibilities of height control according to the principle described above, a model was built for testing in the wind tunnel. This consists of a teardrop-shaped hull, with a diameter at the widest point of 150mm and a length of 650mm. The wings had the profile Göttingen No. 449. The wing width was 400mm, the chord depth 200mm. The total weight was 15kg. The control holes were arranged in five or nine rows. The first row of holes was 25mm from the leading edge of the wing. Each hole had a diameter of 1.3mm."

The little holes were opened and closed using a valve which closed when a current was passed through it. Once the required height was achieved, based on the reading of an on-board altimeter, the holes would close. There was a 10cm tolerance range and once this was exceeded, the holes would be reopened and the bomb would generate more lift. The report states: "Within the tolerance limits, the valve opened and closed in rapid succession, in such a way that, depending on the altitude and wind force, the ratio of the opening and closing times changed. It showed that the working frequency was of great importance for the maintenance of a constant height."

During the testing, different wind speeds

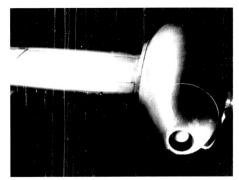

ABOVE: This close-up of the glide bomb shows the tiny holes on the wing through which air would be blown to regulate lift.

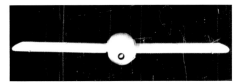

ABOVE: Forward view of AEG's glide bomb.

were tried but the bomb was always able to maintain level flight within its pre-set tolerances. AEG was planning to introduce further course-correcting measures such as flaps to compensate for weight losses "in case of burn-up of the rocket or lift changes due to uneven propulsion", with the blown-air system being retained for fine control.

AEG's innovative, though primitive, remote guidance system never appears to have reached production – perhaps due to the corporate manoeuvring and restructuring in 1941 which saw Siemens transfer its shares in Telefunken over to AEG, making the latter Telefunken's sole owner. AEG's military electronics work was probably consolidated within Telefunken at this point and nothing more was heard of the AEG Gleitbombe.

HERMANN OBERTH FERN-RAKETE
Transylvanian-born rocket pioneer Hermann Oberth, who published The Rocket into Planetary Space in 1923, designed and made the calculations for a new long-range rocket in the autumn of 1941. In a report produced for the Allies immediately after the war, he outlined the project and told them what it was for: "The apparatus under consideration should carry an explosive charge of 1000-3000kg a distance of 6000km (about as far as the distance from Europe to North America). It should be either automatically controlled or brought to its destination by a pilot, who would leave later in a supersonic glider, as in the case of the British designed 'Comet'."

In other words, in 1941 Oberth had designed an inter-continental ballistic missile. By comparison, the V-2 carried a warhead of 1000kg.

The fuel was to be a mixture of 74% alcohol and 26% water, and was to be pumped by gas turbine-driven pumps from the magnesium-aluminium alloy fuel tanks into the rocket's combustion chambers.

Regarding his rocket's flight, Oberth wrote: "HAP [the Army establishment at Peenemünde] succeeded in causing recoil-propelled projectiles to attain supersonic speeds in the following manner: a gyroscope was built into the rocket and so placed that its axis was not dependent upon the position of

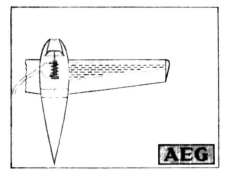

ABOVE: Diagram showing the system for operating the glide bomb's blown wings.

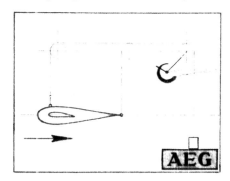

ABOVE: AEG's goal in designing its glide bomb was to create a weapon which would regulate its own altitude remotely.

the rocket. Whenever the axis of the rocket deviated from its predetermined position (the so-called program), a potentiometer began to function, which supplied electrical currents in proportion to the deviation and actuated the rudder in such a manner that it directed the projectile back to its position."

To achieve the necessary range, Oberth outlined what he called the 'step principle', which we know today as 'stages': "The speed of a rocket can also be increased by catapulting it before combustion, or carrying it as payload with a large rocket, and thus reaching a point of definite velocity. Then the velocity attained by combustion is added to that obtained before. For the superposition of rockets, which so far as I know, was suggested by Prof Goddard of Worcester, Mass., for the first time in scientific literature, the name 'step principle' has been adopted."

He said one rocket could be carried on top of another, so that when the base rocket's fuel was exhausted, it could be jettisoned and the rocket engines of the upper 'step' ignited. Oberth said he had investigated this process in a confidential report of 37 pages entitled On the Best Division of Step Aggregates and "in this connection, I should like to mention briefly that I have developed (in Vienna and Reinsdorf) a simple method for fastening rockets together, and easily separating them at the proper moment".

Skin temperature during the final phase of the missile's flight was likely to rise dramatically, he wrote, "in the case of the A-4, for example, the skin temperature after returning was 1200°C, while attaining a landing speed of 800-900m/sec".

Having made his calculations in 1941, Oberth apparently worked out that the largest explosive charge his missile could carry was 1.815 tons and "I said then that I considered the

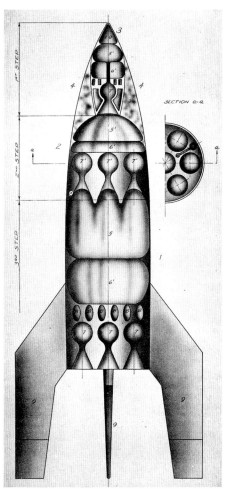

ABOVE: Hermann Oberth's Fern-Rakete of 1941 was effectively a multi-stage intercontinental missile intended for attacks on America.

design a failure, whereupon it was shelved".

On the design itself, illustrated with a picture of the missile, he wrote: "There is not much to say regarding this. I naturally don't remember all the individual details any more. The rocket should be about 4m thick, about 18m long without fins, and 20m with fins. (1) was the lower rocket, (2) the middle rocket, (3) the upper rocket. A fireproof cap (4) was placed over the upper step (3) and the middle step (2). Parachutes could be placed in the space between (3) and (4) in order to land the most important parts of the middle step, or tanks for liquids could be put there in case parachutes of the middle step burned during the test while landing.

"The lower step could be saved in the event that the individual parts fell apart after flight, and were landed by parachutes, which could be kept in the spaces under the tanks between the combustion chambers. The oxygen tanks are (5) and the tanks containing the alcoholic mixture of the three steps are (6). The combustion chambers are (7). I have designated the fuel pumps and fuel turbines as (8). The lower step should be held steady by means of find (9), and be controlled chiefly by control surfaces."

The explosive load was shown as (10). Oberth acknowledged that his design was probably not workable given the technology available in 1941, but the idea of firing huge multi-stage missiles at America from Nazi Germany must have been quite appealing when the Americans finally joined the war in December of that year.

▶

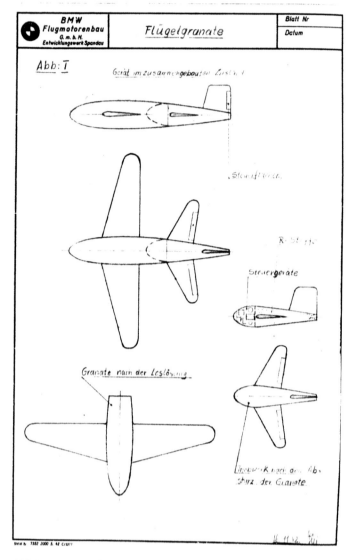

ABOVE: The BMW Flügelgranate was an ingenious two-stage weapon which could separate in mid-air, with the valuable control mechanism housed in the tail being returned to base despite the destruction of the bomb-carrying forward section.

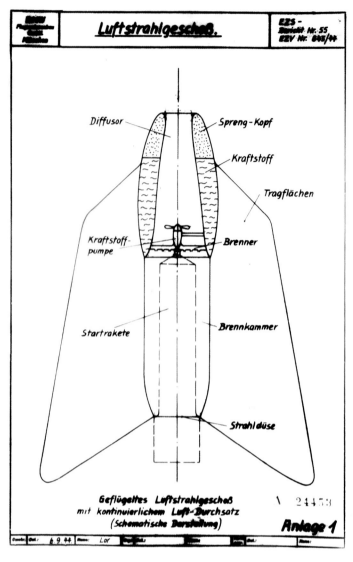

ABOVE: BMW's Luftstrahlgeschoss was an attempt to produce a weapon similar in destructive effect to a V-2 but powered by a ramjet.

BMW FLÜGELGRANATE

On November 16, 1942, BMW Ingenieur Friedrich Fleischhauer came up with a design he called the Flügelgranate or 'Winged Grenade'. This was essentially a complex two-part flying bomb. With both parts joined together, the Flügelgranate resembled a full-scale unmanned aircraft with wings and an almost conventional tail. When the aircraft was over its target, the forward section would detach and crash down on to it. Meanwhile, the rear section, containing the valuable guidance system, would remain airborne, turn itself around and fly back to base.

His patent application for this innovative design, which referenced a 1923 patent for 'improvements in or relating to wireless controlled aircraft' by Elmer Ambrose Sperry and a 1924 patent by the Sperry Gyroscope Company for 'improvements relating to wireless control systems for aeroplanes and like aircraft' was entitled 'return of the control units of self- or remote-controlled projectiles'.

Under 'invention description', he wrote: "One known effective means for delivering large quantities of explosive over substantial distances is the use of winged

grenades, which have either received an initial speed by catapulting and with this help can cover a larger distance or are self-propelled. To achieve good results such grenades are usually equipped with quite valuable control devices.

"In the usual execution of the grenades, these devices are destroyed with the entire control mechanism in the explosion of the grenade. The high consumption of valuable instruments in this case would represent a bottleneck in mass deployment of such grenades. In order to avoid this, according to the invention, the entire control system is to be accommodated in a unit detachable from the grenade, which can be separated from the grenade at a desired time and, by using the existing control system can be returned to the starting point.

"The detachment of the grenade above the target can be done by explosive bolt or mechanical release device, which can be triggered by means of the remote control. Simultaneously with this, the vehicle's remaining thrust can be used to return the control unit. The change of centre of gravity after the release of the control carrier leads to the crash of the grenade and thus to the impact in the target.

"To check the hit, it is also possible to incorporate a photo device in the control panel, which is operated in the moment of the crash and photographically captures the explosive effect of the grenade in the target. The idea of the invention has the same validity also in the case of a wingless grenade equipped only with tails. Also there, the tail can house the controller as a self-contained, traceable unit."

As a final note, after outlining exactly what he was claiming, Fleischhauer wrote: "The invention arose by my own consideration during the employment with me by my group leader, Dipl.-Ing. Schwinge, who assigned me the task: 'Investigation of range, fuel consumption and aerodynamic quality of grenades'."

Like Daimler-Benz, BMW seems to have frequently dabbled in the design of various aircraft and other devices which went beyond its remit as a renowned engine manufacturer. Fleischhauer's Flügelgranate sits alongside the various BMW jet fighter and bomber designs as an unusual expression of the company's willingness to diversify. Whether the Flügelgranate would actually have worked in practice will never be known but it appears to rank alongside many other early 'drones' being developed at this time.

Not only could the Flügelgranate, as envisioned, fly to its target and drop its payload, it could also take a photograph after the fact to allow its controllers to assess the damage afterwards. Presumably the Flügelgranate's usefulness would be limited to line-of-sight operations and its radio-control system would no doubt have been susceptible to jamming, but the fact that BMW felt it was worth patenting suggests that there was some confidence in the prospect of the technology it embodied, or something like it, one day becoming a practical reality. Which it has.

BMW LUFTSTRAHLGESCHOSS

The longer the war went on, the further BMW seems to have diversified its interests. On September 14, 1944, three of the company's engineers – Huber, Stolzinger and Wendler – produced a report entitled Das Strahlrohr als Geschossantrieb or 'The ramjet as projectile propulsion'. The sort of projectiles they outlined were effectively ground-launched flying bombs in the same vein as the V-1.

However, despite having produced a report on ramjet-powered missiles, they seem to have been curiously unpersuaded as to the benefits of their own invention. Their report begins: "For suitable applications, the transition from the artillery projectile to the powered projectile provides significant benefits in terms of firepower. However, in the case of large firing ranges, the effort is also greatly increased. In particular, the ratio of amount of propellant to quantity of explosive carried rapidly increases to undesirably high levels, with the procurement of fuels becoming a problem."

So when it came to an unpowered gun-fired artillery shell versus a powered missile, fuel was likely to be a problem for the latter – although it was noted that a ramjet could utilise alcohol or gasoline for fuel rather than requiring jet fuel. But it didn't end there. The three engineers wrote: "The ramjet is basically usable for the propulsion of projectiles, but it has the following serious disadvantages compared to the rocket: 1) Strong dependence on air condition and speed, so poor suitability for different heights, climbing and accelerating. 2) Need for propulsion aids at the start. The apparent advantage of just a simple fuel is therefore not fully available. 3) At supersonic velocities small problems in control will be magnified. 4) Due to the above reasons, the projectile must have rather large wings and can only be used against surface targets or with remote control. Defence against aircraft is not impossible, but the wind influence is significant."

The main advantage of ramjet-powered missiles was their relative cheapness and the long ranges they could travel, "however, the considered ramjet projectile is not suitable for replacing the artillery or missile projectile in any way. In general, given the application of the air condition and speed, independent rocket propulsion for missiles seems more appropriate where

the range demand permits, while for long ranges the winged subsonic ramjet missile can be used to advantage."

Being fuelled by alcohol or gasoline meant that "in contrast to the oxygen carriers required for the rocket-drive, there are no special requirements for handling and storage. In addition, the consumption is much lower than in rocket propulsion, since the oxygen required for combustion is taken from the ambient air. However, the drive has a much higher air resistance, so that the conditions are much less favourable when demanding high speeds.

"There is probably a certain range above which the slow-flying ramjet is superior to the rocket, while in the field of smaller shots the rocket propulsion, in many cases with solid propellants, will be preferable. Here are similar conditions, as in the drive issue for fast aircraft, where you are in many cases going to prefer the engine with higher consumption due to resistance advantages and better high-speed suitability.

"However, considerations based on the procurement situation and the manufacturing effort for the fuels can considerably shift the application limit."

The report outlines the workings of a ramjet – the projectile would need to be brought up to speed by some other means before the ramjet itself could be ignited and powered by air literally being rammed into the intake for its combustion chamber by its own forward motion. The missile proposed by BMW would effectively be little more than a ramjet with wings attached "whose shape and size depends on the intended airspeed and should allow the projectile a stable flight in the intended direction and height. For larger firing ranges, these areas can be provided with control devices for independent course control or remote steering. The associated devices are then also to be accommodated in the diffuser jacket".

The explosive charge could be housed either in the area around the intake or within a centrebody in the intake. The fuel would also be housed in a thin layer of bodywork around the ramjet and "to avoid unwanted shifting of the tank contents, one could imagine that the tank space is completely or partially filled by a suitable sponge or foam body, from which the fuel is forced out by evaporation".

Another alternative mentioned would be to fit the warhead with its own booster rocket, which could then separate from the ramjet once the latter's fuel was spent. But "in all cases, one will also use a launch rocket centrally located in the interior of the core, which brings the entire projectile at the intended altitude and airspeed and is then ejected to the rear. This is necessary because the ramjet used does not provide thrust when stationary".

In operation, the BMW Luftstrahlgeschoss would be launched down a ski-jump style slope: "Starting the jet projectile in the manner of an aircraft with relatively small additional thrusts seems inappropriate because of the long take-off distance. The best method of firing is probably the following: the projectile is shot

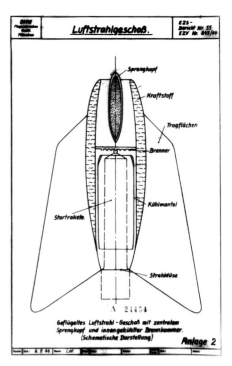

ABOVE: A second version of the BMW Luftstrahlgeschoss with the explosive charge positioned in the intake as a centrebody.

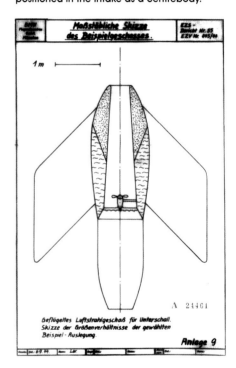

ABOVE: Third version of the Luftstrahlgeschoss with wings intended specifically for subsonic flight.

down a short, thrower-like slide at an angle of about 45. The starting thrust is provided by one or more normal-type powder missiles of about 10 tons overall thrust. Required is a speed of 200m/sec at 1km altitude."

Again, the nature of the weapon being considered by BMW in the autumn of 1944 speaks volumes about Germany's fortunes at this point in the war – fuel shortages were forcing a reappraisal of less attractive means of propulsion such as the cheap but problematic ramjet. Although rockets were deemed preferable, the war situation meant they were beginning to become impractical when it came to expendable weapons. •

Blowing off steam

Heinkel P 1076

At first glance it might look like a relatively conventional piston-engined fighter but on closer examination it becomes apparent that Heinkel's P 1076 was anything but ordinary – with its innovative steam cooling system, contra-rotating prop, offset engine and forward-swept wings.

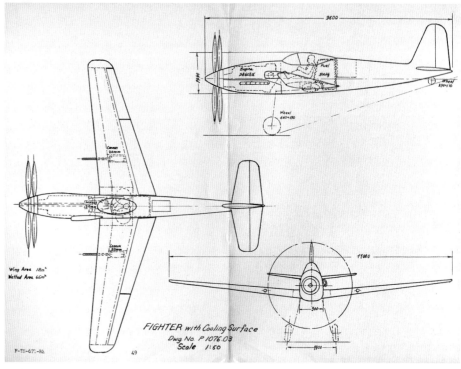

ABOVE: Simple three-view drawing of Heinkel's P 1076 – note the deliberately slightly off-centre position of the engine.

As the Soviets began to surround Vienna in early April 1945, the Heinkel design team based there made a hurried retreat westwards, led by chief designer Siegfried Günter. The 35-strong group surrendered to the Americans and were installed together in a small office at Penzing airfield near Landsberg, west of Munich.

Almost all of their files and drawings had been left behind – to be destroyed or captured by the Russians – so they set about recreating the drawings and reports relating to their final six projects. It is unclear whether this was a result of American pressure to retrieve the projects or, as Ernst Heinkel himself later concluded in his autobiography, a result of Günter's sheer determination to continue his precious work. The chronologically earliest of these 're-creations', dating from mid-1944, was a series of studies related to developments of the He 162 single-jet fighter, originally given the project number P 1073 but included in this final round of design work due to the number

of promising lines of research arising from it.

The other five projects were P 1077, the rocket-propelled interceptor usually referred to as 'Julia' by Heinkel itself; P 1078, the single-jet fighter design which succeeded the He 162 in the late war 1-TL-Jäger competition; Heinkel's entry for the twin-jet night fighter competition, the P 1079; the sketchy and underdeveloped P 1080 ramjet fighter and the piston-engined P 1076 fighter.

The earliest known drawing of the P 1076 comes from a brief outline report completed at Penzing on or around July 23, 1945. This includes brief details and dimensions of five of the six projects, excluding the P 1080, with the drawing of the P 1076 itself having been completed after those of all the others. A full report on the design, in German, was completed on August 31, 1945, and signed by its authors Heerdt and Hohbach, with Günter also signing as their supervisor. A full and direct

translation into English was eventually issued as T-2 report F-TS-671-RE in October 1946.

It begins: "Orders of the RLM. In the beginning of 1945 RLM asked for a project of a very fast single seater fighter with internal combustion engine. RLM preferred projects with pusher propeller similar to the rear driven Do 335. Our numerous projects showed the following: the weight of the airplane with pusher propeller becomes heavier than with tractor propeller because of the following: Nearly 180kg for the long propeller shaft. To obtain the proper centre of gravity a long fuselage is needed, meaning more weight and more resistance. More weight for the necessary nosewheel and for strengthening the lower fin for landing forces. Perhaps 10% more weight means also a 10% larger wing area. We do not believe that the gain of propeller efficiency compensates the weight difference.

"We also believe that the pusher propeller

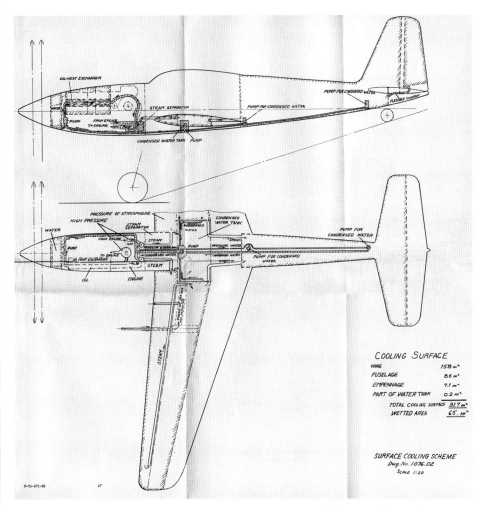

Labels in diagram (top): OIL HEAT EXCHANGER, STEAM SEPARATOR, PUMP FOR CONDENSED WATER, PUMP FOR CONDENSED WATER, FLEXIBLE CONDUIT, PUMP TO ENGINE, CONDENSED WATER TANK, PUMP

Labels (lower): PRESSURE OF ATMOSPHERE, HIGH PRESSURE, STEAM SEPARATOR, CONDENSED WATER TANK, WATER, FROM ENGINE, STEAM, PUMP, PUMP, STEAM, PUMP FOR CONDENSED WATER, TO ENGINE, CONDENSED WATER, PUMP FOR CONDENSED WATER, OIL HEAT EXCHANGER, STEAM, OIL, ENGINE, STEAM

PART OF WATER TANK

COOLING SURFACE

WING	15.8 m²
FUSELAGE	8.6 m²
EMPENNAGE	7.1 m²
PART OF WATER TANK	0.2 m²
TOTAL COOLING SURFACE	31.7 m²
WETTED AREA	65. m²

SURFACE COOLING SCHEME
Dwg. No. 1076.02
SCALE 1:20

ABOVE: Diagram showing how the P 1076's elaborate and unusual steam cooling system was intended to work.

improves performances only of tailless airplanes. We did not decide on this type of airplane because in our opinion the tailless airplane is only possible with a counter rotating propeller which would perhaps be available and then at a later date.

"The control of the angle of attack before take-off would also be difficult because of a high landing gear. It seemed best to us for the purpose of home defence to rely on our experiences with the He 100."

This appears to overtly state that the RLM issued a requirement for a high-speed piston-engined fighter in early 1945, yet the P 1077 'Julia' dated from October 1944, if not earlier, and Heinkel's project numbering was chronological, which suggests that the P 1076 dated from earlier still. So what were its competitors? The paragraphs above would tend to suggest that whatever they were, they used the pusher propeller layout that the RLM 'preferred' since Heinkel is at pains to reject this arrangement.

One explanation might be the little-known and even less well understood Hochleistungsjäger competition of mid-to-late 1944 (see also p36-41). This appears to have been loosely contemporaneous with the 1-TL-Jäger competition but was intended to produce a fast piston-engined fighter rather than a jet. A Focke-Wulf report on the Hochleistungsjäger design comparison conference held on September 18-20, 1944, shows three entries for the contest – one from Focke-Wulf itself, one from Dornier and one from Blohm & Voss. All were to

be powered by the Jumo 222 E/F driving a pusher prop. The latter was certainly working on a Jumo 222 E/F powered fighter in late 1944 in the form of its P 207. Focke-Wulf's entry was known simply as the Hochleistungsjäger and Dornier's entry does not appear to match any known design. Blohm & Voss followed up the P 207 with the P 208, which was powered by a DB 603 N.

It is not inconceivable that Heinkel designed the P 1076 in 1944 to 'shadow' the Hochleistungsjäger competition, then pitched it as a full entry during the early part of 1945.

The P 1076 report gives an explanation of how it was inspired by the He 100 – a monoplane piston-engine fighter design dating from the late 1930s, which made its first flight on January 24, 1938. This aircraft was able to achieve remarkable speeds for its time by doing away with a drag-inducing radiator and using an internal evaporative cooling system instead. This involved piping the water coolant, heated into steam by the He 100's running DB 601 engine, out on to the wings where it would rapidly condense back into water and would then be electrically pumped back into the engine.

The report states: "Experiences with the He 100. The airplane (first flight 24.1.38) with wing area 14.5sqm and DB 601 A with 1000hp at 5000m altitude, with armament, attained a speed of 690km/h which was over 100km/h faster than the Me 109 with the same engine. The steam cooling worked well.

"However, the cooling system was still somewhat more complex than desired

particularly because of the oil system alcohol heat exchanger. At the time it was decided that a faster airplane than Me 109 would not be needed for the next few years and an order for a faster airplane would be given later on. Even if it would be slower, the decision was to first build a single-seater fighter with an air-cooled engine (Fw 190). Moreover in 1939 RLM already was of the opinion that the development of a new propeller fighter would be outdated by new turbojet fighters (280/262) on order at that time (the He 100 with a slightly smaller wing (11sqm) and 1800hp made a record fight of 746km/h near sea level).

"The advantages of steam cooling in addition to reduction of drag: automatic temperature control for both water and oil without thermostat and any moving parts; very rapid heating of the oil after starting; de-icing of leading edge is positive. The water loss with battle damage is not rapid because the steam is at outside atmospheric pressure. Further, the loss of condensed water is decreased by spanwise structural members, or added pieces, that are riveted to the skin such as hat, angle, etc. stringers. For home defence this damage is of little consequence as it is possible to reach an airfield after sustaining several hits. Spare water which will be consumed can be carried in lieu of the weight of the conventional cooling system.

"The Heinkel firm did not offer the He 100 again at a later date because the cooling surface was too small for increased engine power."

This explanation of why the He 100 was never put into full production – because the Luftwaffe would not need a faster fighter for several years, and the He 280/Me 262 was the future of fighters anyway – appears somewhat doubtful, while the note about the system's complexity seems to offer a more likely explanation. The report also says: "The first construction of surface cooling had a double skin cooling cell scheme. The disadvantages were wrinkling of the skin with heat, rough wing surface and high steam pressures because the cells were too narrow, and the steam and condensed water piping were complicated. The tight riveting of the wing structure, which later on has been used for the He 100 and He 119, proved to be a simple and good construction and was therefore chosen for the P 1076." But whereas the He 100 had a 1000hp engine to cool, the new project would be equipped with a 2100hp DB 603 LM, requiring some substantial modifications to the original design: "Improvements beyond the He 100. To reach higher speeds than the He 100 it is necessary to considerably increase the cooling surface area. This increase is accomplished by: placing the fuel tanks in the fuselage instead of the wings as formerly done; new landing gear; using the whole aft part of the fuselage, stabiliser, fin, rudder and the side of the oil tank surface next to the airstream for cooling. This, together with the somewhat greater dimensions of the airplane, gives 2.3 times the cooling surface of the He 100.

"The water cooling system is made more dependable by the use of the already tested injector type water pump rather than the formerly used electric driven membrane type pump which failed due to short circuits. ▶

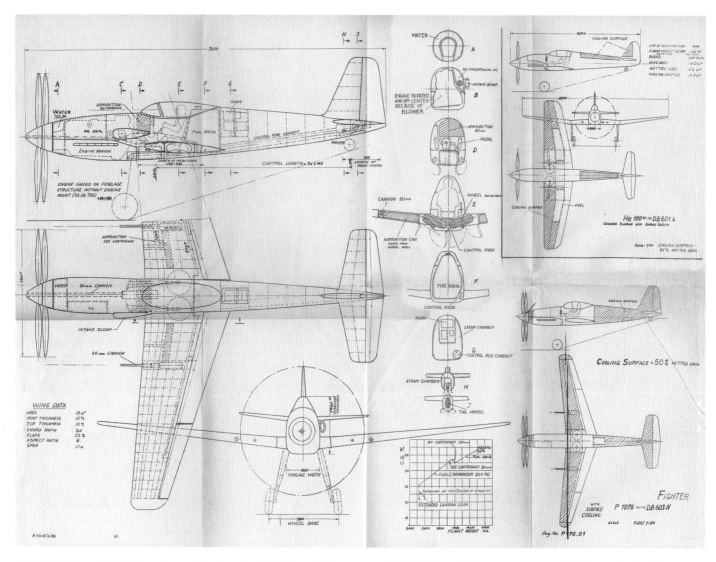

ABOVE: This huge drawing from the original postwar P 1076 report shows a wealth of detail, including a comparison with the earlier He 100.

The wing dihedral simplifies the collection of condensed steam and reduces the number of pumps to three in the fuselage. The oil cooling of the Jumo 213 by water indicated the way to considerably simplify oil cooling. Because the separator is at atmospheric pressure, the temperature of the condensed steam is low enough to cool the oil. All cooling water first passes through the oil cooler before going to the engine.

"The He 100 engine was hung directly on the extended fuselage structure in order to save weight and space. This proven design adds the possibility of incorporating the oil tank in the extended structure. As the oil heat exchange takes place in the combination tank-cooler, piping is simplified. It would be best to place this unit in the system between the existing engine water pump and the engine, but this would require a minor modification of the engine."

The report notes that the cooling surface area had been increased from 25% on the He 100 to 49% of the entire surface for the P 1076. In fact, "the total increase of cooling surface is 127% due to the somewhat larger airplane".

This cooling system was ideal for level flight and relatively sedate manoeuvring, but during a fast climb the Heinkel team admitted that it would not be entirely effective: "During climbing, especially for emergency output, the total heat of the engine cannot

be transmitted by the cooling surface. To provide sufficient cooling for take-off and best rate of climb with full throttle and for compensating steam losses in case of hits, we have provided 150kg of cooling water."

Slacking off the throttle just a little, however, or reducing the rate of climb would help to moderate the use of valuable coolant: "With an unimportant reduction of rate of climb the cooling water consumption can be greatly diminished or almost totally avoided. In the most unfavourable case, for emergency output (permissible for only five minutes), and for the speed of the best rate of climb at 7km to 10km altitude, 4kg per minute cooling water is used.

"This quantity can be diminished by 2kg per minute by an unimportant reduction in the rate of climb, for example, 10% at 9km altitude, the most unfavourable altitude. During the best rate of climb with combat power and injection of methanol-water MW50, 2kg per minute of cooling water is used in 7km to 10km altitude. With a little reduction of rate of climb (10%) at the most unfavourable altitude of 9km, for example, cooling water consumption can be totally avoided."

The aircraft's propeller type was also dictated by the installation of a DB 603 LM: "Another very desirable improvement for single seater fighters with powerful engines would be a counter rotating propeller

because the great torque is dangerous if full throttle is applied at low speeds after a poor landing approach. A counter rotating propeller unit with a hollow shaft (for 30mm, MK 103, engine shaft cannon) was under construction at VDM. Without a counter rotating propeller it would be best to take a not too large diameter propeller with higher rpm and not use high manifold pressures at low speeds as, at low speeds, no greater thrust can be given by high manifold pressures than with medium pressures."

The Heinkel team noted that drag from the DB 603 LM's air scoop had been taken into account when making performance calculations and that the greatest possible diameter for the type's propellers would be 3.3m. Evidently "the breadth of the blades was chosen as a good compromise between fast level flight and best climbing speed for emergency output at the rated altitude of 10.8km. Therefore a blade breadth of 10% of the diameter at 0.7 radius was chosen. Regarding the high flight speed and the Mach number resulting from flight speed and tip speed of the propeller, the thickness of the profile at 0.7 radius was fixed at 5%".

As if the DB 603 LM was not enough, a second and much more powerful version of the engine was also considered for installation. The report states: "Variation of the project P 1076 by using the 3000hp engine DB 603 N.

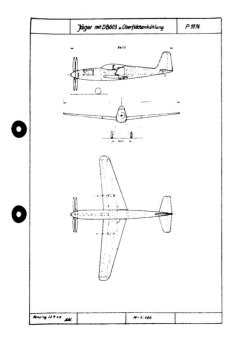

ABOVE: July 23, 1945 sketch of the P 1076 from an early report compiled by the Heinkel team at Penzing. For years, this appears to have been the only known contemporary depiction of the design.

In March 1945 Daimler-Benz promised in a letter to develop further the DB 603 LM (2100hp) with nearly the same overall dimensions. This engine, DB 603 N, would attain an emergency output of 3000hp by increasing the speed and the blower pressure.

"The question is now how the single seater fighter P 1076 is to be designed if we take the 3000hp engine instead of the 2100hp engine.

The condition is that the new airplane has to transmit at least the same part of the engine heat by surface cooling. Therefore, the cooling surface must be increased by 40%.

"The project with the 2100hp engine at the rated altitude of 10.8km with emergency output has a horizontal maximum speed (855km/h), which is nearly the same as the critical speed where the steep increase of resistance begins. The further gain of speed by greater engine power would be unimportant for this type of airplane. Therefore, the dimensions of the airplane could be larger without considerable loss of speed, and with larger dimensions we also get the necessary cooling surface.

"A part of the increased drag is due to the necessary enlarging of the fuselage (14% of the linear dimensions) because the airplane needs 48% more gasoline than before for the same endurance. By this the drag of the fuselage increases 30%. With an enlargement of the wing area to 26sqm and by including the tail surface, the cooling surface is increased by the same ratio of heat increase. With the same flight endurance and military load the more powerful engine attains a considerably greater rate of climb. However, the gain of speed is unimportant."

In terms of armament, the report text only mentions a single MK 103 30mm cannon mounted within the engine, firing through the spinner. However, the drawings show an additional pair of MG 151 20mm cannon - one in each wing - with space around the gun barrels for cooling air to enter the wing plus a small extra inlet for still more cool air to prevent overheating of the guns themselves and their ammunition.

It is interesting that what has appeared in modern works to date concerning the P 1076 seems to have been written without the benefit of the final report, which must surely represent the last word on the project. Details shown elsewhere are sketchy and the only previously known drawing appears to be the one shown in the July 1945 report. One modern account suggests a choice of three engines - the DB 603 M, Jumo 213 E or DB 603 N. There may be some truth in the inclusion of the Jumo 213, since the July 1945 report does mention it as an alternative engine alongside the 'DB 603', even though the final report only mentions it in passing. One aspect of the design missing from all modern accounts is the rotated position of the engine, which results in the propeller actually being slightly offset from the aircraft's centreline and giving the aircraft a slightly 'bent' look, particularly when seen from above.

Armament is generally given as an MK 103 and two 30mm MK 108s but this seems to be a simple inaccuracy - perhaps resulting from close study of the July 1945 report drawing and guesswork. One particularly outlandish article has suggested that the P 1076 might have been fitted with the DB 609 - a design which was cancelled in 1943.

Had it been built, and had the necessary engines also been built, the P 1076 might potentially have ranked among the world's most powerful piston-engine aircraft. But the 'simple' cooling system developed by Heinkel still seems rather complex and Daimler-Benz's claimed output figures for its engines seem rather high. Even in the most favourable circumstances, the two companies would still have struggled to make it work as planned. ●

AIR CRAFT DATA

Hersteller:			Heinkel		
Baumuster	162	Julia	P 1076	P 1078	P 1079
Bauform:	Schulterdecker	Hochdecker	Tiefdecker	Schwanzlos	Mitteldecker
Bauart:	M.tall-Holz	Holz	Metall	Metall-Holz	Metall-Holz
Verwendungszweck:	Jäger	Jäger (Senkrecht.)	Jäger	Jäger	Nacht j.Zers
Motoren:	BMW 003;HeS 11	Walter-Rakete	DB 603;Jumo 213	HeS 11	HeS 11
Besatzung:	1	1	1	1	2(3)
Besondere Merkmale:		Pulver-Startraketen			
Abmesungen:					
Spannweite (m)	7.20 | 8.00	4.60	11.00	9.00	13.00
Länge, größte (m)	9.05	6.74	9.60	6.00(Rumpf5,0)	14.00
Höhe, größte (m)	2.55	1.00	2.90	2.40	3.40
Radspur (m)	1.50	Kufe	1.90	2.00	2.60
Bereifungsart					
Reifengrösse (mm)	660 x 190	-	660 x 190	740 x 210	1015 x 380
Radbremse					
Bugradgrösse (mm)	380 x 150	-	290 x 110(3porn)	465 x 165	770 x 270
Inhalt d.Kraftstoffbehälters(L)	1310 | 1530	900	700	1500	4000
Inhalt d.Schmierstoffbehälters (L)	-	-	70	-	-

ABOVE: Data on five of the final six Heinkel projects compiled for the Americans. The only one missing is the P 1080 ramjet fighter.

Heinkel P 1076

Late 1944 (see p76-79)

Artwork by Luca Landino

COMMENTS

Forward-swept wings, contra-rotating propellers and an engine slightly offset to one side are the key visual features of the P 1076. What's not so visible is the advanced steam cooling system hidden just beneath the skin of its fuselage and wings.

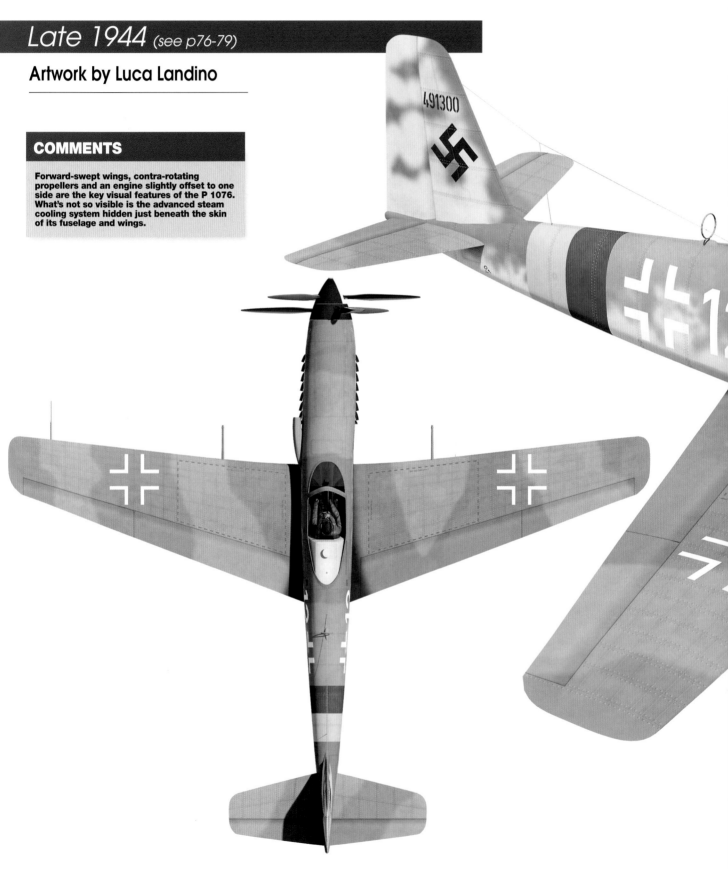

491300

Only memories

Hs P 75 *(Juli 194*

Henschel projects

Thanks to the Russians seizing its Berlin headquarters on April 22, 1945, and destroying or taking away almost all of its documents, the British and Americans knew very little for certain about the advanced aircraft projects worked on by Henschel during the war. What they did know came from an authoritative source, however...

ABOVE: Factory model of the Henschel P 75, the photograph of which was glued into Friedrich Nicolaus's post-war report. The date is partially cropped off in the original but according to Nicolaus it was 1941.

Berlin may have fallen and with it the Henschel factory at Schönefeld but the company's chief designer Friedrich Nicolaus was captured by the British. At some time during the next 18 months he compiled a report entitled Bericht über die Entwicklung der Henschel Flugzeugwerke or 'Report on the Development of the Henschel Aircraft Works' for the Ministry of Aircraft Production (MAP).

MAP was merged into the Ministry of Supply (MOS) in April 1946 and Nicolaus's report was finally published by the MOS as Reports and Translations No. 730, Reports and Monographs list XIII,36 in October 1946.

Almost everything that is known today about Henschel's projects comes directly from this 49-page document, which includes a total of 22 glued-in photographs and seven drawings. Some of Nicolaus's words sound oddly familiar, having appeared elsewhere, while other aspects of the report appear never to have been seen before or else were ignored in other accounts.

While some of the report refers to types that were actually built, such as the Hs 121-130, it also makes reference to a number of projects. Some of these are referred to by their official designation – the Hs 132 jet dive bomber, P 75 tail-first aircraft, P 130 piston engine fighter, P 135 jet fighter and P 136 rocket-powered fighter – but others are merely listed and their features described without a designation being given. Some Henschel projects that are known of aren't on that list – the P 87 and P 90 tail-first aircraft and the P 122 tailless twin-jet aircraft. These do seem as though they might match up to some of the unnamed projects, but others are previously unknown.

At the beginning Nicolaus states: "Preliminary remarks: The report could only be kept to a condensed form as a result of the circumstances. The records and sketches are made according to memory, since all files and drawings were destroyed or removed. Only a few photos were available. Numbers were only given where they

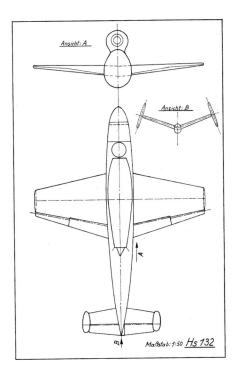

ABOVE: The Hs 132 single-jet ground attack aircraft as it is depicted in Nicolaus's report. The fuselage cross-section here is not oval and the twin-fins on the V-tail are small.

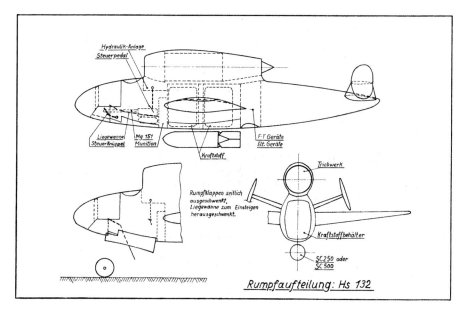

ABOVE: Side views of the Henschel Hs 132 from the postwar report.

could be binding. Value judgments are only made from the military point of view."

He then divides the report up into six sections: introduction, aircraft used at the front, aircraft for use at the front that were under development, experimental aircraft, selected projects and comments on what development programmes he envisions going forward, adding: "If one or the other is of interest, we will try to supplement the explanations."

The introduction outlines the company's background – founded in 1933, making it the youngest of the major players, and lavishly funded thanks to its association with the vast Henschel family industrial empire. Apparently, "as a new firm, the company was not welcomed by the RLM, and was initially regarded by the rest of the industry with strong jealousy".

However, the company managed to attract sufficient contracts to make it a viable proposition and carved out a niche building other firms' aircraft in large quantities while working on less lucrative projects of its own – particularly specialised ground-attack types such as the Hs 123 and Hs 129, and high-altitude aircraft such as the Hs 128 and Hs 130.

This specialisation would ultimately lead to Henschel designing the prone-pilot pressure cabin for the rocket-propelled DFS 228 high-altitude research aircraft and a prone-pilot jet-propelled ground-attack aircraft, the Hs 132. The latter is explained in some detail.

HENSCHEL HS 132
Nicolaus writes: "The dive attack with the Hs 123, Ju 87, and later Ju 88, which had been carried out at the beginning of the war with great success, had come very much to a degree of disrepute because of the increased ground defence at the front.

"However, the good prospects that were to be expected in the dive attack made it desirable to resume this type of attack by modern means. Thus, the task was as follows: a large horizontal speed, the greatest dive speed as close as possible to the target, the smallest intercepting radii, the smallest dimensions of the aircraft, restriction in payload, range and weaponry and maximum protection of the pilot. The Hs 132 was created from these conditions.

"Hull: light metal construction, pilot on his belly lying in the tip of the fuselage, protected against bombardment by a large, 75mm thick disc of armoured glass, extended by an armour plate (15mm), a couch pressed out of armour (8mm). The cabin opened downwards as a normal entry and exit opening and as an emergency exit in the air. This also provides the best protection for belly landings, with an opening on the upper side serving as an emergency exit in this case. The two fuel tanks, which were provided with heavy rubber protection, were protected to the rear."

The aircraft was to be built mainly of wood and steel, with the use of light alloy kept to a minimum. Steel and wooden components were to be joined by an "intermediate layer" of glued dural and wood, which was to be riveted to the steel part and glued to the wooden part. According to Nicolaus: "The direct gluing of steel with wood was sought but was not yet reliable enough."

Flaps and ailerons were to be made using a "new construction (corrugated wood)". The wings themselves were to have a very smooth plywood skin similar to that of the He 162.

A V-tail with end-plate rudders was to be fitted which were to be made entirely of wood. The engine, lying on the back of the aircraft, was to be either a BMW 003 or Jumo 004 with the HeS 011 replacing whichever was chosen when it became available. The position of the engine would give it an "easy-to-clean air inlet" and an "exhaust jet free from the fuselage via the blower". In addition to the fuselage fuel tanks, the wing roots would also be designed to house

an additional unprotected tank each.

The hydraulically actuated undercarriage was a tricycle arrangement and the main legs were to be of "very wide gauge", folding into the wing roots. The nosewheel at the forward tip of the fuselage turned sideways while retracting to lie flat under the pilot's legs.

Equipment was to be "normal fighter equipment with regard to flight and engine control, location, radio etc." while armament varied according to the engine fitted. With a BMW 003, it would feature just two MG 151 cannon with 250 rounds each, plus a bomb load totalling 1250kg or 1500kg under the fuselage. The greater thrust provided by the HeS 011 however, would

ABOVE: The cover of a Henschel brochure for the Hs 132.

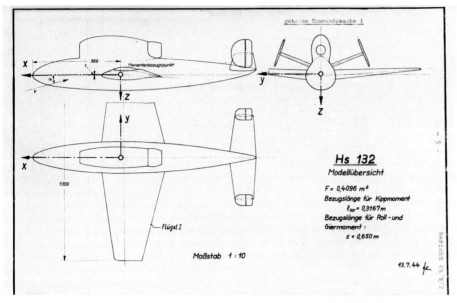

ABOVE: The AVA reported on wind tunnel tests of the Hs 132 on January 20, 1945. At this point the design had an oval cross-section and large twin-fin plates, suggesting that either the postwar report's design was simply an approximation or that the design had changed by April 1945.

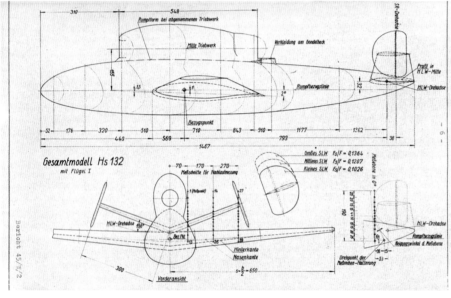

ABOVE: Another drawing of the Hs 132 model tested by the AVA.

allow for four MG 151s with 250 rounds each and a bomb load of 1500kg or 2000kg.

The aircraft's "safe dive speed" was to be 950km/h (590mph). Top speed in level flight with a BMW 003 was to be a relatively meagre 650km/h (403mph) carrying a 500kg bomb load, or 780km/h (484mph) without the bombs. With a HeS 011 the only figure given is for level flight without a bomb load – 830km/h (515mph).

Nicolaus continues: "In construction were three prototypes, of which the first was to make a flight test at the beginning of May 1945. The completion had been delayed by relocation of the construction office to Silesia and bomb damage to sub-contractors. Preparations for the start of the series were made."

DFS 228

On the DFS 228, listed under 'partial developments', Nicolaus writes: "On occasion, we were entrusted with urgent tasks by the RLM for the exploitation of our special experiences ... for other companies.

A not very large but constructively very interesting task was, in 1944, a commission to find a better solution for the pilot cabin of the DFS 228 in construction, visibility, and safety. The DFS 228 was designed as a high-altitude reconnaissance aircraft.

"It was to be towed as high as possible, then reach its maximum ceiling by means of a Walter rocket drive, then glide as flat as possible, again reach the now larger peak height by briefly switching on the drive, and so on again. Heights of up to 25km were expected. Our solution, which came to work, was: a prone arrangement of the pilot, similar to Hs 132, without armoured glass of course, which gave a clear view of the task at hand."

He then explains how the pressure cabin was to be fixed on to the completed fuselage of the DFS 228 and the parachute escape mechanism, oxygen and air conditioning systems worked, and how there was "protection from fogging of the viewing windows by double discs with silica gel cartridges". Evidently "the first cabin of a small series had just

been finished at the end of the war".

Incidentally, Henschel's part in the development of the DFS 228 seems to have been almost completely overlooked. The aircraft's designer Felix Kracht is generally given credit for the DFS 228 V2's prone pilot pressure cabin – the V1 had a normal seated pilot position.

MAJOR PROJECTS

After sections concerning Henschel's work on the Jumo 222 engine, a late-war heavy fighter version of the Ju 88/188 and numerous experimental aircraft – particularly the Hs 130 series – the next section of Nicolaus's report concerns pure project work, rather than designs that had been or were being built.

He writes: "Our project work has always been very active. My ambition was to provide myself with a permanent picture of the probable military and technical requirements and to put forward the corresponding development tasks (in retrospect, I can say that even without premonition our suggestions were always right).

"Although many at the RLM were aware of this, there was very little enthusiasm in this regard. The management of the Technical Office would only wait for the wishes of the General Staff. And they would come only with their wishes of the moment, when the military situation that the aircraft or the engine or the weapon etc. was needed for had already come about. The equipment of the front was thus decisively behind their real needs.

"In the following, I have only listed a few major projects, which we have worked on in at least detailed drafts and a detailed calculation of the performance. They are separated into themes and arranged in a chronological order."

The themes picked out by Nicolaus are: single-seat fighter with four projects, heavy fighter with three projects, ground-attack aircraft with five, bomber with three, battlefield reconnaissance with one, long-range reconnaissance with three, commercial or transport with four and special aircraft with five. A total of 28 projects, some with numbers given but most without.

SINGLE-SEAT FIGHTERS

The first project detailed is a fighter from 1938. According to Nicolaus: "Design concept: Concentration of all internals (e.g. weapons, fuel tanks) and aircraft parts which need special maintenance and therefore have access hatches, or have doors which open and close (e.g. undercarriage), in the fuselage, because these features cause unavoidable roughness and discontinuities of the surface, the area of which on the fuselage is less than that of the wing.

"Completely clean air surface, static structure undisturbed, so a large wing of low profile and with effective landing aids was made to improve the start, the landing and in particular the maximum altitude. To lower the landing gear and achieve a large angle of attack during landing, two design options: 1, rotating wing or 2, buckling of the fuselage tail similar to Hs 124. Drafts were largely

ABOVE: Photograph of the AVA-tested model of the Hs 132.

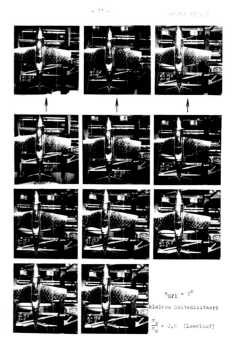

Gesamtmodell Hs 132 mit F)6ral 1

ABOVE: Evidently several subtly different wing and twin-fin shapes for the Hs 132 were tested by the AVA.

worked through. Despite the interest of the technical bodies there was no order, since the design deviated too far from the usual."

The second fighter project was the radical tail-first or 'canard' P 75, dated 1941. Today this is a relatively well-known design, but the version presented by Nicolaus differs significantly in having a vertical control surface on each wing rather than a single large fin on the aircraft's underside.

"Design concept: further development to aerodynamic cleanliness and thus reaching higher speeds while maintaining the control effect; possibility of accommodating large motor forces using opposing airscrews, at the same time improvement of the flying characteristics.

"Possibility to accommodate heavy weapons in the fuselage by means of a rear-facing motor in the central fuselage, since obstruction due to airscrews, which would otherwise be very large, would be eliminated.

"In the absence of a single, more powerful engine, the DB 603 twin-engine was to be used, as a side-by-side with gearbox,

as in He 177 A. Nose wheel gear. Wind tunnel tests with a central and a double lateral wing had been concluded with very favourable results and the drafts had been worked so far that the contracts could have been signed and work begun.

"Despite the advocacy of the technical bodies, the design was rejected on the grounds that 'the pilots could not get used to the fact that the propeller was at the rear and the tailplane was ahead'."

Two projects are then presented as tailless single-seat fighters – the P 130 and P 135, the date given for both being 1944/1945, since they were worked on in parallel.

"Design idea: Achievement of the best aerodynamic shape of all and thus with given driving power of the maximum achievable speeds. This makes it very difficult to minimize the incidence of changes in the centre of gravity and to keep reasonable landing speeds.

"Two paths were pursued simultaneously: 1) Proj 130: aircraft with gasoline engine, high-performance Jumo 213 and counter-

rotating airscrews in the rear, built-in cooler in the fuselage, air flow supported by injector effect of the exhaust. Position of the aircraft pilot is determined by careful inspections of the airflow with the utmost regard to the smallest frontal resistance, in view of the turning warfare and attack, the carrying out of large accelerations which occur when the aerodynamically possible narrow curves and radii of interception are utilised."

In other words, Henschel attempted to minimise the impact of g-forces on the pilot during the extreme manoeuvres of combat in highly manoeuvrable aircraft.

"For combat, the best arrangement was an almost supine position with slightly angled head, sitting half-erect for the journey. Emergency exit in flight by catapult seat and lateral discharge on the ground. Armament: 4 x MG 151 with 250 shots each, or rockets, or combination. For the additional bombs possible. Nose wheel gear. Central fin.

"Hs P 130 can be described as a powerful final solution of the piston-engine fighter. Compared to the jet fighter, it has the advantage of considerably better start and acceleration ratios and throttling ability, although by its very nature not reaching its top speed. It was expected to have a top speed of 820km/h. The project was very far-reaching, wind tunnel trials were prepared.

"The proposal found strongest interest in the Technical Office, but was not widely propagated by us, as the solution with jet engine (see below) seemed to us to be more viable."

No drawing of the P 130 appears to have survived. Nicolaus then describes the jet-powered P 135: "2) Hs Proj 135: aircraft with one jet engine, initially BMW 003, later HeS 011. Jet engine centrally arranged in the fuselage tail, straight cylindrical air supply from fuselage tip with lowest friction losses. Pilot arrangement as before with ▶

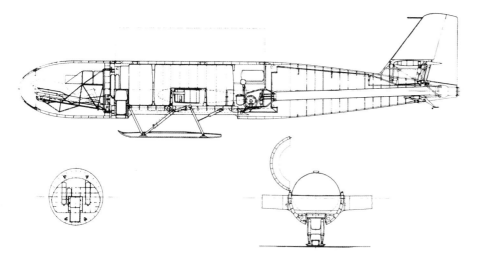

ABOVE: The DFS 228 high-altitude reconnaissance aircraft – with Henschel-designed prone pilot pressurised cockpit. Henschel thought little of the rest of the fuselage and had plans to marry the cockpit up with the fuselage of the P 135.

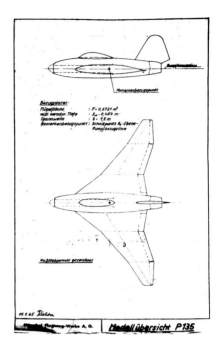

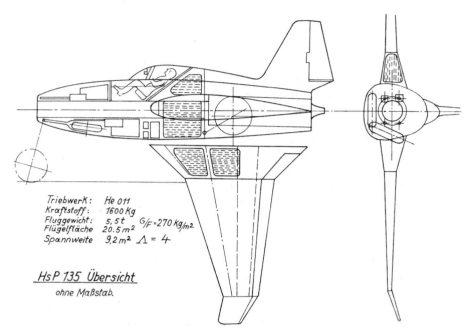

Triebwerk: He 011
Kraftstoff: 1600 Kg
Fluggewicht: 5,5 t   G/F = 270 Kg/m²
Flügelfläche 20.5 m²
Spannweite 9,2 m² Λ = 4

HsP 135 Übersicht
ohne Maßstab.

ABOVE: The Henschel P 135 as the design stood on January 11, 1945. As with the Hs 132 it seems the design changed between this point and the war's end.

ABOVE: The P 135 as shown in Nicolaus's report. Note the forward-swept wingtips.

the Hs P 130, armament the same. Nose wheel, gear only in the fuselage so that the wing smoothness was not disturbed.

"Wing with double kink, outer parts for the improvement of the rolling behaviour again kinked forward. The V-position of the outer parts should be adjustable in flight in the case of the prototype aircraft, in order to obtain the most favourable arrangement with respect to the design."

Top speed with the BMW 003 was expected to be 930km/h or 1010km/h with the HeS 011. Maximum ceiling with both was 14-15km (46,000-50,000ft).

Nicolaus concluded his summary of the P 135 with: "Large flight time due to strong throttling capability and good aerodynamics at high cruising speeds. Wind tunnel tests were concluded with very favourable results, the work advanced very far. The construction contract was expected."

It has been suggested that the P 135 was Henschel's entry for the 1-TL-Jäger competition to find a new single-jet fighter for the Luftwaffe – but that the entry was too late to be considered.

The competition began in July 1944, with an outline specification for a new single jet fighter. The first companies invited to supply designs to this specification were Messerschmitt, Focke-Wulf, Heinkel and Blohm & Voss. The spec was then refined with a new version issued on December 4, 1944. At this time, Messerschmitt, Focke-Wulf, Heinkel, Blohm & Voss and Junkers were invited to tender designs. Henschel was not included, nor was it invited. It was simply not a part of the formal competition.

However, according to the March 5 to March 15, 1945, section of the war diary of the Chef der Technische Luftrüstung or 'Head of Technical Air Force Armament', the office of General Ulrich Diesing, under the heading of '1 TL-Projekt': "FL-E required the following projects: 1) Junkers, B&V, and modified FW project. 2) Mtt.

Optimal solution. Recently, EHK proposed that in addition to 2) Fa. Henschel be used as a second solution for the optimal solution (based on the work of Dr Zobel)."

The outcome of the February 27-28 1-TL-Jäger meeting had been Focke-Wulf's Nr. 279 design being chosen as an 'immediate solution' and shortly thereafter awarded the designation Ta 183, with Messerschmitt's design, presumably the P 1111, being chosen as an 'optimal solution' for longer-term development. Now it appeared that Junkers' EF 128 design, the Blohm & Voss P 212 and the Ta 183 were all being regarded as 'immediate solutions' with Henschel being tacked on alongside Messerschmitt's fighter as a development for the future. Perhaps this was why Nicolaus was so confident that the P 135 was about to receive a construction contract.

HENSCHEL'S FLYING WING
The earliest listed heavy fighter or destroyer design was dated 1936, after the construction of the Hs 124 fighter-bomber. Nicolaus says: "We had made proposals which resembled the later Me 110, but we had a greater aspect ratio and a somewhat more favourable situation in the way the engines were arranged. When we then dealt more intensively with the high altitude designs, we also worked on the most powerful destroyer, and at the same time 'light combat aircraft' in a series of projects."

The second destroyer, as previously mentioned, was based on the Ju 88/188. "The superiority of the escort protection of the bomber units, which became increasingly important in 1944, prompted us to propose a variation of the Ju 188 as a destroyer in which we wanted to take over the wing, the landing gear and the fuselage, and the engine of ours – the developed Jumo 222.

"The fuselage and the trunk part contained a heavily armoured cabin with a heavy weapon (cannon and rockets), including a set of weapons for an oblique shot, and a strong armoured base. The

gunner, like in the Hs 130 E, would have a periscope with a view of the top and bottom of a twin MG 131 on the rear of the hull and on the fuselage side, in addition to a MG 151 in the fuselage. The large fuel tanks had strong rubber protection."

The third heavy fighter, from 1944, was a flying wing based on the Horten IX but powered by a pair of linked Jumo 213s driving contra-rotating propellers. Nicolaus' description of this project leaves many questions unanswered however, particularly the enigmatic first line. He writes: "In 1944, certain hopes of a timely and efficient nature were linked to the completion of the Horten IX, which, however, we had to dash on the basis of the tests we carried out. After all, Lippisch seemed to have a time advantage. We therefore, following the wishes of the RLM, projected a destroyer to the wing of Ho IX. This had a pilot and a radio operator, both under armour protection, with heavy offensive armament, but no defence. The engine was a twin-engine Jumo 213 with counter-rotating airscrews in the fuselage. The maximum speed I could expect was 780km/h. Contrary to the Horten design, we had provided a central fin."

GROUND-ATTACK AIRCRAFT
Almost from the outset, Henschel had attempted to find a niche for itself among its more established rivals by designing aircraft that no one else was particularly keen to work on – specifically high-altitude and ground-attack types. It therefore comes as little surprise that Nicolaus outlines, albeit very briefly, five ground-attack projects worked on by Henschel. He writes: "This aircraft category was always pursued by us with the greatest interest, since it was decisive for the war in the East. The following variations of the theme were worked on in many different ways (1939-1943): a) similar to Hs 123: Single-engine, small, agile, not too heavy weapons, single-seater, used for armed reconnaissance. b) similar to Fw 190: Single-engine, single-

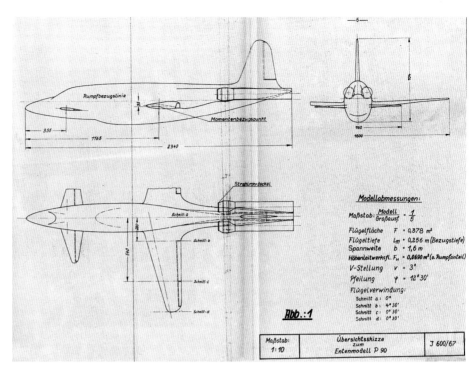

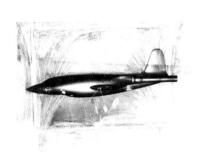

ABOVE: Original drawing of the P.90 wind tunnel model, this time with small canards.

ABOVE: Wind tunnel models of Henschel's version of the Me 328, the twin pulse-jet P 90. The page is shown upside down in order to show the models the right way up.

seater or two-seater, strong armour of crew and fuel. c) similar to Hs 129: Two-engine, single and double-seater, best visibility, strong protection for crew and fuel, largest cannon and rocket calibre, not as 'set-up' but organic. Projects were also implemented as a combination of assemblies of existing machines, e.g. new Hs 129 armoured cabin, Hs 129 armament, wing, tailplane and landing gear of Me 210, engine Fw 190.

"d) twin-jet aircraft, high flight control. Limited in flight duration, weapon calibre and number. Single-seater. e) Similar to 'V-1' as the 'poor man's attack aircraft'. Enhanced Argus jet tube, not too heavy weapons, manoeuvrable, used in large numbers, single-seater. There was no clear decision on a dedicated attack aircraft or demands from the General Staff. In addition to the use of Hs 123, Hs 129, and Ju 87, only the fighter-bomber and ground-attack equipped fighters were used as attack aircraft. The failure rate, especially due to poor targeting, was exceptionally high, and there was hardly any success against tanks."

The only one of these projects which, on the basis of its layout description, potentially matches a known Henschel project is d), the twin-jet aircraft. It is one of two that resembles the P 122, although the P 122 was a two-seater.

BOMBERS
Although it did not win the competition that resulted in the He 177, Henschel seems to have been awarded contracts for both its high-altitude work and for the development of a four-engine bomber. The design Nicolaus outlines is intriguing: "Four-engine design with Jumo 210 for large

ranges (4000km) and loads (3000kg) (1936). The contract was awarded on the basis of a design competition, which was initiated by the then-Chief Development Officer in the RLM, Oberstleutnant von Richthofen.

"Four to five-man crew, full-view cockpit, strong defensive armament by mechanically operated twin turrets on the back of the crew cabin and the underside and stern. Internal motors sunk in the wing with remote shaft for propeller. Exterior engines in the wing. Large protected fuel tanks can be exchanged for bomb magazines.

"Large bomb load in magazines and individual attachment points in the fuselage and wing roots. Mock-up finished, drafts very far advanced, construction precautions taken. After the departure of von Richthofen there were differences with Udet and work was immediately aborted, since the tactical assumptions for a bomber were 'nonsense'."

The second bomber project detailed had a tail-first configuration and was based on the same considerations as the first. It was "carried out as a study only for us, to investigate the improvement of the defences". Finally, in 1944, Henschel worked on "c) tailless with four BMW 018, range 2000km, 2000kg bombs, three man crew, remote controlled rear weapon, internal engines in the wing root, air intake can be covered. Project completed, wind tunnel tests in preparation". None of these three fits the description of any known Henschel project, although some lists describe the P 25 as a long-range bomber with four Jumo 210s and the P 26 as being the same as the P 25. Perhaps the P 26 was the tail-first version Nicolaus outlines.

BATTLEFIELD RECONNAISSANCE
Just one project in this category is described, a version of the Hs 129 ground-attack aircraft: "In all Luftwaffen this was the most unloved breed. This was the type Hs 126, 'Lysander' or similar. The task could not have been done by them any longer, and

had been transferred to the fighters. But in the sense of a better 'eyes-on' view, which is not possible with the single-seater, we suggested a variation of Hs 129 (1940), in which the weight of the bombs and some of the weapons was taken up by an observer, who was to be protected by armoured glass and armour, and a defensive shield, which was also to be placed under armour."

REMOTE RECONNAISSANCE
The three recce projects outlined are novel but sketchy in their description. First is a 1942 tail-first design with engines built into its wings for better aerodynamics. It had "Two men in the cab, one man in the tail booth, pressure chambers, hull in the smallest dimensions, two side fins close to the engine nacelles. Project completed."

The second, from 1943, was also a canard design – but powered by three jet engines. It had "a jet in the fuselage, two in wing root, each intake can be covered, so could be flown with three, two or just one engine. Two man, project completed". Lastly, there was a tailless version of the second project, dating from 1944, which was also 'project completed'. The vagueness of the latter description may leave room for it to be interpreted as another 'fit' for the tailless P 122 – albeit with a different engine configuration.

COMMERCIAL AIRCRAFT AND TRANSPORTER
Like most of the German aircraft companies, particularly during the early years of the war, Henschel anticipated a German victory or at least a peace that did not leave Germany utterly devastated. As a result, it was making plans for a time when military aircraft would no longer be in such high demand: "On the basis of a series of in-depth discussions with Deutsche Lufthansa (DLH), we considered how to get involved in the DLH procurement programme, which was expected after the war." The civil projects were: "a) a two-engine ▶

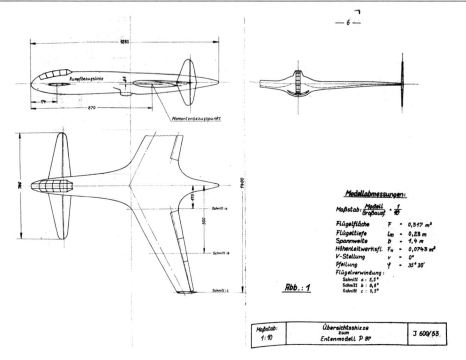

ABOVE: The highly unusual Henschel P 87, from a report which immediately preceded that on the P 90.

ABOVE: Again, this page is shown upside down so that the P 87 models can be viewed more easily. The upper model here has a central fin, whereas the lower one has wingtip plate control surfaces, as shown in the drawing.

high-speed aircraft with a BMW 801 A (1941), a range of 1500km, 20 passengers, an overpressure cabin for medium altitude. b) a four-engine transatlantic high-speed craft with BMW 801s (1942) for mail and valuable cargo, capable of maximum altitude to exploit the most favourable winds. Drafts were very extensively worked through, a detailed mock-up built. c) a Diesel version of b) as a two-engine design."

During 1942, Henschel had worked on designs for a military battlefield transport too: "For the Luftwaffe, the project of a two-engine, tactical transporter with BMW 801 A (1942) was dealt with very extensively. In particular, extensive studies have been carried out on the design of the landing gear and landing aids in order to achieve the best possible use in the worst and smallest places."

HENSCHEL'S ME 328

Finally, Henschel had worked on five projects that fell into the 'special aircraft' category. The first of these was a small bomber, worked on in 1941, that appears to have been very similar to the Me 328 B.

Nicolaus writes: "While the previously mentioned types of aircraft were trying to meet the variety of the war zones and their often different conditions, an Allied invasion seemed ever more probable to me, and I felt there would be a need to fight the invasion fleet with special aircraft. From these considerations a small aircraft, equipped with the most primitive engine, the Argus thrust tube, was built and kept as simple as possible without a landing gear, only skids, without firearms, only equipped with large-scale bomb or torpedo.

"The mission should be carried out from land or ship with catapult launch as a cheap form of long-range artillery, or from a carrier aircraft (He 177) using crash or torpedo attack some 100km off the coast. The design was carried out as a standard aircraft and tail-first with two Argus thrusters at the fuselage tail. The wind

tunnel tests were concluded with favourable results, the designs worked through. They were submitted in 1941, but found no interest because 'an invasion was unlikely'."

One Henschel project matches this description almost exactly: the P 90. One wind tunnel test model drawing, labelled 'P 90' and two wind tunnel photos are known to exist, from a full DVL report, UM 1127, on the associated wind tunnel tests. The drawing also bears the description: "Übersichtsskizze zum Entenmodell P 90" or 'Overview of the canard model P 90'. It also includes the reference "J 600/67" in the bottom right hand corner, beside the description.

The following sheet of the report states: "Introduction. In the UM 1126 report, extensive 3- and 6-component measurements were reported at Henschel Flugzeug-Werke AG's canard project P 87. This report provides the 3- and 6-component measurement of a further project, the P 90.

"The most important differences between the two versions are the ratio of the wing area to the fuselage cross-section area, the wing sweep back, and the jet nozzle drive of the P 90, in contrast to the propeller drive of the P 87."

J 600/67 was Henschel's account number for the project with the DVL. Previous descriptions of what has been incorrectly known as the 'J 600/67' do seem accurate in detailing its date and purpose, but they also state that the aircraft was built and that the project was halted or cancelled by the RLM. The inclusion of the design in the unbuilt projects section of Nicolaus's report makes it clear that the type was not physically constructed and although Henschel submitted the idea, no contract was forthcoming from the RLM due to lack of interest.

INTERCEPTOR TRIO

The problem of how to catch and destroy waves of American bombers as they overflew Germany was given serious consideration by Henschel from

1944 right up to the end of the war.

According to Nicolaus's report three different potential 'solutions' were looked at. He writes: "The tactics of the Americans to protect their bomber units during daytime deployment involved strong defensive associations between their aircraft and resulted in the proposal for the development of a special interceptor to be distributed along the incoming routes and near particularly important areas.

"Its characteristics were to be: exceptional ability to climb, maximum speed in the attack, which should be carried out on each target only once (not a turning fight), and weapons with devastating effect."

Flight time would be relatively low and provision would need to be made for catapult launches.

Henschel's first solution was to marry a rocket-propelled missile similar to the Hs 117 to a tiny manned glider. This combination would be fired at the bomber stream overhead from the ground and once it got close enough the pilot would detach his little aircraft from the missile and glide it back down.

Nicolaus: "Three solutions were worked out by us (1944-1945): 1) A proposal to replace the remote rocket 8-117 with its technical sources of error with a combination of a projectile (with drive but without control) and a pilot controlled aircraft of small scale and weight and without own drive.

"The aircraft should be moved as close as possible to the target by the projectile's

3.) Modellbeschreibung :
A) Hs-1 oberer Einlauf

Die ideale Form eines TL-Einlaufes mit Nusen wäre die nach Abb.1

Auf demselben Blatt befindet sich eine Kurve über den Verlauf des Verlustbeiwertes, wenn der Einlauf des Modells Hs-1 in der aus Abb. 1a zu erschenen Weise geändert ist.

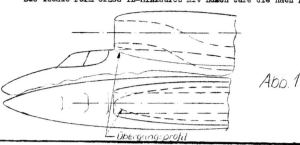

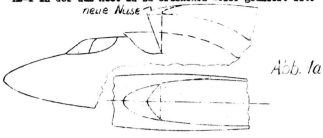

neue Nase

Abb. 1

Abb. 1a

Übergangsprofil

ABOVE: Slightly stylised side views showing intake arrangements for the Henschel P 108's single BMW 003 turbojet. The dorsal intake version of the P 108 was given the arbitrary name 'Hs-1' by BMW.

Blatt: 14

Hs-1

Hs-1

+cc 32

Abo 3c

Abo 3o

ABOVE: Two views of the Henschel P 108 'Hs-1' version, showing the type's straight wings and dorsal intake.

ABOVE: Forward view of the P 108 'Hs-1' model.

drive, the projectile should be triggered, and the carrier aircraft should then be taken out of the danger area even in a dive. A Walter unit similar to 109/509 of the 8-117 with a controllable thrust between 135kg and 1100kg was planned. The tailless aircraft had an area of 4sq m and a span of 4m. The starting weight would be 900kg, the landing weight 360kg."

Climbing speed was to be around 200m per second with a top speed at sea level of 990km/h or 960km/h at an altitude of 10km.

"Disadvantages of this solution are that

only a single attack can be flown, and the low flight time, which does not allow an attack to be missed. The duration of the flight would have been approx. 50 sec."

This missile/manned glider combination was intriguingly similar to Karl Stöckel's MGRP design (see p6-7), though not Blohm & Voss's P 214.

The second solution to the American bomber problem was similar to the first but rather than a missile/glider combination, this would involve something similar to the Bachem Natter. This

manned rocket-launching interceptor was designated P 136 and it would allow "greater flight time and the ability to attack multiple targets in succession".

According to Nicolaus: "Its features were: tailless aircraft with a prone pilot (= Hs P 135), Walter R-drive with full thrust, armament consisting of 12 x 5cm rockets, which should be shot from two rocket launchers. No landing gear, only land skids.

"The dimensions and the duration of the flight were determined from detailed comparisons between top speed,

ABOVE: Wind tunnel model of the P 108 'Hs-2' model, with side intakes.

climb speeds and the required amount of fuel. Top speed should be on the ground from the start = 1000km/h."

Some basic data is then given – starting weight 3100kg, fuel 1840kg, wing area 11.2sq m, maximum thrust 2400kg,

minimum thrust 300kg. Climb to 10km (32,800ft) altitude was to take 60 seconds, at which point the P 136 would still be climbing at a rate of 200m per second.

The third solution involved combining the thrust and speed of a rocket engine with a ramjet or 'Lorin drive' to lower fuel consumption and provide additional thrust. This would involve a thorough reworking of the P 136's rear section.

"The disadvantage of all rocket engines, the high fuel consumption, and therefore the aircraft's low flight time, led us to investigate the possible applications of the Lorin drive in connection with the rocket drive. Here in the last months of the war a cooperation with Dr Zobel, Braunschweig," writes Nicolaus. Zobel was a ramjet pioneer working at the Luftfahrtforschungsanstalt or 'Aeronautical Research Institute' (LFA), at Braunschweig.

"The possibilities seemed to us to be the following: a) The combustion chamber of the rocket drive falls away and is replaced by a Lorin drive, which is placed circularly around the stern of the fuselage. Rocket and Lorin drives operate independently of each other.

"The operation of the Lorin device should be effected by C-Stoff and T-Stoff. By the complete redesign of the fuselage tail, we expected a favourable influence on the interference resistance between the fuselage and wing. By experiment, it should be clarified whether a sheathing of the rocket's cone, so that air can be sucked in, brings a thrust increase.

"The Lorin drive should be arranged in a ring-shaped manner about this so-called 'mixing' tube, so that we were already expecting air through the Lorin tube and thus an additional thrust when the rocket drive was started.

"Next, it was thought to design the mixing tube so that it could simultaneously operate as a Lorin drive. We expected that the hot rocket jet would improve combustion in the Lorin drive. The large overall length of the Lorin drive appeared as a fundamental disadvantage in these considerations, which would have given rise to great static difficulties. This point should be given particular attention in the further development of the Lorin drive."

DFS 228/P 135 HYBRID

The 28th and final design outlined by Nicolaus at the end of the 'special aircraft' section involves the unholy marriage of two other Henschel projects – the rocket-powered DFS 228 high-altitude reconnaissance aircraft and the turbojet-powered P 135 fighter.

"Inspired by the task of the DFS 228, to which we developed a new pressure chamber for the pilot, we also attempted to examine the fuselage, which we considered weighty and aerodynamically unrefined. This led to a project of tailless design taking over the characteristics of the wing of Hs P 135, combined with our pressure cabin. A variation of this design was likely to occur as the basis for a record aircraft

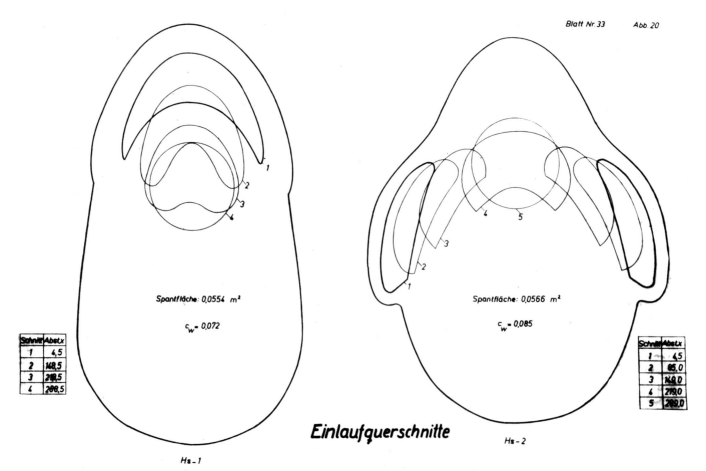

ABOVE: The differing intakes of the P 108 'Hs-1' and 'Hs-2' are depicted in this drawing dated July 5, 1944.

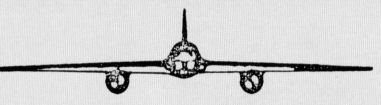

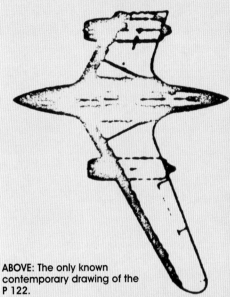

ABOVE: The only known contemporary drawing of the P 122.

One of the best known but most elusive Henschel projects of the war is the twin-jet P 122. It was featured in Luftwaffe: Secret Wings of the Third Reich and appeared in an artwork by Ronnie Olsthoorn on the contents pages.

Although British postwar report German Aircraft: New and Projected Types gives a few scant details of its vital statistics, including a range of 1240 miles at an altitude of 55,700ft – making it a high-altitude type, probably equipped with a pressurised cabin – there is only one known original drawing available, from the same report, and nothing else. Nicolaus makes no direct reference to it in his postwar report either.

Ronnie already had a basic model of the P 122, created some years ago, but I asked him to revisit the cockpit canopy. A single clear bubble covering most of the nose's upper surface, as depicted by some artists, or a single large strip of Perspex as shown in Ronnie's original render did not seem right to me as part of a pressure cabin.

Looking at the original drawing, it was obvious why most artists had chosen to go for a large area of Perspex. At a cursory glance, that would appear to match what's

shown in the drawing. Examining the P 122's nose in extremely high resolution, I noticed a curve which appeared to be the rear wall of the pressure cabin, confirming the high-altitude aspect of the design. However, when Ronnie looked at the drawing close-up, he saw that the upper surface of the nose had two shapes on it which appeared to be windows running down the centreline of the aircraft. These are not immediately apparent but once they have been pointed out you may well wonder why you had not seen them before.

He noted that the 'smudging' on the drawing appeared to be the remains of shading, and postulated that the two crew may well have originally been depicted but had faded off almost entirely due to successive generations of copying from the original drawing. Shapes on the side of the nose were likely to be evidence of sighting windows, allowing the pilot to see what he was doing during landing, despite the poor visibility from the rest of the pressure cabin's small windows.

Perhaps one day the original P 122 document will be discovered, but for now this unusual design remains largely 'unknown'.

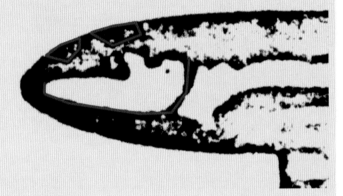

ABOVE: Looking closely at the P 122's cockpit area, it is possible to discern two shapes on the upper surface which appear to be windows. Below them is the curve of a pressure cabin wall.

with regard to altitude and speed."

P 87 AND P 108

Although he mentions many projects which are otherwise unknown, Nicolaus also fails to mention a number of Henschel projects which are known about. The P 87, tested by the DVL immediately prior to its work on the P 90 and reported on in UM 1126 of November 22, 1943, Konto J 600/53, was a large canard design with what appears to be a pusher-prop arrangement similar to that of the P 75. Unlike the P 75, the cockpit was in the nose.

The very brief DVL report attached to the numerical results of its wind tunnel testing, states: "Commissioned by Henschel Flugzeug-Werke AG, 3- and 6-component measurements were carried out on the model of the canard project P 87. The model was measured in different variations. The results are communicated in the form of numbers.

"Introduction. In order to obtain aerodynamic documentation for the implementation of a canard project,

numerous wind tunnel measurements were carried out on a model of the type P 87. The various model arrangements have been extensively studied so that a good overview of the results is available.

"Models. The model was made of wood on a scale of 1:10, the surface was polished. The model was built on a modular basis, so that the different variations could be measured without significant modifications."

Only two arrangements are actually detailed in the report – one with the control surfaces as wingtip plates and a second with a central conventional tail fin. Nothing else is known about the P 87.

Last of all, on July 19, 1944, BMW produced a report entitled ET-Bericht Nr. 22 detailing work it had undertaken with Henschel on the Henschel P 108 – a small aircraft to be powered by a single centrally mounted BMW 003. Two different arrangements were tried – one with engine intakes positioned on either side of the cockpit, one with a single dorsal

intake – with work having evidently got under way during November 1943.

As with the P 87, little further information is given about the P 108. Both models used by BMW, designated Hs-1 for the dorsal intake and Hs-2 for the side intakes, had completely straight and unswept wings and neither is shown with any sort of tail arrangement though it would undoubtedly have required tail surfaces of some sort. Whether this would have been a V-tail like that of the apparently similar Hs 132 or a conventional tail arrangement is unknown.

Given the vast amount of well-funded project work undertaken by Henschel, it must have been a bitter disappointment to Nicolaus that so little of it apparently survived. How much was destroyed and how much was salvaged from the rubble in Berlin by the Soviets and taken away remains to be seen – but beyond this, all that remain are scraps and the memories of Friedrich Nicolaus recorded in his report for the victorious Allies. ●

Henschel P 108

July 1944

Artwork by Luca Landino

COMMENTS

The Henschel P 108 design presented here is one of two possible arrangements studied for the aircraft. The other would have had a significantly different rear fuselage, with twin side intakes feeding the single BMW 003 turbojet rather than a large dorsal inlet. No details of the intended tail plane arrangement exist so the layout shown here is speculative, as is the armament depicted.

251003

Junkers photo J.46281 shows a display model of the EF 116 in one of its many different guises – as an Ar 234-sized twin jet with a conventional cockpit and radically swept wings and tail surfaces.

The chimera

Junkers EF 116

At a time when state-owned Arado was undertaking the first test flights of its Ar 234, the other major state-owned aircraft manufacturer, Junkers, was wind tunnel-testing its own twin-jet design. But where the Arado was conservative in every respect, the Junkers embodied a host of radical ideas.

ABOVE: The earliest known photo in the EF 116 sequence, J.43337, shows a basic cylindrical fuselage shape with forward-swept wings.

ABOVE: J.43338, the second photo in sequence, shows the same EF 116 model from a different angle, revealing a conventional tail arrangement.

ABOVE: A third photo of the early EF 116 model, J.43582, shows a side view.

ABOVE: This rear view of the EF 116 model, now fitted with backwards-swept wings, has caused some confusion. Some have stated that it shows the postwar EF 132 but here it has been left uncropped to retain the original Junkers caption.

ABOVE: This photo shows the sharply forward-swept wing angle tried on some EF 116 models.

ABOVE: One of the more unusual arrangements tried with EF 116 was to give its wings an anhedral angle of 15-degrees, shown here in photo J.43659.

The EF 116 has tended to be seen as little more than a stepping-stone on the way to the EF 122 and then the Ju 287, but it deserves closer examination in its own right – without the baggage of what would come later.

Junkers' 004 jet engine was given its first flight test on March 15, 1942, attached to an Me 110 and on July 18 of the same year it powered the Me 262 V3 for a successful 25-minute flight. The Arado E 370, work on which had begun as early as 1940, received the official designation Ar 234 in February 1942 and approval was given for the construction of prototypes. Everything about the Ar 234 was 'safe' – straight wings, straight tail planes, an unremarkable cigar-shaped fuselage, and its engines hung beneath its wings for easy and uncomplicated access.

However, it was evident to the Arado team that the new ideas on aerodynamics

coming out of Germany's numerous research establishments were likely to afford greater performance to a jet-propelled aircraft. So the company embarked on a new experimental programme in November 1942 under the designation E 560 to assess what gains might be made by using swept-back or 'pfeilflügel' shapes and different engine arrangements. It was thought that the development of the Ar 234 might well benefit from this work but the company was also keen to determine what the next generation of jet aircraft might look like.

Since Arado lacked its own wind tunnel facilities, it engaged a series of contractors to carry out research on its behalf, including Messerschmitt, the Luftfahrtforschungsanstalt (LFA) at Völkenrode near Brunswick in central Germany, the Flugtechniche Versuchsanstalt (FVA) at Prague in Czechoslovakia, and the Aerodynamische

Versuchsanstalt (AVA) at Göttingen.

Junkers had received much of the same early data on swept wings as Arado, dating back to 1940, but only seems to have followed up on it once Arado's work was already well on its way to completion. But where Arado, which already had a 'safe' design close to its first flight tests, saw distinct advantages in swept-back wings, Junkers considered that swept-forward wings might be less risky and therefore commenced its own tests, using its own wind tunnels, with wing shapes that were swept-forward, swept-back and even in crescent form. Swept tail planes and unusual engine installations were also examined as part of the process, which was given the project number EF 116.

Precisely what prompted Junkers to commence this programme is ▶

ABOVE: J.45184 begins a sequence of photos showing the EF 116 model being tested without a tail piece fitted.

EF 116, Mod. Antsor. Mosch. C.83 Variert.

ABOVE: Compared to what would eventually emerge as the Ju 287, the EF 116 was remarkably slender and elegant.

ABOVE: Another view of the EF 116 undergoing tests without a tail.

ABOVE: Hard to see from this angle, but the EF 116 has now been fitted with a different fuselage. This one has a cockpit 'bulge' on its upper surface.

ABOVE: J.45186 shows the clutter of scaffolding and equipment around the EF 116 model being tested.

unclear, but it seems likely that the company's designers were aware of the work being undertaken at Arado.

The EF 116 wind tunnel models were chimerical: a selection of different parts that could be put together in a variety of combinations. This meant that the aircraft had many different forms; it could have its wings set at various angles, its engines attached at various points and even different arrangements of cockpit.

The EF 116 programme commenced on March 19 in Junkers' high-speed wind tunnel, with tests intended to determine the best

shape for its wings' aerofoil section. Next, low-speed testing of swept wing arrangements took place between April 28 and June 30. This included wings that were swept-back, swept-forward and unswept. One design had wings with a 15-degree dihedral to create a shallow 'V', another had swept-back wings with tips that were swept forward – a W-wing configuration. In straight swept-back form, seen from the rear, the EF 116 resembles a later jet bomber such as the Boeing B-52 – which may have led at least one historian to label this 1943 design as an example of Junkers' work for the Soviet Union after

ABOVE: An unusual view of the EF 116 model with cockpit fuselage from above.

ABOVE: Here a large set of forward-swept EF 116 wings is tested without a fuselage.

ABOVE: A set of straight wings being tested without a fuselage as part of the EF 116 project.

ABOVE: Junkers photos J.45745 and J.45746 each show the same table full of EF 116 test pieces from a different angle.

ABOVE: Three views of the EF 116 display model, which featured three alternative attachment points for the aircraft's twin Jumo 004 engines.

Germany's defeat, the EF 132 bomber.

Since it was evidently inspired by the Ar 234 and Arado's follow-on work with high-speed multi-engine aircraft designs, it seems likely that the EF 116 was conceived with similar roles ultimately in mind – as a fast bomber or reconnaissance platform. Attempting to provide some scale is difficult since although some of the models were evidently intended to match the Ar 234 in relative size, others appear to have represented what would have

been somewhat larger aircraft designs, just as Arado was working on scaled-up versions of the Ar 234 as the E 395.

With in-house facilities to call upon, Junkers seems to have quickly surpassed Arado's work on swept-back designs, generating huge quantities of data in a relatively short time. The project came to an abrupt end on September 29, 1943, at about the same time that the RLM issued a new requirement for a Strahlbomber or 'jet-bomber'. This requirement was issued

to both Arado and Junkers, with outsider Blohm & Voss also being allowed to tender, but excluding the big private companies – Focke-Wulf, Heinkel and Messerschmitt.

The day after EF 116 was concluded, EF 122 commenced. This was based on the data generated by the earlier project and less than three months later would be redesignated Ju 287 – a four- or six-jet bomber with forward-swept wings. Without the EF 116, the Ju 287 might never have existed or might have taken a less radical form. ●

Junkers EF 116

September 1943

Artwork by Luca Landino

COMMENTS

A huge number of different configurations were possible for the twin-engine Junkers EF 116, including W-wings, swept-back wings and even inverted crescent-shaped wings. The version depicted here features a long slender fuselage with the engines directly attached to it. Artist Luca Landino also prepared an alternative with the engines fixed beneath the wings.

Flying sharks

Lippisch P 15 Diana

When asked to come up with a single-jet fighter which built upon his own aerodynamic research, Me 163 designer Alexander Lippisch came up with some of the wildest aircraft designs ever seen in the Third Reich...

At the end of February 1945 Alexander Lippisch, foremost advocate of tailless aircraft in Germany, was facing up to the fact that his long-cherished ramjet fighter concept, the P 13, was unlikely ever to be built.

Beginning in November 1944 efforts had been made to construct the P 13a V1 prototype as a glider through the efforts of enthusiastic student workers – who dubbed their creation the DM-1 – but Lippisch had already largely given up on the P 13a by that stage and was instead considering what he called the P 13b. Where the P 13a had been a flying arrowhead of an aircraft, with a delta wing and the cockpit built into a large

vertical fin, the P 13b was somewhat more conventional; a cross between the P 13a and the broad delta-winged twin-jet P 11, another promising Lippisch design that had been largely abandoned due to lack of resources.

His thoughts were turning towards yet more conceptual designs – the elongated slender delta P 14 for high-speed flight – when in early March 1945 he was visited at the Luftfahrtforschungsanstalt-Wien (LFW) in Vienna by Oberst Siegfried Knemeyer,

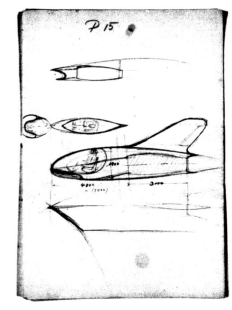

ABOVE: This was evidently Alexander Lippisch's first attempt at the P 15.

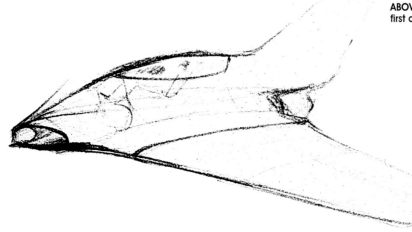

ABOVE: Lippisch's second P 15 exhibits an odd, almost beak-like, split nose intake.

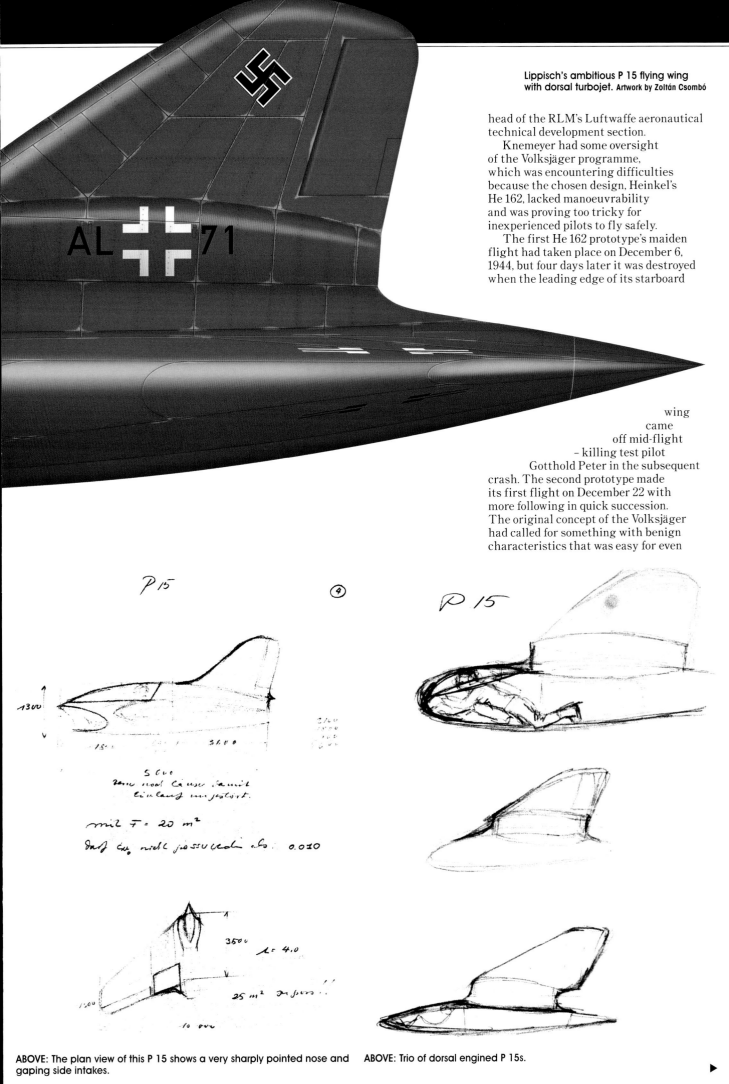

Lippisch's ambitious P 15 flying wing with dorsal turbojet. Artwork by Zoltán Csombó

AL ✠ 71

head of the RLM's Luftwaffe aeronautical technical development section.

Knemeyer had some oversight of the Volksjäger programme, which was encountering difficulties because the chosen design, Heinkel's He 162, lacked manoeuvrability and was proving too tricky for inexperienced pilots to fly safely.

The first He 162 prototype's maiden flight had taken place on December 6, 1944, but four days later it was destroyed when the leading edge of its starboard wing came off mid-flight – killing test pilot Gotthold Peter in the subsequent crash. The second prototype made its first flight on December 22 with more following in quick succession. The original concept of the Volksjäger had called for something with benign characteristics that was easy for even

ABOVE: The plan view of this P 15 shows a very sharply pointed nose and gaping side intakes.

ABOVE: Trio of dorsal engined P 15s.

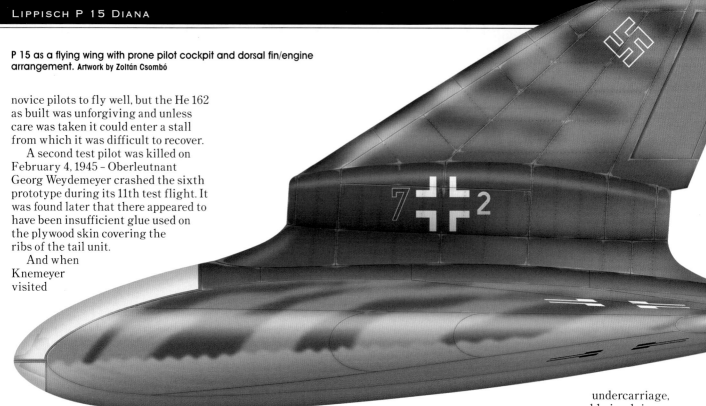

P 15 as a flying wing with prone pilot cockpit and dorsal fin/engine arrangement. Artwork by Zoltán Csombó

novice pilots to fly well, but the He 162 as built was unforgiving and unless care was taken it could enter a stall from which it was difficult to recover.

A second test pilot was killed on February 4, 1945 – Oberleutnant Georg Weydemeyer crashed the sixth prototype during its 11th test flight. It was found later that there appeared to have been insufficient glue used on the plywood skin covering the ribs of the tail unit.

And when Knemeyer visited

Lippisch, he was also aware that the 1-TL-Jäger competition to find the Luftwaffe's next front line jet fighter was making only slow progress. A meeting on February 27-28, 1945, intended to pick a winner in the contest had ended without any real decision – apart from the effective elimination of Heinkel as a competitor. Messerschmitt and Focke-Wulf had both come away believing that they would soon receive development contracts for their designs, as 'optimal' and 'immediate' solutions respectively, while the remaining two companies, Junkers and Blohm & Voss, seem also to have thought that contracts for their designs might well be forthcoming.

With the Volksjäger programme rapidly turning into a disaster and with no clear end in sight for 1-TL-Jäger, it appeared as though drastic action was needed to provide the Luftwaffe with the single-jet fighter it so desperately needed. Lippisch had evidently acted as a consultant during the design and development of the He 162 – suggesting the downturned wingtips which cured a problem with longitudinal instability.

So during his visit to Vienna, Knemeyer asked Lippisch if he could design a new single-jet aircraft based on proven aerodynamics. According to Lippisch's autobiography, Erinnerungen or 'Memories': "After the 'Blitzaktion' Volksjäger He 162 had unreasonable flight characteristics for the young pilot, at the suggestion of Colonel

Knemeyer we designed a jet fighter P 15 'Diana' consisting of existing components: the proven Me 163 airframe, the cockpit and armament of the He 162, and the modified hull of an Me 163 derivative (the Ju 248 = Me 263) with built-in jet engine. The project did not go beyond sketches."

But it seems that this was not Knemeyer's first suggestion. Initially, Lippisch began making sketches showing entirely new designs. These appear to have been based on aspects of various designs from earlier in his career, with shades of his early jet fighter work for Messerschmitt showing through in some designs, and others depicting what amounted to a P 13a fitted with a turbojet in place of its ramjet combustion chamber.

In all, there were around 10 different designs loosely based on three different configurations. The first configuration was something akin to his Messerschmitt P 01 designs, with the pilot seated in the tailless aircraft and the turbojet's intake passing him to feed the engine, mounted in the rear fuselage. There was a single large tail fin and no

undercarriage, presumably implying a trolley take-off and skid landing.

The first of these P 15s had the pilot seated in the aircraft's nose with the intake passing beneath and to either side of him in a U-shape. The second had the pilot seated centrally in the aircraft with a sharp beak-like mouth intake in the nose.

For the third design, the pilot sat in a very narrow cockpit in the nose with gaping whale shark-like intakes on either side of him. For this design, the fin was only gently swept.

Next, Lippisch changed tack. He moved the turbojet out of the fuselage and mounted it on the aircraft's back where the fin had previously been. The fin itself was positioned above the turbojet, like an enormous shark fin. Three designs were drawn up in this layout, the first with the pilot lying prone in the aircraft's nose, unhindered by engine intakes, the second had

ABOVE: Flying wing P 15 with seated cockpit. Artwork by Zoltán Csombó

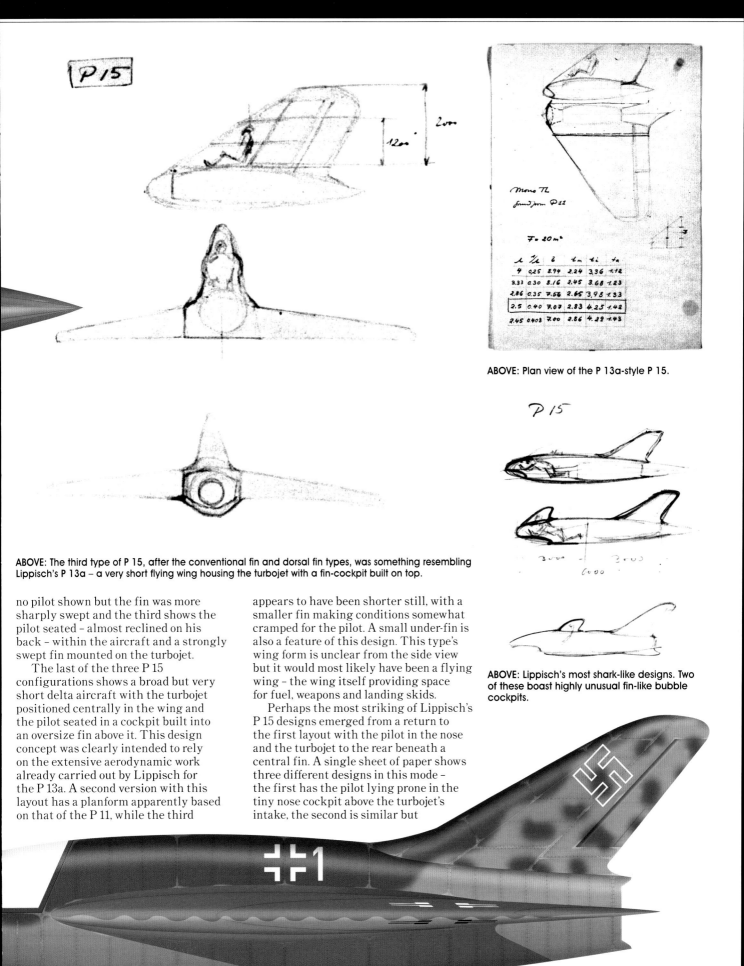

P 15

*Mono TL
frond form P 11*

$F = 20 m^2$

l	l/c	b	lm	li	la
4	0.25	8.94	2.24	3.36	1.12
3.33	0.30	8.16	2.45	3.68	1.23
2.86	0.35	7.56	2.65	3.98	1.33
2.5	0.40	7.07	2.83	4.25	1.42
2.45	0.408	7.00	2.86	4.28	1.43

ABOVE: Plan view of the P 13a-style P 15.

P 15

ABOVE: The third type of P 15, after the conventional fin and dorsal fin types, was something resembling Lippisch's P 13a – a very short flying wing housing the turbojet with a fin-cockpit built on top.

ABOVE: Lippisch's most shark-like designs. Two of these boast highly unusual fin-like bubble cockpits.

no pilot shown but the fin was more sharply swept and the third shows the pilot seated – almost reclined on his back – within the aircraft and a strongly swept fin mounted on the turbojet.

The last of the three P 15 configurations shows a broad but very short delta aircraft with the turbojet positioned centrally in the wing and the pilot seated in a cockpit built into an oversize fin above it. This design concept was clearly intended to rely on the extensive aerodynamic work already carried out by Lippisch for the P 13a. A second version with this layout has a planform apparently based on that of the P 11, while the third

appears to have been shorter still, with a smaller fin making conditions somewhat cramped for the pilot. A small under-fin is also a feature of this design. This type's wing form is unclear from the side view but it would most likely have been a flying wing – the wing itself providing space for fuel, weapons and landing skids.

Perhaps the most striking of Lippisch's P 15 designs emerged from a return to the first layout with the pilot in the nose and the turbojet to the rear beneath a central fin. A single sheet of paper shows three different designs in this mode – the first has the pilot lying prone in the tiny nose cockpit above the turbojet's intake, the second is similar but

ABOVE: P 15 with conventional prone pilot cockpit. Artwork by Zoltán Csombó

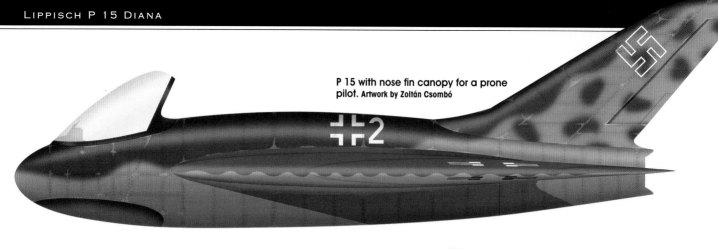

P 15 with nose fin canopy for a prone pilot. Artwork by Zoltán Csombó

P 15 with central fin canopy for a seated pilot. Artwork by Zoltán Csombó

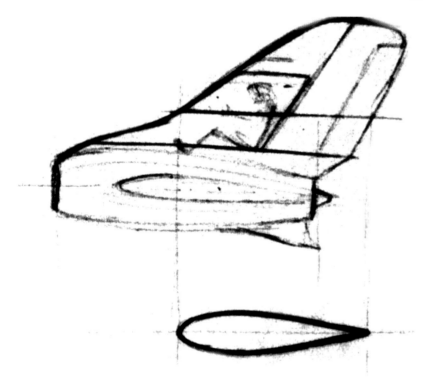

ABOVE: This tiny P 15 is little more than a turbojet mounted in a small flying wing with a small cockpit-fin bolted on top. Whether it would have even been capable of flight is questionable.

introduces a fin-shaped bubble canopy for the pilot. The third retains the oddly fin-like bubble canopy but sees the pilot moved to a seated position in the centre of the aircraft. The fin is strongly swept back and an under-fin is also present.

'SHARKS' REJECTED
Lippisch's shark-like original P 15 drawings do not appear to have met Knemeyer's expectations – primarily because he was looking for something that could be built quickly and each of the new sketches would have required a ground-up new design. Therefore Lippisch quickly came up with an alternative that utilised the components mentioned as the P 15 'Diana'.

He wrote a brief two-page outline of the project on March 4, 1945, entitled Flugtechnische Grundlagen für Projekt P 15 'Diana' or 'Aeronautical Fundamental

for Project P 15 'Diana'. This began: "The highest speeds were met with the tailless aircraft Me 163 (constructed by Dr Lippisch). Investigations in high-speed wind tunnels clearly show the superiority of this design in the high-speed range. The flight characteristics are significantly better in all flight areas than those of the most normal modern aircraft. This finding has been consistently confirmed by all testing stations.

"The development of high-speed fighter aircraft based on the normal aircraft does not lead to the necessary tactical speeds (1000km/h). It therefore seems obvious to use the results already available and the existing tailless designs for these new developments. The present draft is determined by demands resulting from the need for the shortest development time and the fastest production start. Therefore, the task was set so that from the components of the model Me 163 B and C, He 162 and Ju 248 and 263 could be put together in a new pattern.

"The demands are: Flight weight 3.6 tons, flight time 45 minutes, maximum speed 1000km/h, armament and equipment such as He 162 and Me 163 B, nosewheel chassis like the He 162, engine HeS 011 (BMW). The following modules are to be used unchanged: Me 163 C swept wing, cockpit He 162, main undercarriage He 162 or Me 109 G, controls Me 163 B, weapons installation He 162 or Me 163 B."

The P 15 was to have a wingspan of 10m and a wing area of 20sqm but an increase in wing area in a ratio of 1:1.8 was possible, as was an increase in wingspan by 1:1.4. However, "compared to the He 162 or similar designs based on normal

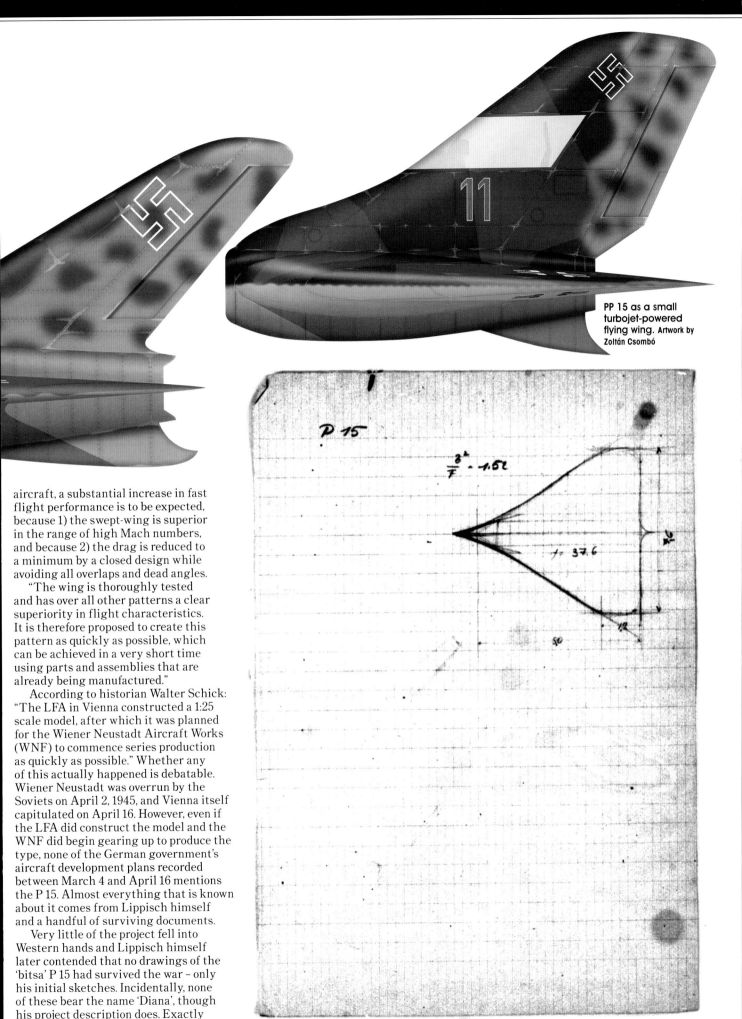

PP 15 as a small turbojet-powered flying wing. **Artwork by Zoltán Csombó**

aircraft, a substantial increase in fast flight performance is to be expected, because 1) the swept-wing is superior in the range of high Mach numbers, and because 2) the drag is reduced to a minimum by a closed design while avoiding all overlaps and dead angles.

"The wing is thoroughly tested and has over all other patterns a clear superiority in flight characteristics. It is therefore proposed to create this pattern as quickly as possible, which can be achieved in a very short time using parts and assemblies that are already being manufactured."

According to historian Walter Schick: "The LFA in Vienna constructed a 1:25 scale model, after which it was planned for the Wiener Neustadt Aircraft Works (WNF) to commence series production as quickly as possible." Whether any of this actually happened is debatable. Wiener Neustadt was overrun by the Soviets on April 2, 1945, and Vienna itself capitulated on April 16. However, even if the LFA did construct the model and the WNF did begin gearing up to produce the type, none of the German government's aircraft development plans recorded between March 4 and April 16 mentions the P 15. Almost everything that is known about it comes from Lippisch himself and a handful of surviving documents.

Very little of the project fell into Western hands and Lippisch himself later contended that no drawings of the 'bitsa' P 15 had survived the war – only his initial sketches. Incidentally, none of these bear the name 'Diana', though his project description does. Exactly where the name came from and its significance, if any, remains a mystery. ●

ABOVE: The final drawing of Lippisch's P 15 sequence is a plan view, presumably related to the earlier sketches.

Lippisch P 1

March 1945

Artwork by Luca Landino

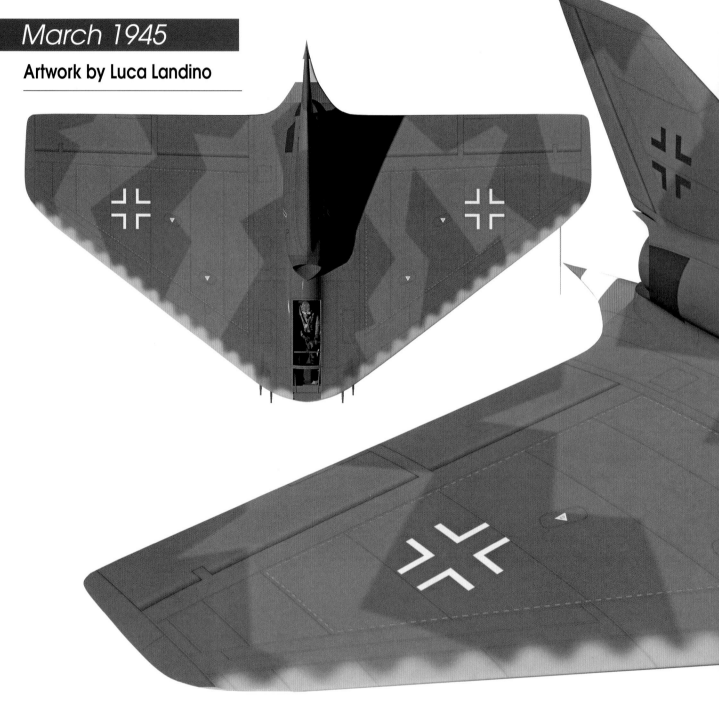

5 Diana

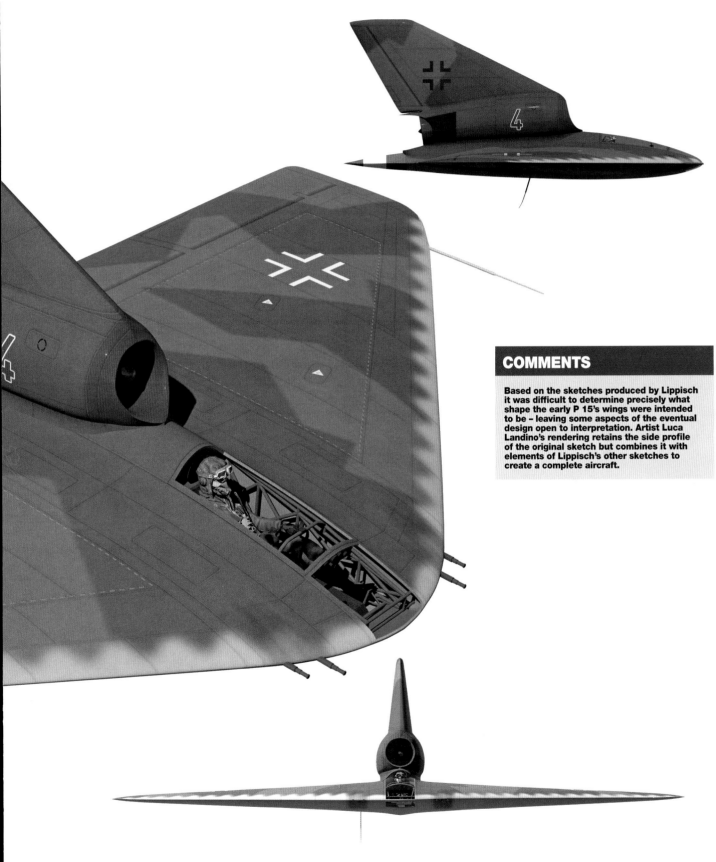

COMMENTS

Based on the sketches produced by Lippisch it was difficult to determine precisely what shape the early P 15's wings were intended to be – leaving some aspects of the eventual design open to interpretation. Artist Luca Landino's rendering retains the side profile of the original sketch but combines it with elements of Lippisch's other sketches to create a complete aircraft.

Schnellstbomber

Messerschmitt Me 109 Zw, Me 309 Zw and Me 609

Having been disinclined to enter the Schnellstbomber competition at first, as it drew to an end Willy Messerschmitt found his company's design was a front-runner. Only one other project really stood in its way...

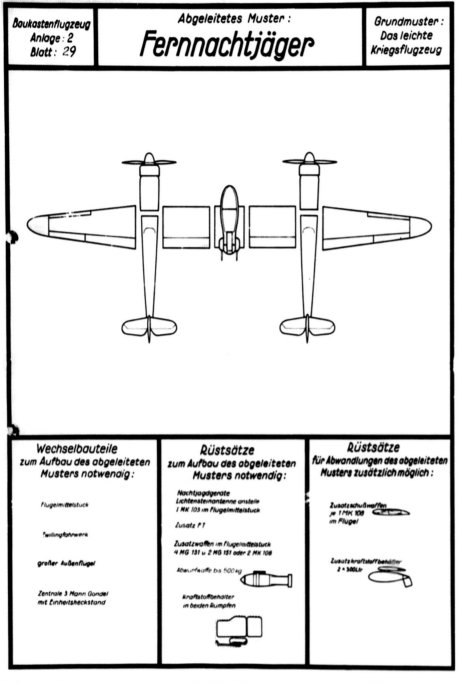

Baukastenflugzeug Anlage : 2 Blatt : 29	Abgeleitetes Muster : *Fernnachtjäger*	Grundmuster : Das leichte Kriegsflugzeug

Wechselbauteile zum Aufbau des abgeleiteten Musters notwendig :	Rüstsätze zum Aufbau des abgeleiteten Musters notwendig :	Rüstsätze für Abwandlungen des abgeleiteten Musters zusätzlich möglich :
Flugelmittelstuck	Nachtjagdgeräte Lichtensteinantenne anstelle 1 MK 103 im Flugelmittelstuck	Zusatzschußwaffen je 1 MK 108 im Flugel
Twillingfahrwerk	Zusatz FT	
großer Außenflugel	Zusatzwaffen im Flugelmittelstuck 4 MG 131 u 2 MG 151 oder 2 MK 108	Zusatzkraftstoffbehälter 2 × 300Ltr
Zentrale 3 Mann Gondel mit Einheitsheckstand	Abwurfwaffe bis 500 kg	
	kraftstoffbehälter in beiden Rumpfen	

ABOVE: While other companies were working on proposals for a Schnellstbomber or 'fastest bomber', Messerschmitt was drafting proposals to reduce the number of aircraft types in production by using existing components in modular construction. This 1942 design shows a long-range night fighter composed of Jumo 213 power-egg engines, faired-over Me 109 fuselages, Me 110 outer wings and a new three-man cockpit gondola with symmetrical central wing sections.

During an RLM development conference in May 1942, it was decided that a new type of bomber was required – one that could fly as fast as, or faster than, existing fighters using only existing and readily available inline piston engines. It would be a single-seater with a range of 2000km and a bomb load of 500kg. The fuel tank would be armoured and a maximum speed of 800km/h was required. The requirement's catch-all title was simply Schnellflugzeug or 'fast aircraft'.

Evidently Junkers' technical director Heinrich Hertel, on receiving this specification, suggested that if the very fastest aircraft was required, then an uncompromising solution was called for, with no weapons or armour to slow it down. He was then asked to come up with a design based on this ideal.

At the same time, Heinkel was given a contract to carry out a similar study. Messerschmitt's Alexander Lippisch appears to have had some involvement from the outset too, perhaps thanks to his May 1942 proposal for a Schnellbomber, the P 10.

During this period, Focke-Wulf also appears to have been asked to submit its own thoughts on the possibilities for a Schnellflugzeug and Blohm & Voss submitted one too, although whether it was asked to do so or simply submitted a proposal loosely based on the specification is unclear.

During the autumn, Messerschmitt published a proposal which offered a radical solution for a perceived shortfall in German aircraft production. The document, which apparently survives only as an undated, untitled draft, states: "The last few months have clearly demonstrated that we do not have enough aircraft. The question arises why? The work capacity available to us in Europe should be big enough in order to keep pace with the production figures of the US and Russian aircraft industry to some extent.

"We also do not assume that the quality of our workers is worse than that of the Americans or even the Russians. Nevertheless, we build much fewer aircraft than our opponents. Thus, it is only possible that our aircraft industry works catastrophically uneconomically.

"The task of this memorandum is to

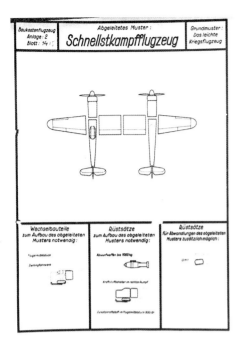

ABOVE: Modular fast bomber design – the earliest double Me 109 designs retained their original tail units.

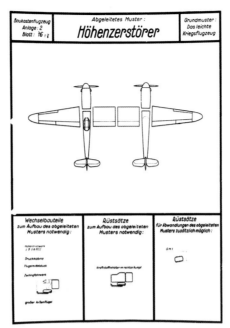

ABOVE: High-altitude heavy fighter powered by a pair of Daimler-Benz DB 622 engines.

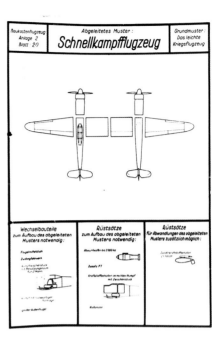

ABOVE: This larger fast bomber design features an extended cockpit to allow a second crewman, seated with his back to the pilot, presumably to act as radio operator and/or rear gunner.

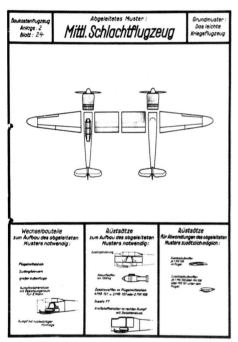

ABOVE: Modular Messerschmitt attack aircraft powered by a pair of BMW 801s.

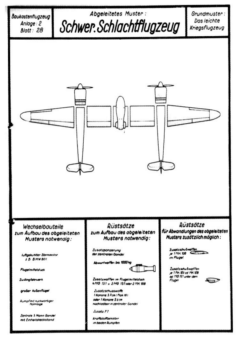

ABOVE: Heavy attack aircraft with central gondola cockpit and BMW 801 engines.

propose measures which are suitable for directing the work capacity available to the German armaments industry by planning on the crucial tasks in such a way that a multiple of today's production capacity is achieved. Project investigations, as well as all aircraft types that are still operating at the front, but are no longer in mass production, are out of consideration.

"This instructive overview and graphical comparison makes it easy to see the gaps in the previous planning at first glance. While on the one hand certain sectors are not covered at all, other tasks are often overcrowded. This is especially true for the area of two- to three-seater heavy fighters, night fighters and fighter aircraft.

"So today we build and develop 53 different basic aircraft types. The fact that

these 53 developments are happening at the same time is the reason why we do not get enough aircraft out. The ceiling of our work capacity is too low to build these 53 basic patterns at the same time. That is why the programmes have to be overturned constantly, none of these patterns are really ready for production and the distribution of the existing work capacity and the raw material is affected. Incredibly precious working hours are lost for these reasons.

"Unimaginable failures appear in the form of waiting times, scrapping of equipment, parts and devices and not least in a loss of labour due to the demoralising effect of such frequent changes. And this not only with the company that assembles the airframe, but multiplied by all the subcontractors."

The report suggested that the number of different aircraft types in production needed to be urgently reduced and "we propose to make the necessary deletions on the basis of the modular principle, which offers unprecedented freedom in disposition from a strategic point of view".

In other words, bits of existing aircraft types could be put together to create aircraft suitable for different missions. On this basis, just 16 basic aircraft 'patterns' would be needed – each consisting of interchangeable modular components, including the fuselage, wings, engine and tail unit. Different equipment packs could then be used to customise the aircraft for particular roles, such as extra fuel tanks for long range, camera equipment for reconnaissance or extra weapons for destroyers or ground-attack variants.

Among these basic patterns were a number of types formed by putting two existing fuselages side by side, connected by two straight wing sections. In some instances a new three-seater cockpit gondola was inserted between the two sections to form an even larger aircraft.

In all, the proposal offered 32 different modular patterns – slightly at odds with its own claims – 21 of which involved double fuselages. The benefits of creating new aircraft from a multitude of modular parts included faster production, commonality of parts and reduced costs. Naturally, all the examples given were composed of Messerschmitt parts. Nothing appears to have come of this lengthy proposal document at the time, but it was not forgotten.

EARLY COMPETITORS
On November 13, 1942, six months after the initial decision to pursue the development of a Schnellflugzeug, some of the possible designs were discussed at another RLM ▶

Schnell – Kampfflugzeuge

Geheim

Typ	Motor	PS bei N_k	Geschwindigkeit/Höhe bei N_k	N_{Not}	N_k mit GM1	Fläche m²	Fluggewicht kg	Kraftstoff kg	Reichweite VReise/H
1. Normal-Bauweise.	Jumo 211	2×1060/5.3	685/6.8	700/6.5	920/8.9	24	7700	1240	2000/500 /6
	BMW 801E	2×1390/6.3	745/7.7	770/8.4	764/10	28,9	9380	1500	
	DB 603 G	2×1475/7	750/8.4	760/8.4	767/10.5	28,5	9290	1500	2000/650 /6
2. Doppelmotor im Rumpf.	DB 610 C	2500/6.5	725/7.7	735/7.7	735/10	26	8500	1400	2100/635 /7.5
	DB 613	2950/7.0	760/8.2	772/8.2	770/10.5	29,7	9590	1500	
3. 3-motorig.	Jumo 211	3×1060/5.3	710/6.8	725/6.5	742/8.9	33.7	10875	1780	
	BMW 801E	3×1390/6.3	770/7.7	795/8.4	786/10	41.3	13135	2150	2000
	DB 603G	3×1475/7.0	773/8.4	785/8.3	790/10.5	40.2	12845	2100	
4. Zwei-Rumpf-Bauart.	BMW 801E	2×1390/6.3	760/7.7	785/8.4	777/10	28,5	9300	1500	2000/640 /6.0
	DB 603 G	2×1475/7.0	762/8.4	775/8.4	780/10.5	28	9140	1500	2000/650 /8
5. Schwanzlos-Einmotorig.	DB 603 G	1×1475/7.0	750/8.4	770/8.4	—	25	5100	960	2000
6. Einmotorig.	DB 603G	1×1475/7.0	727/8.3	740/8.3	748/10.5	16	5140	830	2000
	Jumo 222	1×2060/5.0	750/6.5	765/6.5	772/8.6	18	5800	950	
7. Strahl-Triebwerk (TL).	Jumo TL	2×925 kg	dauernd 712/8	810/9	—	26.4	8800	3150	1690/700 /9
8. 3-motorige B.u.V.-Bauweise.	BMW 801E	3×1390/6.3	765/7.7	790/8.4	—	44	13.500	2800	2400/620 /6
9. Junkers. Ju 288 Sonderprojekt	DB 610	2×2500/6.5	660/7.3	680/7.5	700/9	66	16.920	2560	2100/585 /9
10. FW 190	DB 603 G	1475/7	735/8.0	765/8.4	—	18.3	4340	—	—

Die Flugzeuge Nr 1 bis 7 sind in gleicher Auslegung gerechnet: 1 Mann; 500 kg Bomben; ohne Bewaffnung; 2000 km Reichweite.

Die Flugzeuge Nr 8 u. 9 sind mit 2 Mann Besatzung u. 1000 kg Bomben gerechnet. Ju 288 mit B-Stand MG 131 Z.

GL/C-E2
2/10. 42.
neu überarbeitet am 5/11. 42.

FACING PAGE: A selection of Heinkel designs intended as potential entries for the Schnellstbomber competition dated November 1942. At the bottom are some earlier entries – the Blohm & Voss P 170, and alternative versions of the Fw 190 and Ju 288.

development conference. First among these was the Blohm & Voss P 170 triple-engine Schnellbomber, a design created in late September 1942. Next was an unnamed large tailless type submitted by Lippisch. Luftwaffe test stations chief Oberst Edgar Petersen said that he was in favour of a tailless configuration because "the tailless machine is so agile, it moves around, makes a defensive movement. The other fighter then has to start a new attack, and he is not quick enough to do that. Personally I would therefore prefer the tailless design".

DVL chief Friedrich Seewald said: "I do not think all the qualities that the Me 163 undoubtedly has should be attributed to the fact that it is tailless. For the most part, it's because it does not have a propeller."

Generalfeldmarschall Erhard Milch said: "You know what kind of job I gave Lippisch with his Schnellbomber. I also believe that you can do all kinds of things in this area. But when I look at it in time, I have to agree with Professor Hertel that you have to act without compromise, and then I reject everything in which I still see the unknown."

He said Lippisch regarded the issue of tailless versus conventional aircraft as "solved" but "the question as it is with a very large tailless type is still unclear today. It will still be there, but it will probably take two or three years to work. I think we should strongly support the issue of the tailless aircraft, but not an ad-hoc project with the shortest possible deadline. We cannot afford that".

Then there was a design put forward by Kurt Tank on behalf of Focke-Wulf. A twin-engine fighter was mentioned first – probably the Ta 154 – then Walter Friebel, from the RLM's technical office, said: "Focke-Wulf had indeed submitted a project Schnellbomber. But we dropped that."

A month later, on December 12, 1942, the Lippisch, Blohm & Voss and Focke-Wulf projects were gone and Hertel presented his findings at the RLM development conference. In the meeting's minutes, this section has the heading 'Schnellstbomber' or 'fastest bomber'.

Friebel began the meeting by outlining the requirement for single seater, 500kg bomb load, 2000km range aircraft using existing engines, then after a brief discussion with Milch about the climb rate he said: "The reworked designs – three-engine, four-engine and one-engine – showed that the most useful thing to do is to make a two-engine aircraft, a two-engine twin-fuselage aircraft, where the pilot sits in the left fuselage. One would have something like a double fighter."

Hertel then presented the Junkers design for a Schnellstbomber: "We have reworked the project of a two-fuselage aircraft with the aim of getting a fast-paced aircraft. It has been shown that the basic assumption that you have an airplane of about 7.5 tons is

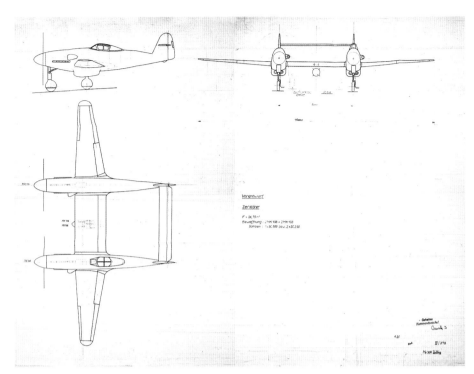

ABOVE: The Me 309 Zwilling – abbreviated to Me 309 Zw in the report text – and never referred to as the Me 609, which was something else entirely.

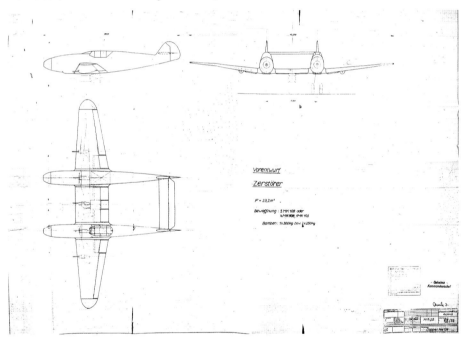

ABOVE: The double Me 109 eventually entered for the Schnellstbomber competition was a refinement of the earlier modular designs. Wind tunnel testing demonstrated the need for a narrower central section and a single tailplane to join the two fuselages together.

correct. Maintaining the demand of 500kg bombs, the aircraft would weigh about 7.3 tons and reach a speed of 760km/h. This project has now been thoroughly studied.

"This results in the requirement that the bombs must be housed in the fuselage and a solution is found, which is aerodynamically high quality. The result is laid down in this drawing. The bomb lies pretty much directly under the wing. On one side the pilot sits above the bomb bay, on the other side this space remains free. The undercarriage is folded right back and disappears here behind the wing."

Milch asked whether the Junkers design, the designation and appearance of which is unknown today, used any elements of

existing fighters and was told that it did not.

Three days before the meeting Messerschmitt had drawn up plans for a twin-fuselage Me 309, based on the principles of the earlier proposal, and submitted them to the RLM just in time. Questioning Hertel, Wolfram Eisenlohr, head of the RLM's engine development section, said it would surely be easier if the 'doubling' involved "the finished engine of the 109, the armament of the 109, the whole hull."

Milch cut in: "You said '109'."

Eisenlohr: "No, the 309, pardon, I misspoke myself there. This solution could come from the 309 relatively quickly. It would be, as I said, built on the 309. I could ▶

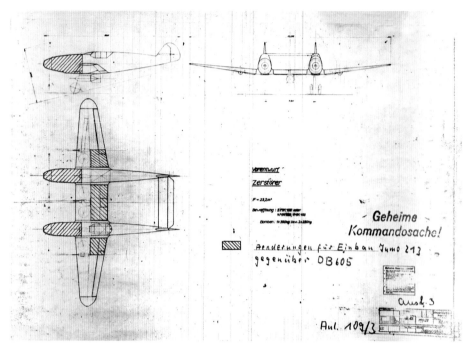

ABOVE: Modified drawing of the Me 109 Zw, showing sections that would need to be changed if the DB 605 of the original design was to be replaced with a Jumo 213.

imagine that would make a very quick solution possible. This way could lead very quickly to operational service. The engine and everything else would be there; that would not be a substantial matter."

Freibel said: "But what would have to be redone would be the tail and the middle piece; where Messerschmitt forgot to mention the undercarriage. The width here at Messerschmitt is not enough to get in the undercarriage."

After the meeting, it was decided to hold a follow-up conference on January 8, 1943, where the companies now involved – Junkers, Heinkel and Messerschmitt – could formally present their proposals. However, it soon became apparent that other firms were eager to participate and had suitable designs. Dornier and Arado were allowed to put forward proposals and the date of the presentation meeting was pushed back to January 19, 1943, at 10am.

PROJECT COMPARISONS

When the day came, Claude Dornier brought along the P 231, Willy Messerschmitt brought the Me 109 Zw – the Me 309 Zw evidently having been shelved, Hertel brought his unnamed twin-fuselage Junkers aircraft and another unnamed Junkers design with two engines in the fuselage driving a contra-rotating prop in the nose, Arado had submitted the E 530 but no one from the company appeared to present it, and Siegfried Günter presented three unnamed Heinkel designs – a twin-fuselage fighter, a twin-engine contra-rotating prop design and a twin-jet design.

The Messerschmitt submission had originally been drafted on December 9, 1942, and included both the Me 109 Zw and Me 309 Zw. It began: "According to the proposal to unify the warplanes on a few basic patterns, preliminary designs were carried out for the development of a fast aircraft from two single-seat fighters. The main use of this combined aircraft is use as: destroyer

with strong armament and possibly small bomb load up to 500kg or fast bomber with reduced armament, but larger range and bomb load up to 2000kg. As a starting pattern, the preliminary investigations were based on the Me 109 and Me 309.

"Compared to a new development for the same task position, such a combination of existing aircraft has the advantage that the start of production is much faster. In addition, the cost of redesign and fixtures is only about 30% of the necessary for an entirely new design. Another advantage of the use of existing patterns is the accelerated testing, since experimental patterns can be created in a short time and in case of need even in larger quantities. In addition, most essential components already have been endurance tested in the initial aircraft.

"Basically, this design also allows a two-seater version, but at the expense of lower fuel stock. Furthermore, for this twin aircraft, as well as in the basic pattern, the possibilities of increasing the power available, e.g. special fuel or additional injection, apply. For the preliminary designs Me 109 and Me 309 the following picture emerges: A) Double Me 109. A quick solution on the basis of Me 109 G with DB 605 is the best option in terms of scheduling. The Jumo 213 (possibly unit drive unit) and new landing flap are equipped with further development options with greater construction costs."

The double Me 109 would involve the use of the two fighters with alterations limited to "creation of a new wing piece between the two hulls (simple production, as rectangular), laying the landing gear connections and using larger wheels, change of the wheel housing in the wing, extension of ailerons and slots, installation of additional containers instead of the second pilot's seat, new tailplane (simple production, because rectangular)".
Weaponry as a destroyer would be five

MK 108 cannon, or four MK 108s and one MK 103. The bomber would carry two MK 108s and 1500 litres more fuel.

For the second option, "B) Double Me 309. The preliminary drafts show a combination of two Me 309 with DB 603 G, albeit still in the initial stage basically the same possibilities as the combination of the two Me 109. According to the built-in, more powerful engines, the performances are better". The necessary changes were the same as for the Me 109. Armament as a destroyer was two MK 108s and two MK 103s, although two further MK 108s could also be accommodated if need be.

A second document, of January 6, 1943, focused solely on the "Schnellbomber Me 109 Zwilling". This time the engine was given only as the Jumo 213 A or B, either of which could apparently easily be fitted to the Me 109. Everything else remained the same and presumably it was this version which Messerschmitt presented at the January 19 conference.

Milch was unavailable for the meeting, so it was chaired instead by Luftwaffe General der Flieger Egon Doerstling. Generalleutnant Wolfgang Vorwald, chief of the RLM's development department, spoke first after Doerstling's introduction, saying: "The only point to be dealt with is the question of fast bombers. The last session was on December 12. It was supposed to be repeated on the 8th of January with the necessary additions to the submitted projects. Meanwhile, the circle of tendering companies has been expanded, and today the individual projects are to be discussed. I ask that Oberst Pasewaldt discuss the projects in detail."

Head of the RLM's technical office, Dr Georg Pasewaldt said that representatives of the companies concerned would present lectures on their designs in alphabetical order. Friebel then said: "Once again, I would like to send you a brief explanation of the call for tenders. In previous meetings, the project has been handled by a variety of companies, which included the following task: 500kg bomb at 2000km route and a speed of at least 750km. There were a variety of types on this occasion: single-engine, twin-engine, three-engined, tailless, twin-fuselage, and it turned out that more designs could be interesting, namely a single-fuselage twin-engine aircraft with propellers front and rear, and single-fuselage twin-engine with two counter-rotating propellers, with the power of the rear engine being delivered through the cannon hole through to the front propeller, and finally, based on the current state of jet engine development, the solution based on the jet engine.

"These tasks have been tackled by the companies Heinkel, Messerschmitt, Dornier, Junkers and Arado, and it is probably best that the gentlemen present now. The company Arado has not appeared at the moment."

With no Arado, Claude Dornier went first, discussing his P 231. The alphabetical sequence did not apply to Hertel, because Milch had given him the task of assessing the others, rather than presenting the

Junkers project – which evidently had been dropped by this point. Dornier said: "We got involved in the work on this task at a later date, but have been able to fall back on earlier work. We assumed that the normal fighter in the arrangement of the lateral engines is actually obsolete, and as a solution have brought the tandem order: a motor with tractor prop, normally installed, as in the fighter, and an engine behind the pilot, via a shaft extension driving a propeller located behind the tail."

He said work on the design had actually begun in 1937 and had been submitted to the RLM but that at that point it "was probably ahead of its time".

Heinkel was next and Günter said: "We worked on the Schnellstbomber with propeller propulsion and jet propulsion. We soon realised that higher speeds were definitely calculated with the jet propulsion system. If one still concerns oneself with the propeller drive, then the question of construction time was urgent in our opinion. It only has purpose if you can do it faster than jet-propelled aircraft.

"For the various options we have considered, we have therefore proposed only the simplest forms, namely a twin plane with two normal single-seaters. We have also dealt with another idea, with an airplane with centrally located engines in the fuselage. But we thought that doing more work for the development means that if we do this work, we'd rather put it in a jet plane.

"The twin aircraft is in construction certainly the simplest thing there is. You can certainly prove that you can achieve the performance of a single-seater, despite the bomb load. That seemed to us the main condition attached to the design."

He said little more about his twin-fuselage prop-driven aircraft and single fuselage contra-rotating prop design, concentrating the rest of his speech on the twin-engine jet, which had three MG 151s installed in the housing above each engine. None of these designs is known today.

THE DOUBLE 109

Willy Messerschmitt went last of the three contenders. He said: "Herr General, I did not really intend to take part in this fast bomber thing. I did it only because I take the view that, with today's load on the aircraft industry and the ongoing recoveries, it is necessary to spare effort and, moreover, that such aircraft, still using Otto engines, must come to the front as soon as possible if they are to have value.

"Therefore, I investigated whether it is possible to build such a plane with a 109, using most of its parts. As Günter has already said, it is quite possible to build a two-fuselage aircraft from the existing fighter, which will fully meet the demands of speed in the near future. Such an aircraft could perhaps fly in half a year and, because of the large-scale production of the 109, of course, can also come to the front in the very shortest time. The savings are about 75% compared to a new aircraft. That does not matter so much in the design, but primarily in manufacturing.

"If you start a new aircraft today

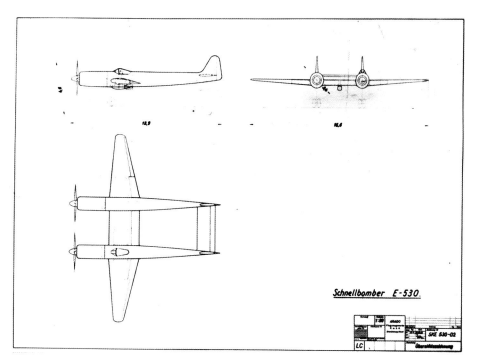

ABOVE: Arado apparently only entered the Schnellstbomber competition towards the end of the assessment process and then was not present to discuss its design. This does not seem to have surprised any of the participants in the final design comparison meeting – the egoless government-owned Arado largely did as it was told without complaint.

with new surfaces, a new undercarriage, equipment, fuselage, tail, then this is a giant process, which requires a structure. But if we take an existing aircraft, if we do not do something which is not even necessary, then we can do it in a very short time. We need to start again practically only on the tailplane, in the simplest way, the middle between the wings left and right, between the two fuselages, the connecting piece and otherwise some changes. As an undercarriage here it is thought it will take the shock absorber of the 110 as it is. So again, no redesign.

"In this way, we would at least achieve the benefits that the companies Heinkel and Junkers would achieve with the twin-hull aircraft. There is certainly no reason to think that the benefits are lower. But we would certainly be there in a year, if not sooner.

"On the other hand, the jet aircraft is coming in the foreseeable future. We fly a jet in Augsburg. This is probably designed as a fighter, but it can also take 500kg bombs. In its characteristics it is reasonably okay, and at least it has already flown at speeds in 6000 to 7000m altitude of about 850km at a climb rate of 13m/sec. You can make a fast bomber out of such a plane without too much modification. Of course, it will not get into production as fast as the double-fuselage 109, because all the devices have to be created and the run-up for the whole plane is to be done."

HERTEL'S SUMMARY

Speaking after Messerschmitt, and providing a technical summary of the preceding projects, Hertel was keen to point out that he too had come to the Schnellstbomber competition late. He said: "Junkers was originally not involved in the development of a high-speed bomber. She has come to this task by the commissioning of the field marshal, that I should subject the submitted drafts of a review and recalculation."

He said that when he had first begun to draw up Junkers' competition entry, the two-fuselage arrangement had seemed the most promising, but "when working through this draft of a two-fuselage aircraft, it turned out that such a solution is quite unattractive and does not really come to terms with the concept of a high-speed bomber, since the second fuselage would have to disappear in a high-speed bomber.

"A project has therefore been developed by Junkers in which two motors are connected in series, the second drives a second propeller via a shaft passing through the gun bore of the first. At the time, this project also looked quite favourable from the engine side after the discussion with Daimler-Benz. However, it has become clear that such a project needs about one to one-and-a-half years more on the engine side."

He said that based on this delay, a design similar to Dornier's Do 231 had been examined, because the single fuselage would have far less drag. Referring back to the other projects, he said: "The two-fuselage projects which have been presented by Heinkel, Junkers and Messerschmitt, are almost identical. What also Messerschmitt said: if such a project is built, then there is the question of the building of a double Me 109. A new design will not be worth looking at, especially since practical testing of a new design will prove to be difficult even with the fastest construction.

"The performance achieved can be stated at 770km/h at the height of 8.5 to 9km. This is the mathematical mean of the three solutions. The details of the projects only fluctuate by 1%. What is very characteristic is that in all designs

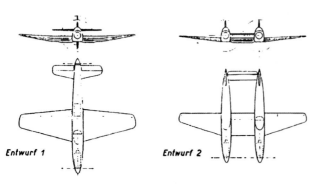

Vergleich zweier Schnellbomber - Entwürfe   DoP 231

Entwurf 1

Entwurf 2

Gegenüber Entwurf 1 ergeben sich für Entwurf 2 folgende Unterschiede:

Rumpf-Oberflächen
(mit Triebwerken)

Rumpf-Stirnflächen

Schädlicher Widerstand
Σ c_w · F ohne Flügel

Höchst- Geschwindigkeit

Dornier-Werke G.m.b.H.
Friedrichshafen a. B.

DoP 231/2-03
T 101 a t as R 5

ABOVE: Dornier presented its P 231 Schnellbomber design with both the 'in vogue' double-fuselage layout and Dornier's own unique tandem push-pull arrangement, which won it a great deal of support.

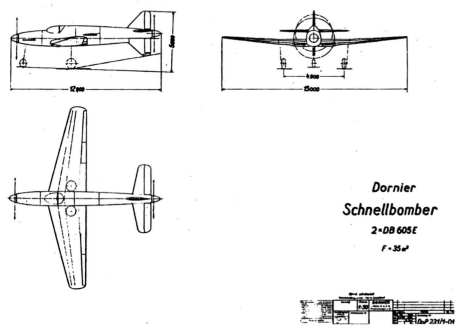

Dornier

Schnellbomber

2 = DB 605 E

F = 35 m²

DoP 231/1-01

ABOVE: The drawing might look simplistic – but the decision-makers at the RLM in January 1943 quickly recognised the potential of the single-fuselage Dornier P 231. It defeated the Messerschmitt Me 109 Zw and went on to become the Do 335.

In essence, the choice boiled down to a slower double fuselage design delivered earlier, or a faster single fuselage design delivered later.

THE LUFTWAFFE VIEW

As the meeting went on, the two young Luftwaffe representatives – General of Fighters Adolf Galland and General of Bombers Dietrich Peltz – came increasingly to favour the Dornier design, expressing some scepticism about the double Me 109.

Peltz said: "Even assuming that the Messerschmitt solution is for 1944 and the Dornier solution comes in 1945, I certainly believe that the performance advantage will make up for that lead."

Given that this would deprive the Luftwaffe's bomber squadrons of a new machine for at least two more years, rather than one, Vorwald said: "You are of the opinion that you could manage with fighter-bombers in the fast-action area for so long?" Peltz replied: "Yes!"

Vorwald went on: "This is a very important statement. May I ask if anybody wants to take the floor on the decision that is now emerging for the Me 109 Zwilling or the Dornier project, or if there are reasons to do both? Is there a demand for making both solutions?"

Doerstling said: "Crucial is the General of the Fighters as a representative of the General Staff. When he says 'I find myself with current conditions until the year 1944 anyway, and when I see the Dornier in front of me I do not think much of an interim solution. It depends on the final solution,' that is very binding. We must strive uncompromisingly for a long-lasting solution. But of course everyone feels a sense of responsibility when he says something like that."

Vorwald said that choosing Dornier's project would not leave the fighter squadrons with an incapable aircraft.

Galland then said: "I do not know if the American did not plan a similar development when he started on the Lightning back then. It's also a double fighter-sized plane after all. At that time, as he now sees, he did not choose very well. He has shipped the plane to Africa and flies it around there now.

"If the performance is actually only 40km higher than a fighter's and the bomb load is nearly the same, the remaining conditions are the same, but the flight characteristics are worse, then you are left wondering whether if it is not better for the fighter to increase the performance with the jet engine until the connection with the double-engine Dornier is there, and see whether that is not faster with less effort."

Doerstling thought Galland was confusing matters by suggesting that the P 231 would be better for fighter pilots.

But Galland said: "I mean it differently. With all its load, the 109 suffers a loss of speed. Now, I wonder if we cannot make it faster before we go and build a plane that is just a tiny margin above it, and then take the next step to a two-engine plane."

Doerstling: "It makes you wonder if we can do that."

the assumption of the surface size is about the same, about 25 square metres, at Messerschmitt somewhat smaller, at the others a little larger. Also, the construction weight is about the same, namely 7.65 tons with 5% fluctuations in the information, so that is quite clear: a new design in this area is not worth it, as Messerschmitt says."

He said that "according to the modular method proposed by Messerschmitt, there will be an extremely fast production startup and the possibility, if it does not prove successful as a fast bomber, to switch to a fighter". He said that the Messerschmitt presentation gave too few details about the bombing ability of the double 109. And "in addition, the external suspension is still unsightly in the current project".

However, he said he believed Messerschmitt would find a solution to this and that "considering the above points of view, I consider the Me 109 Gemini to be the fastest to produce and most appropriate solution".

Regarding the single fuselage designs, he said that the Dornier design looked just like that of Junkers "only that the drive shaft goes directly backwards and drives the propeller. Now that engine development is in place, I have to say that Dornier's project as a high-speed bomber will probably be much faster". He said that a single fuselage would have a smaller surface area, better airflow over the wings and would allow the propellers to operate more efficiently.

From a production standpoint, the Luftwaffe's senior staff engineer Roluf Lucht said: "I think that a twin brings great advantages on the factory side and the performance advantages in the short term are so great that you should make the twin for these reasons, especially since the Me 210 in one and a half years does not have the performance, as this machine brings. When this machine is there, the cry will come for a larger number of them, as well as for higher speed and very good armament, which could still be mounted in the centre section."

Galland would not be dissuaded from picking the P 231 though. He said: "I find it unsustainable that we commit ourselves to the Messerschmitt project, and thus bring even more into a heavily loaded machine. Then that will be only half a solution, which goes quickly, but not without many extra demands on crew and rear armament and additional bomb suspension. In terms of performance, you can not create more weight in the mass as it stands on paper."

Friebel also argued for the double 109 because he believed it could handle a heavier weapons load: "There will be very high demands on fighter development in the near future. Apart from the flight performance, the height and the speed, it demands in the future the accommodation of the 5cm weapon. These are all things that cannot be covered in the single-engine fighter for the near future. I see no other option than to set up the quick combat question and the fighter question in one and the same airframe with equipment kits.

"I see comparatively clearly the solution in the twin 109, because a really heavy weapon can be housed centrally, in the symmetrical plane, where otherwise the bombs would be accommodated. We will not spare these aircraft from use as fighters either. We know perfectly well that the one-engine fighter, with the demands of the fighter pilot's side for the year 1943 and 1944, cannot be built with the 109, even if we incorporate more powerful engines.

"Therefore, I see the fastest solution in the two-fuselage solution, because in 1943, at the latest in 1944, this would bring something to the enemy. I think it quite possible that the Dornier project could also be suitable as a fighter, but it actually comes a little later."

He said that the P 231 would simply not be able to accommodate the necessary weaponry and added: "Personally, knowing that next year I will be under tremendous pressure, I am in favour of making the twin and dropping the other because I am convinced that in 1944 on the fighter side, it will be very close."

Doerstling said that the fighter side and the bomber side should each have something separate but Messerschmitt put in: "Unfortunately, there is the question of capacity, which is now practically such that it brings the collapse of development, if we continue this way. If it continues like this, our development will be lagging behind in a year compared to those abroad because too much is done. Of course, it would be nice to do a variety of tasks."

FINAL DECISION

Pasewaldt said he was in favour of building both in an ideal world but thought that, realistically, Messerschmitt did not have the capacity to build the double 109 unless another major project was dropped: "The desirable solution with regard to deadlines would be the development of the Messerschmitt double 109, and then for the reasons that have been expressed by the General of the Fighters and also by Lieutenant Colonel von Lossberg, under all circumstances, the Dornier solution.

"I have continued to pay attention to the capacities available and they are extremely limited. In the course of our conversations, it turned out that Messerschmitt, as I knew it anyway, was not in a position to carry out this work unless other important projects were to be cancelled. The focus for Messerschmitt is firstly taking care of the fighters, to which a special meeting is reserved tomorrow, and secondly in the advancement of the Me 262. It's not possible to talk about that at all. Up for debate today, as General Doerstling

also emphasised, is the fast bomber.

"The solution of the fast bomber is undoubtedly the Dornier project. As a result, I would like to ask that the Dornier project be decided as the quick response solution, regardless of the fact that the Dornier project can also be used in many ways for the fighter side."

Vorwald said: "I fully agree with this statement, but in the end I would like to ask the General of the Fighters if he agrees with this opinion as well."

Galland and Peltz both answered: "Yes!"

Messerschmitt himself spoke next, saying that he also believed that the P 231 "must be carried through" but asking that some thought be given to building it with at least some existing parts, and to "the industry working better together".

Dornier said: "I agree with the remarks of Professor Messerschmitt. I would welcome it if a community work came about. We've already considered that and tried to use the Arado hub, and so on. What can be saved must be saved. We would be very happy if we could draw on the experience of other companies involved in high-speed aircraft and take these experiences into account."

Vorwald moved that the decision was made: the Dornier P 231 was the Schnellstbomber, adding: "Should we set a number today? About 10 V-pattern aircraft?" This was approved. "So, 10 V-pattern aircraft."

Doerstling then said: "What is the final decision against Messerschmitt?" Pasewaldt, in the background, said: "Quick combat solution!" But no further discussion took place and this appears to have been the end for the Me 109 Zw or Doppel 109. The type appears to have been referred to as the Me 109 Z after the meeting and up to about May 1943.

The push-pull Dornier P 231 was given the RLM designation Do 335 and was destined never to see service. Had the Me 109 Zw been chosen, and had sufficient production capacity been found to assemble it, it might well have entered service in numbers before the end of the war. ●

SO WHAT WAS THE ME 609?

For years, the double-fuselage Me 309 has been referred to by historians as the 'Me 609' but it is quite clear that this is incorrect. Numerous Messerschmitt documents survive which refer to the Me 609 and none of them has anything to do with the Me 309. They tend to be lists of components, and drawings showing the assembly of a twin-jet fighter. In fact, they all show the Me 262. It would appear that 'Me 609' was a designation applied to standard Me 262s from late summer 1944 to the end of the war. Exactly why this was done is unclear, but it has been stated elsewhere that the designation was used to "cover test-ready Me 262s" and there seems no reason to doubt this.

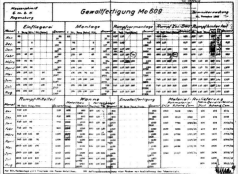
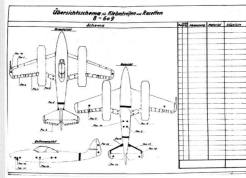
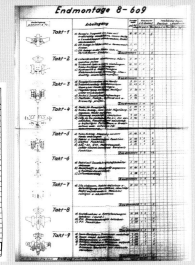

ABOVE: Three pages from three different reports on the Me 609 – each showing assembly details for the Me 262.

Junkers' 163

Messerschmitt Me 163 with canards

The Me 163 was the archetypal tailless fighter but even its creator wondered whether it might have been improved with additional control surfaces. Willy Messerschmitt wanted to fit it with a V-tail and Junkers had another approach in mind...

Alexander Lippisch was always seeking ways to improve the aerodynamics of his tailless designs and on October 11 and 12, 1941, he sketched out a patent application for four potential alterations to the Me 163.

The first involved fitting panels into the sides of its tail which could be lowered to form conventional tailplanes and raised back into the fin when they were not required. The second was for control surfaces which could be extended backwards from the rear section of its wings and a third was for horizontal tail surfaces which could flipped out of the aircraft's rear fuselage on either side.

The fourth patent design was for slightly forward-swept canards which could be flipped out of the aircraft's nose on either side. Retracted, these would sit just beneath the pilot's feet before sweeping out when deployed.

These designs were submitted by Messerschmitt AG on November 14, 1941,

and given the application number PA 811167 by the German patent office on November 18. None of the ideas seems to have found its way into practical tests with the physical aircraft, however.

On July 11, 1942, Willy Messerschmitt himself wrote a patent application for a tailless aircraft, which looked rather like the Me 163, fitted with a V-tail. The sides of the 'V' could be raised together to form a single fin – a similar idea to Lippisch's of nine months earlier.

Messerschmitt wrote: "For tailless aircraft, it is generally necessary to use a vertical stabiliser for stability around the vertical axis. Since the possible moments around the vertical axis are not sufficient to be able to use landing flaps, which lead to a large shift in the neutral point, it is suggested to fit on the tailless machine – a) two smaller tail units, so-called V-tail units, which should fulfil the purpose of landing,

because their inclined arrangement assists with the tailplane. b) The same arrangement, characterised in that the two tails lie on top of each other during the flight with the retracted landing flap, so that they have a surface equal to that of a single tail."

One of the key reasons for installing a V-tail was to provide a larger centre of gravity margin, which would aid stability. It could also be used to provide increased lift. However, the V-tail idea was never implemented.

Following the departure of Lippisch and the dissolution of his Abteilung L, Messerschmitt carried out further development of the Me 163 only reluctantly. Similarly, the main contractor entrusted with series production of the type – Hanns Klemm Flugzeugbau – was very slow to get going since the company had no equipment for building the type's metal fuselage and its workforce required extensive training.

The solution to both these problems was to transfer all responsibility for the Me 163 to a reliable, well-resourced and compliant third party. Junkers stepped in and as of September 1, 1944, assumed full responsibility for both developing and manufacturing the Me 163.

Initially, Junkers assessed the aircraft and decided to make a number of practical changes intended primarily to speed up production but also to save materials. Drawings were revised to ensure that major assemblies could be easily swapped and designed a new skid made of steel which would save on precious aluminium. The company's designers also altered the fuel tank installation, the landing flap mechanism and the canopy jettison system.

But the company went further than changes intended to facilitate production – it also worked on much more fundamental improvements to the aircraft's overall

ABOVE: Wolfgang Späte's bright red (RLM 23) Messerschmitt Me 163 B PK+QL as it might have looked with the experimental Junkers canards-nose fitted. Artwork by Hamza Fouatih

shape. Junkers was also aware of the problems that Willy Messerschmitt had attempted to cure using a V-tail and appears to have tried to solve them using canards and a slightly stretched nose instead.

Two Junkers wind tunnel photos, numbered J.59362 and J.59363 show a glossy model Me 163 fitted with an extended nosecone to which a pair of forward-swept triangular canards are attached. There is some evidence to suggest that another arrangement was tried with rear-swept canards too, though no further documentation on either arrangement has yet been discovered. It seems likely that Junkers had seen the Lippisch/Messerschmitt patent of 1941 and was now trying out one of Lippisch's ideas.

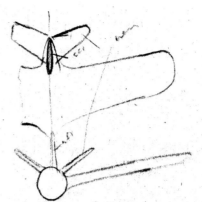

11.7.42 Mtt/El.

ABOVE: Hand-drawn sketch from a letter signed by Willy Messerschmitt showing his idea for a 'tailless' aircraft with a V-tail.

However, these tests apparently did not show sufficient merit to warrant further action but Junkers did not give up on its attempts to improve on the Me 163 B design. Just six weeks after Junkers had taken on the design, on October 11, 1944, the company put forward a proposal to build a new aircraft which embodied a host of changes to the original while still retaining large sections unaltered – particularly the wings. Evidently modifying the existing Me 163 B was simply not enough.

This proposal was refined in a document entitled Kurzbaubeschreibung 248 on November 3, 1944. This stated: "The 248 is a further development of the 163 B. It originated from the effort to create a new series in which the identified weaknesses of the 163 B are removed, but the components running in production are largely carried over without modification. The main defects of the 163 B are considered to be: 1) Too little flight time and thus too little possibility of enemy engagement. 2) Unsatisfactory solution to the start problem with detachable undercarriage. 3) Unsatisfactory landing characteristics of the skid solution (lateral danger of overturning, too low ground angle). 4) Lack of manoeuvrability and thus obstruction due to skid solution. 5) Maximum possible lift on landing unavailable due to inappropriate centre of gravity.

"The 248 has the following essential features: The outer wing surfaces of the

163 B are carried over. There are only a few minor modifications required as a result of enlargement of the wing attachment point. Due to a broadening of the hull (see below), the span increases by 0.2m. The subsequent attachment option of an unbound, high-speed profiled surface is taken into account in the fuselage construction.

"To eliminate the shortcomings of a skid solution, a nosewheel assembly is installed. Main undercarriage and nosewheel are pneumatically retractable. The nose wheel is in the retracted position under the bottom of the pressure cabin, the main bogie in the fuselage between wing beams I and II. This was designed with the aim of creating a construction that also allows landing on extended wheels without risk of breakage, in order to prevent damage to the fuselage. The main bogie and nosewheel systems were therefore chosen so that the longitudinal forces are transmitted via rocker arm directly into the fuselage spars and the lateral forces are deposited on the fuselage frame via a soft strut with low suspension damping."

The Ju 248 was designed with a longer rear fuselage too, so that the centre of gravity could be altered more easily. So after the abandonment of a bolt-on stretched nose and canards for the Me 163, the more substantial redesign that was the Ju 248 was approved for development – albeit too late for anything more than a cursory series of flight tests on a single prototype. ●

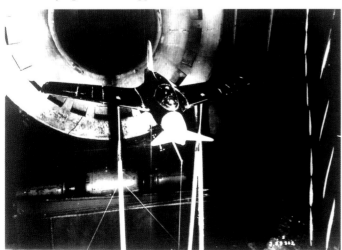

ABOVE: Junkers wind tunnel model of the Me 163 B fitted with an extended nosecone and forward-swept canards.

ABOVE: A side view of the Junkers Me 163 B model with canards.

The anti-Me

Messerschmitt P 1079

During the first half of the war, Messerschmitt had two project offices. While Abteilung L worked on tailless jet- and rocket-propelled types, the general project office came up with a rival pulsejet contender...

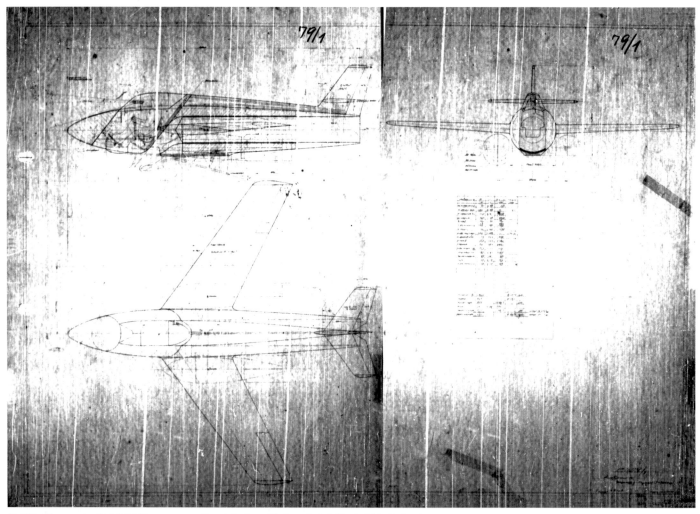

ABOVE: Messerschmitt P 1079/1 – a conventional design with its pulsejet fitted within its fuselage.

Preparations for the first powered flight of the Messerschmitt Me 163 were well under way during the early summer of 1941. This was practical engineering work and there was little more that designer Alexander Lippisch's project office could do to help. Therefore, he returned to the P 01 project series he had established on joining Messerschmitt in 1939 and continued working on it.

At the same time, the main Messerschmitt project office under Woldemar Voigt had plans of its own. Earlier in the year, the Messerschmitt company

had begun talks with engine maker Argus about the pulsejets it was working on with inventor Paul Schmidt. There had been tentative plans to use pulsejets to power the P 65, which would later become the Me 262, but now Voigt's team were working on a project intended to produce a pulsejet aircraft of a similar size to the Me 163.

During May 1941, at least 21 designs were drafted by the project office under the umbrella designation of P 79, also written as P 1079 as the Messerschmitt project numbering system changed around this time. A report was produced

at the end of July which detailed P 1079/1 to P 1079/17, with /10 and /13 being subdivided into /10a-c and /13a-c.

The report, entitled simply 'Aircraft with jet tubes', compared the projected performance of the Argus pulsejet against that of an unspecified BMW turbojet and concluded that while the former provided only 500kg thrust compared to the latter's 600kg, the pulsejet weighed only 80kg, compared to the turbojet's 600kg. On a very small aircraft, the pulsejet's light weight made a big difference – although its fuel consumption

163

was almost twice that of the turbojet.

According to the report, under the heading 'design and task': "For the time being only generally required: high maximum speed, good climbing performance with comparatively large loads (bombs up to 2000kg)." The pulsejet could apparently guarantee a high maximum speed so "the consideration of the ascending attributes should be omitted here". The P 1079's swept wings were also designed with high speed in mind.

It was hoped that Argus would be able to develop the pulsejet into an 800kg thrust variant but "considering that the largest device currently under development produces 500kg of thrust (it is not yet possible to specify an enlargement of the device)" the fuselage had been kept as small as possible in the designs examined. It was hoped that even with a pair of 500kg thrust engines, the P 1079 would be able to fulfil five different roles "1. Fighter – high-speed good climbing ability, range up to 800km. 2. Reconnaissance – good climbing performance and maximum altitude, sufficient ranges to fly over large oceans. 3. Interceptor – high climb rates with low flight times. 4. Bomber – sufficient speed with enclosed bombs to escape today's fighter aircraft. 5. Parasite aircraft (as bomber or fighter) – small dimensions."

The P 1079 document, as it has survived, includes only 11 of the maximum 21 designs. Each is presented with a single drawing and a very brief typed description – often including critical comments.

For P 1079/1, a relatively conventional design, it says: "Accommodation of the fuel in two containers; one of them is executed as a ring tank (fire hazard). Fuel quantity 1200 litres. Unfavourable air intake for the engine. Bad opportunity to enclose the bombs. Unfavourable for engine upgrade. The engine is also the tail carrier."

The second design, P 1079/2, looked unusual with the pilot in the nose and a very long fuselage behind. According to the comments: "Division: Cockpit – fuel tank space – fuselage with engine. Fuel quantity 1200 litres. Unfavourable air intake."

P 1079/3 looked somewhat similar to P 1079/1, and with good reason: "Further development from 79/1. Slightly improved air intake. Improved visibility. Fuel storage in a tank (ring tank). Fuel 1200 litres. Unfavourable centre of gravity position."

Although it doesn't say so, P 1079/4 appears to have been another improvement on the same theme: "Fuel storage in a saddle tank. Residual fuel in the tip of the fuselage underside. Engine on the fuselage underside (improved upgradeability). Lateral air intake.

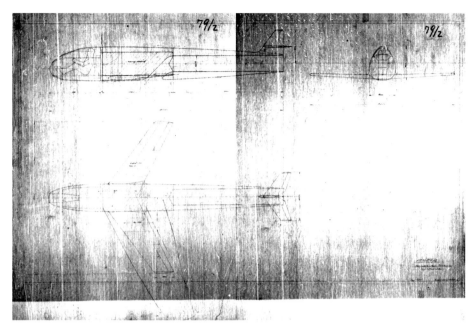

ABOVE: The bizarrely elongated P 1079/2 with its pulsejet at the extreme rear. The P 1079 series appears to have been an exercise in working out where best to place the engine and intakes.

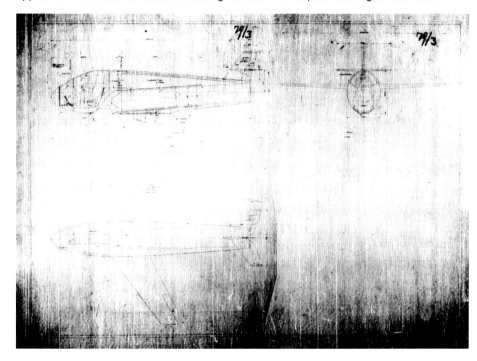

ABOVE: P 1079/3 was a development of P 1079/1.

The P 1079/5 again took a similar layout but this time it was an opportunity to try scaling the wings: "Fuel accommodation in the wing. Large wing thickness 10-25% while the following amounts of fuel can be accommodated: wing area 5sqm approx. 330 litres, wing area 8sqm approx. 640 litres, wing area 10sqm approx. 920 litres. Engine = tail unit."

The sixth design is entirely missing and nothing is known about it. P 1079/7 features a radically repositioned engine – right up on top of the fuselage and to the rear: "The engine is laid free on the fuselage and serves as a tail carrier. Air intake significantly improved. Inadmissible load changes with gas take-off."

Designs eight, nine, 10a and 10b are then missing, with P 1079/10c being next in the series: "Engine installation in the fuselage end, the rear part of the tube

protruding freely. Unfavourable air intake. Fuel content 800 litres. Unfavourable bombing, especially with two bombs."

Designs 11, 12 and 13a are missing, then arguably the most important known design is outlined – P 1079/13b. The report provides a slightly longer description of it too: "Use of two engines. Air intake significantly improved. Fuel content 900 litres. Unfavourable arrangement of the engines. Clear and cheap construction. Easy interchangeability of the engines. Uncertainty in the stability. Good chance to enclose it even when using two bombs. Relatively simple solution of the dive brake. Better flight performance than single engine design."

P 1079/13c and 14 are missing, then comes the remarkable asymmetrical P 1079/15: "Impeccable air intake for the engine. Large amounts of fuel – 1540 litres

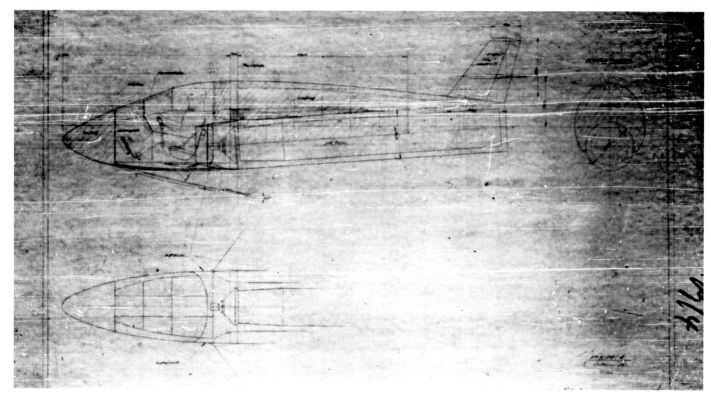

ABOVE: Another development of the /1 – the P 1079/4.

or, when using the entire left fuselage space, 2375 litres. Possibility of two-man crew. One-man crew bad visibility. Possibility to enclose the bombs as in draft 79/13b."

P 1079/16 was similar to 15 but more slender: "Modification of the draft 79/15 (omission of the left fuselage half). Fuel quantity 770 litres. Unbalanced, otherwise like design 79/15." And finally there was the somewhat more conventional P 1079/17: "Modification of the draft 79/16. Improved visibility. Improved stability around the transverse axis. Fuel content 800 litres. Possibility to install fixed weapons in the fuselage tip. Engine side same as draft 79/16. No possibility to reasonably arrange and enclose the bombs."

Graphs then show various values for P 1079/4 to 10, then 10c-13a, then 14, then 13b and finally 15-17. This was followed by a full construction description of the P 1079 (given as the 'P 79') evidently based on the P 1079/13, dated August 1, 1941.

Under 'usage', this states: "The aircraft is designed as a jet bomber for use on short routes. The deciding factor here is that the aircraft with the highest bomb load still reaches high airspeeds when

climbing, which ensure that it escapes the enemy fighter aircraft with certainty. The take-off takes place by being released from a parent aircraft (Me 323, Do 17). By replacing the bombing raid equipment with a weapon, the aircraft can be used as a fighter and interceptor. Because of its small dimensions, it is also possible to accommodate it inside a parent aircraft as an on-board aircraft (fighter or bomber)."

In other words, right from the outset the P 1079 was designed to be launched from another aircraft – although whether it was to be towed aloft, carried under a wing, carried on the back of the 'parent' or even launched inside it is unclear.

In physical design, it was to be a "self-supporting, twin-engine high-decker all-metal construction with retractable landing skids and enclosed pilot's compartment".

Also, under a heading of 'construction': "In the design, the

highest priority was given to cheapness and simple construction in view of the early war effort of the aircraft." The airframe consisted of the cockpit, fuel tank mid-section and fuselage tail section. The tail was split with twin end-plate rudders. It seems much of the P 1079's design was intended to help it reach front line service as quickly as possible: "As immediate solution the standard cabin has primitive equipment which can later be replaced without significant changes to the rest of the aircraft if a fully equipped pressurised cabin is provided. The forward canopy is made in bulletproof glass."

The mid-section had a rectangular cross section and was shielded against radiated heat from the 500kg thrust engines on either side. According to the report: "The engines are arranged on both sides of the fuselage converging towards the rear. The installation is carried

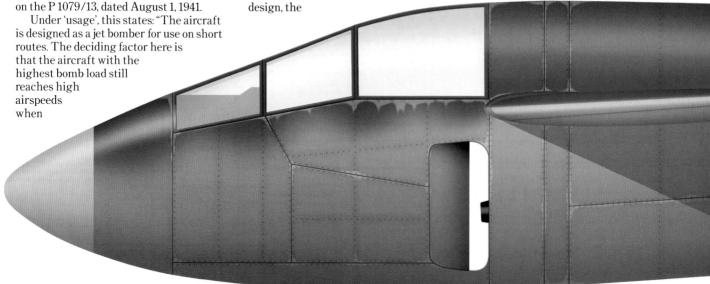

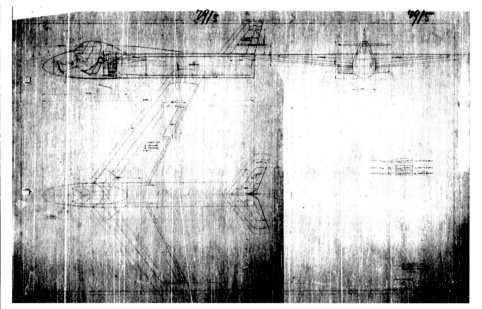

ABOVE: The P 1079/5 was used as a basis for exploring different wing lengths.

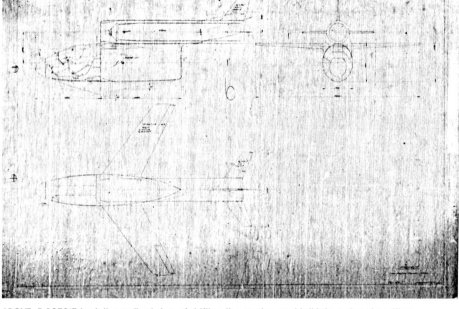

ABOVE: P 1079/7 took the radical step of shifting the engine and tail into a dorsal position.

out by attaching them to the fuselage side walls, thus allowing them to be changed rapidly. The possibility of installing engines of other sizes without any significant change in the airframe is also given."

The fuel tank behind the cockpit could be enlarged by extending the fuselage forward meaning "it is possible to revert to longer ranges. An additional fuel tank can be housed under the fuselage in the bomb shroud. Four container pumps with a delivery rate of 1000 litres per hour each are provided. Quick release is considered".

The report gives a considerable level of detail on the P 1079. Each pulsejet was to have its own power lever with a quick stop function, and other pilot equipment included a pressure gauge, fuel gauge and fuel flow meter on the left-hand side of the cockpit. On the right were controls for power distribution and safety devices as well as a toggle switch for operating the bomb payload. On the dashboard would be an airspeed indicator, variometer, altimeter and turn indicator. And the pilot would also get a light pistol, shoulder and waist belt, back parachute, oxygen system, clock, compass or gyro and a map pocket.

There was a wind-powered generator on board, FuG XVI Z and FuG XXV radio equipment with aerial housed in the rear cabin structure, and an intercom system so that the pilot could communicate with the crew of the carrier aircraft.

Evidently "the aircraft can be optionally equipped with one or two 1000kg to 1800kg bombs housed under the fuselage in a drop-down fairing". Alternatively the fairing could be used to house an additional fuel tank. Finally, "to allow for perfect bombing in the dive a dive brake is provided".

Also appended to

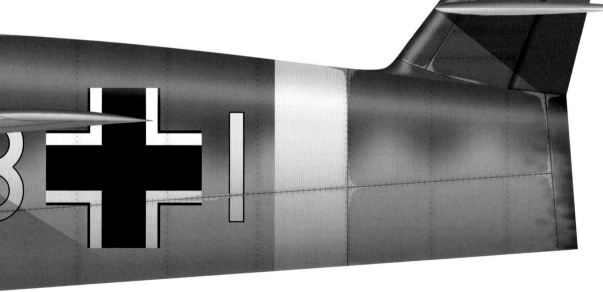

ABOVE: Messerschmitt P 1079/4. From this angle it would actually have been possible to see right through the fuselage. Artwork by Zoltán Csombó ▶

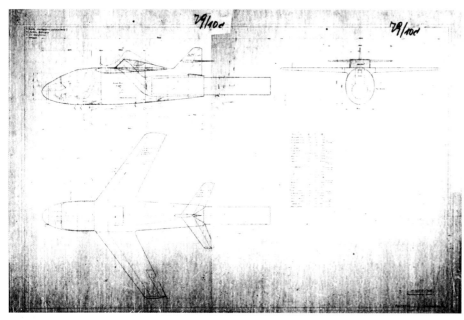

ABOVE: Another /1 development, the P 1079/10c shifted the engine somewhat to the rear and introduced a dorsal intake.

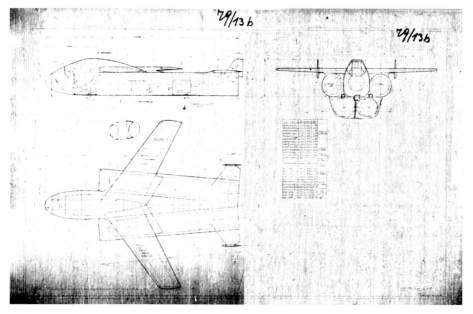

ABOVE: It may not look it, but P 1079/13b was the design chosen for further development and a similar layout, P 1079/10c, would become the very different-looking Me 328.

the document are a comparison between the P 1079 and the Me 109 D, dated July 31, 1941, and a comparison between the P 1079, the Me 109 F and the Me 262 – this being dated July 28, 1941.

FROM P 1079 TO ME 328

The Messerschmitt P 1079 was given the official designation Me 328 in March 1942. But a great deal of discussion and redesign work seems to have taken place from August 1, 1941, up to that date.

During a meeting at the RLM in Berlin on August 29, 1941, to discuss the Me 163 and recent events at Messerschmitt, Flugbaumeister Hans-Martin Antz mentioned an encounter he had had with Woldemar Voigt. The minutes of the meeting state: "Mr Antz said that project office Voigt had now also submitted projects to the office, which were strongly inspired by the drafts of project office Lippisch. He had received draft P 1079/13c dated August 11, 1941, and remarked that this was not the tailless machine, but a machine with strong sweep and jet propulsion. Mr Antz further commented that Mr Voigt had stated that the project would be handed over and that this would make the development of the Me 163 and the Interceptor superfluous.

"Director Hentzen remarked that Prof. Messerschmitt considered the strong sweep of fast aircraft to be necessary on the basis of investigations by Prof. Betz and therefore gave corresponding instructions for the project planning. Brigadeführer Croneiss said that in the meantime Prof. Messerschmitt would not speak on it until the meeting of the 28th but emphasised that he had expressly forbidden the project and development of tailless aircraft to the Voigt project bureau, as this was and should be the work of the Lippisch project bureau."

This same section of minutes from the same meeting was previously quoted in Luftwaffe: Secret Wings of the Third Reich but subsequent research has unearthed the original hand-typed German account which clearly states that the design handed to Antz, which

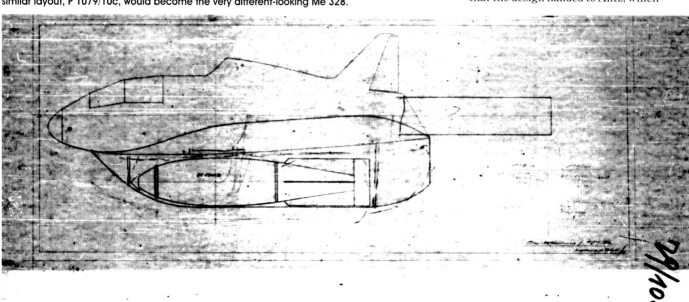

ABOVE: Another view of the P 1079/10c, this time fitted with the bulbous bomb shroud Messerschmitt seems to have intended for the series.

was to form the basis for the Me 328, was the P 1079/13c – not the P 1079/13a, as suggested by the later English translation.

In any case, although no drawing of the P 1079/13c has yet been unearthed, it appears to have been little different from the 13b. This means that although the basic premise of a small airframe with pulsejets slung under the wings on either side was retained – almost every detail was altered until a new and somewhat more basic design emerged – what today is known as the Me 328.

Over six months after Antz received the P 1079/13c design from Voigt, on February 17, 1942, RLM technical office chief General-Ingenieur Gottfried Reidenbach wrote a letter to Willy Messerschmitt headed 'P 1079', saying: "As reported by the DFS, constructional work on the three P 1079 test aircraft will now be carried out by the DFS at Ainring on the basis of a discussion with the Messerschmitt company. I agree with this, but please look after the work in Ainring with the gentlemen of your project office.

"In view of the remaining final uses of the P 1079, I think it is right to make these three experimental aircraft as simple as possible, in tubular steel and wood construction. At the same time, this makes it possible to produce this aircraft with the help of the DFS production and operating resources, and to relieve the experimental design department of your plant. Incidentally, I will try to accelerate the work in Ainring by temporarily presenting some designers who have experience in this type of construction."

Messerschmitt wrote back on February 24, 1942, saying: "We have agreed with the DFS to design and construct as many parts of the aircraft as possible, under the supervision of a master of our project office. With us only the hull and the landing skids are constructed and built. These parts were already too advanced, so switching to DFS Ainring would have led to unnecessary delays."

The following month, the type received the Me 328 designation and work on the three prototypes commenced, but as Voigt told his Allied interrogators on September 7, 1945: "The flight testing of the prototype without engines gave good results. The pilots blamed the low towing speed of the Me 110 and the bad field of view from the 328 at high angles of attack. Special devices were necessary to shorten the landing run on wet lawn.

"With engines no satisfactory results were obtained until the development was stopped; the engine itself did not work satisfactorily and did not give the expected thrust; the noise of the engine was hardly bearable without a sound-proof cabin; the vibrations of the engines were detrimental to the strength of the airframe; there was no unanimity between the RLM and our firm as to the economy of the take-off methods.

"The Me 328 was not ordered in series; the development was stopped when the turbojet engine proved to be reliable and the Me 262 was given higher priority. The Me 328 was the only model designed and constructed during the war by Messerschmitt which was not ordered in series." ●

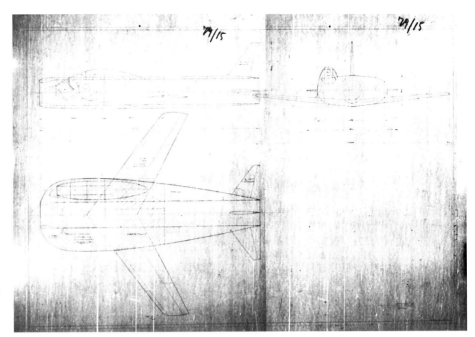

ABOVE: Giving the P 1079/15 a bulbous fuselage meant it had tremendous fuel carrying capacity but resulted in a very odd-looking aircraft.

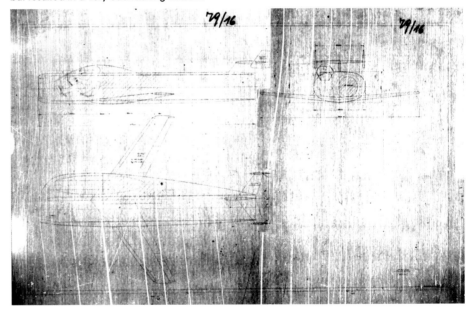

ABOVE: A development of the /15, the P 1079/16 had part of the fuselage removed to create an even more asymmetrical design.

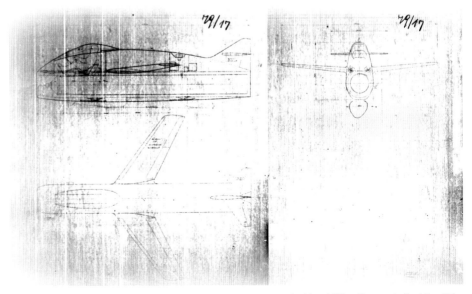

ABOVE: The final design in the sequence, P 1079/17, was created by shifting the cockpit of the /16 up on top of the pulsejet.

The least resistance

Messerschmitt Schnellstflugzeug

Having gained a reputation for building some of the world's fastest aircraft, Messerschmitt was keen to go one step further and design one capable of supersonic flight. The result, surprisingly, was a straight-winged layout with the pilot seeing out through a periscope.

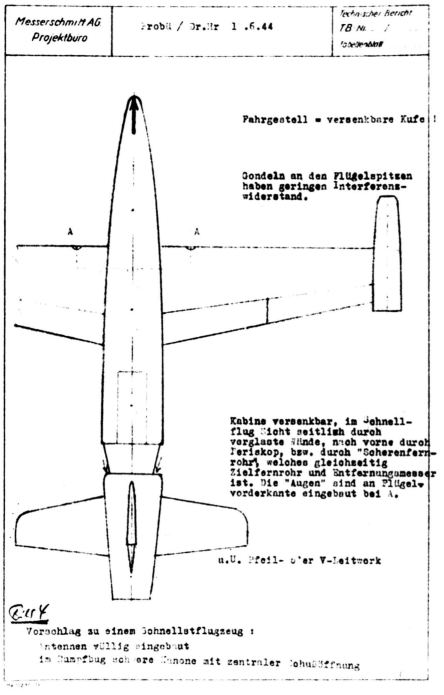

ABOVE: Dr Sighard Hoerner's design for a Schnellstflugzeug – with wingtip engines, a third engine mounted to the rear, a retractable cockpit and a periscope vision system.

Three months before Arado and the DFS reported on their Überschallflugzeug projects, Messerschmitt AG too was working on tentative designs for an aircraft capable of breaking the sound barrier.

On June 12, 1944, research aerodynamicist Dr Sighard Hoerner produced a report entitled Steps to a Fast Aircraft. Like many other reports of the period, this examined how different shapes performed at high speed, the effect of boundary layer flow and compressibility – but with the goal of producing the right shape for a jet-propelled aircraft that could go supersonic.

Hoerner noted that attempts to create a high-speed design had so far concentrated on designing aircraft with swept-back wings, with the disadvantages of complicated spar construction, tendency to roll and relatively high drag at greater speeds. And "finally, the sweep only has significant utility if it is performed sufficiently strongly. For example, a mild sweepback has only minor effect but sweepback of 60-degrees or more may be very difficult to control.

"Our aircraft at the moment are not critical because of their wing profile as such, but in the corners of the cockpit canopy and on the fuselage. In connection with the wing profile, we propose an unswept wing or a straight leading edge. This wing can be designed without slats. The most important points of attack in terms of drag and critical Mach number are the corners on the fuselage and on the cockpit canopy.

"Means for the reduction of this risk are: a) Mid-wing design, especially for the cockpit. b) Design of fuselage cross-section (oval?) and outline. Also here we use application of the laminar flow principle. c) Positioning the engine in the tail.

"Special research should start here! Point c) has the advantage that the sensitive part of the aircraft's surface is entirely spared from engine malfunctions. In addition, extraction of the boundary layer, to gain in efficiency in the wake."

A single drawing was appended to Hoerner's report, showing the jet aircraft that he was proposing. The least unusual thing about it was the skid undercarriage. The turbojet was positioned at the extreme rear of the aircraft, with an annular intake drawing in the air flowing around the stretched-bullet shape of the fuselage.

The thin laminar flow wings had a dead straight leading edge and each was tipped with a pod, which, according to the report, could house either a rocket booster or another turbojet. The aircraft's most unusual feature,

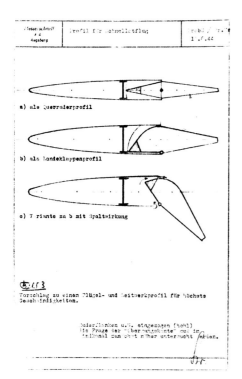

ABOVE: Wing profiles for the Messerschmitt Schnellstflugzeug.

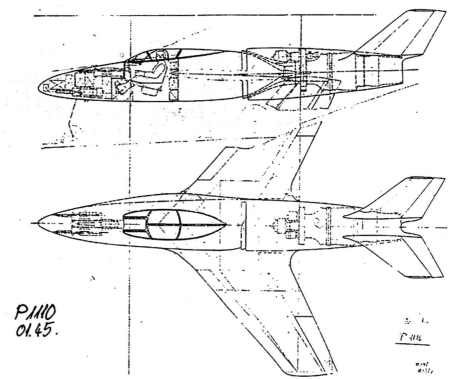

ABOVE: The Messerschmitt P 1110 single-jet fighter design circa January 1945 – with an annular engine intake similar to that devised by Sighard Hoerner.

however, was a retractable cockpit. Precise details of how this was to be designed are not provided, but during high-speed flight, with the cockpit flush against the fuselage, the pilot would only be able to see out "laterally through glazed walls, forward through a periscope, or through a 'scissors telescope', which is at the same time a rifle scope and rangefinder. The 'eyes' are at the leading edge of the wing installed at A".

The diagram shows that the 'scissors telescope' was similar to a set of split binoculars, with the lenses set into the wings and the view being reflected back to the pilot. The drawing's annotations even go so far as to suggest that a heavy cannon could be installed in the fuselage

nose, with the barrel positioned centrally.

It would appear that Hoerner's conclusions about fuselage drag and the unimportance of sweepback were rejected – because from mid-1944 onwards Messerschmitt turned increasingly towards sharply swept-back wings as the best means of achieving high-speed flight. The Überschallflugzeug project submissions utilised none of Hoerner's ideas and instead took more familiar high-speed forms.

However, a feature that does appear to have been carried forward for at least a little while was the annular intake for the rear-mounted turbojet. In January 1945, when Messerschmitt was working on early versions of the P 1110 single-jet fighter,

an annular intake was part of the design. However, even here, work carried out on the annular intake determined that it was not a particularly efficient or effective means of feeding air to a turbojet and the arrangement was dropped in favour of larger and more straightforward side intakes.

Despite the rejection of his work on fast jets, Hoerner was widely recognised as one of Germany's leading experts on aerodynamics and after the Second World War he emigrated to the US as part of Operation Paperclip. He wrote two books on his theories – Fluid-Dynamic Drag and Fluid-Dynamic Lift, which were apparently steady sellers, and died in New Jersey in 1971. ●

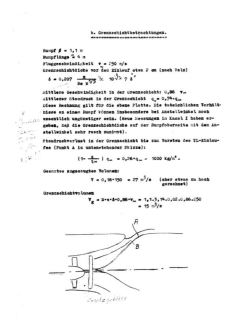

ABOVE: Page from a Messerschmitt report on experiments and calculations relating to the annular intake for the P 1110. It was found to be less effective than expected.

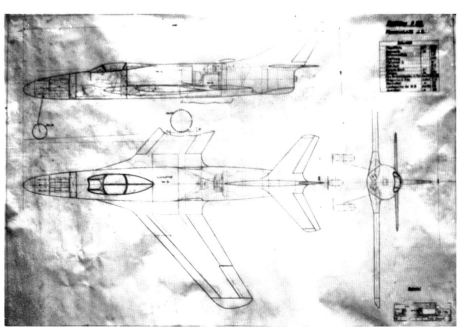

ABOVE: The revised P 1110 with Hoerner's annular intake replaced by a pair of more conventional side intakes.

Messerschmitt S

June 1944

Artwork by Luca Landino

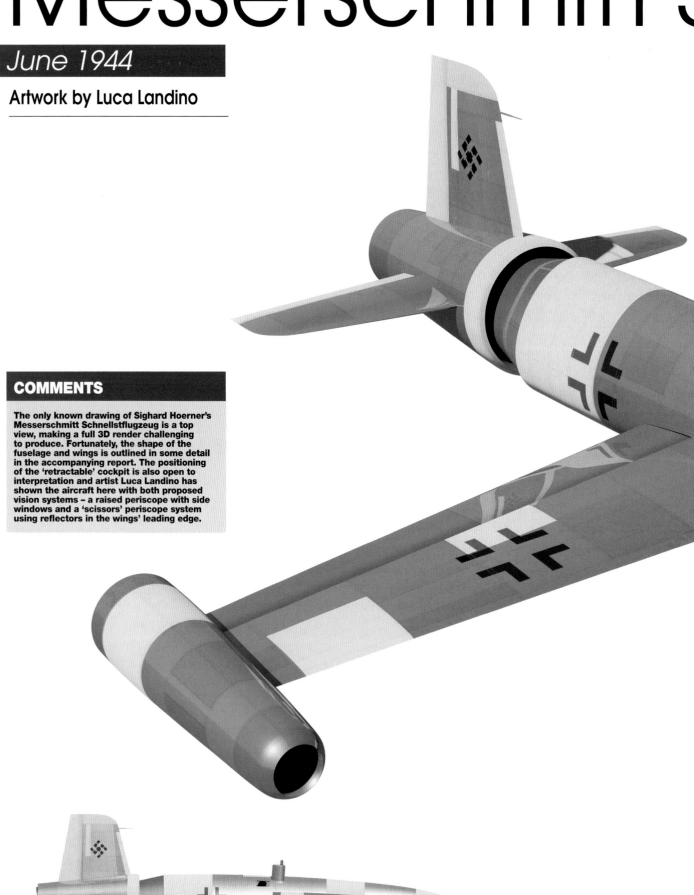

COMMENTS

The only known drawing of Sighard Hoerner's Messerschmitt Schnellstflugzeug is a top view, making a full 3D render challenging to produce. Fortunately, the shape of the fuselage and wings is outlined in some detail in the accompanying report. The positioning of the 'retractable' cockpit is also open to interpretation and artist Luca Landino has shown the aircraft here with both proposed vision systems – a raised periscope with side windows and a 'scissors' periscope system using reflectors in the wings' leading edge.

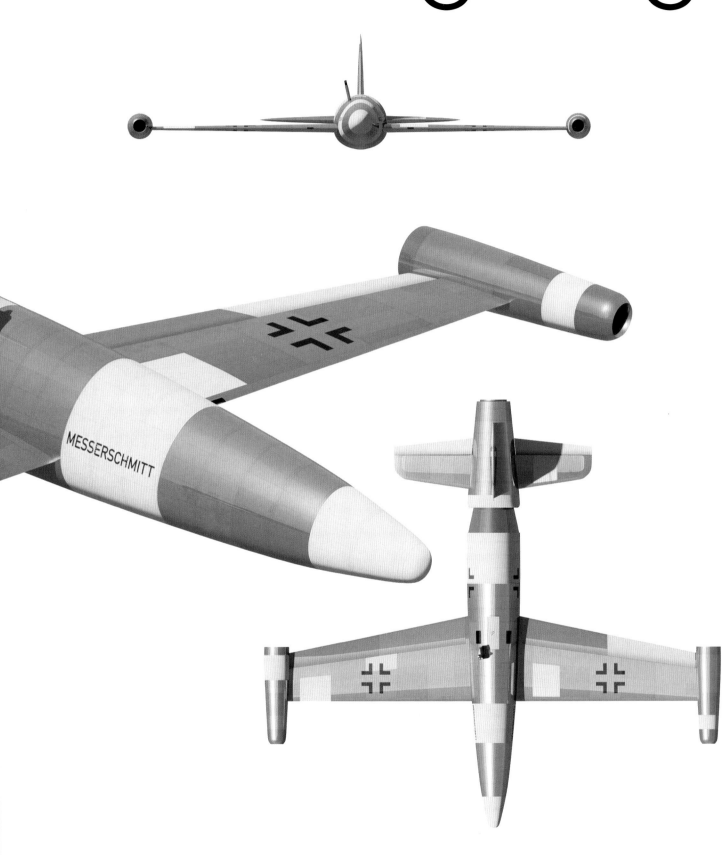

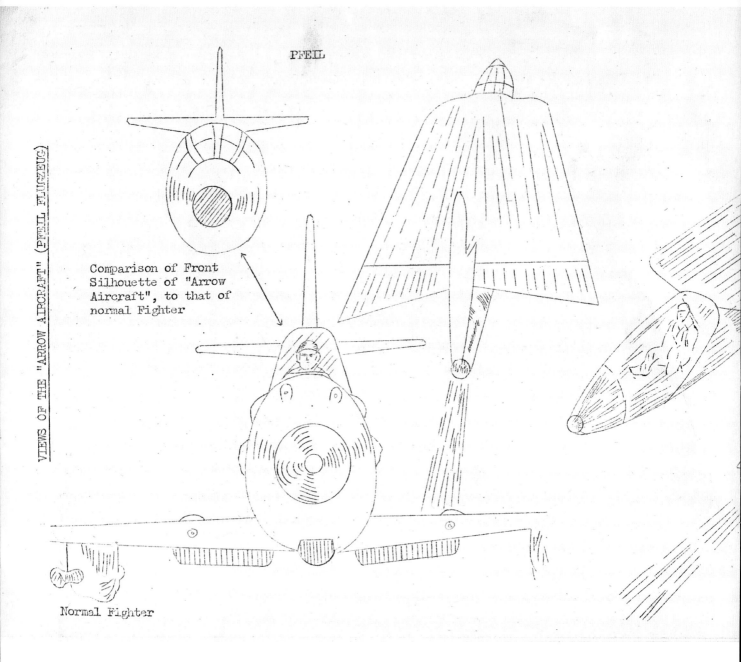

PFEIL

VIEWS OF THE "ARROW AIRCRAFT" (PFEIL FLUGZEUG)

Comparison of Front
Silhouette of "Arrow
Aircraft", to that of
normal Fighter

Normal Fighter

The Arrow Aircraft

Zippermayr's Pfeil Flugzeug

One of the more unusual aircraft designs worked on during the war owed its existence to experiments with winged torpedoes...

Italian-born Austrian scientist Mario Zippermayr carried out industrial and aeronautical research at his laboratory in Vienna until August 1939 when he was drafted into the Luftwaffe.

Having served with Luftgaukommando XVII, the air defence organisation of Vienna, until April 1942, he was then asked by the RLM to re-establish his lab to

investigate and find answers to a number of aviation-related engineering problems.

To begin with, he was supplied with equipment by various firms in the city and received military personnel to act as his staff. His initial work was on developing more reliable brushes for aircraft electricity generators and devising a means of tracking enemy bomber

formations using radio equipment.

However, at the beginning of 1943 he was able to recruit experienced scientists to his staff and was tasked with developing a means of stabilising air-launched torpedoes during their flight from an aircraft until they hit the water. In addition, he had to find a way of increasing the speed, altitude and angle at which torpedoes could be launched without suffering damage when they impacted on the water's surface.

In ordinary circumstances, torpedoes had to be launched at low level, close to the intended target and with the aircraft flying slowly and horizontally. Zippermayr's twofold solution to this was

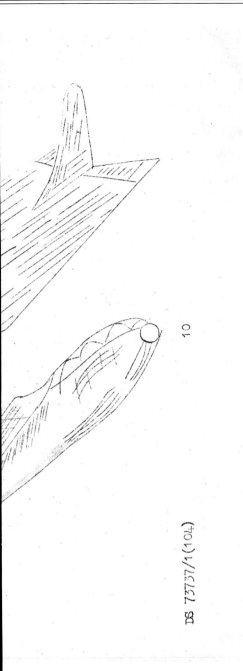

10

ABOVE: A page of sketches accompanied BIOS Interrogation Report No. 267 on the activities of Dr Mario Zippermayr. These illustrate the remarkable shape and size of the Austrian's proposed Pfeil Flugzeug with its incredibly low aspect ratio wings.

to equip torpedoes with both gyroscopes and very deep but also very narrow wings – extremely low aspect ratio. The result was a torpedo that was apparently automatically – and extraordinarily – stable when launched, no matter how fast or how high the launch aircraft was flying.

According to BIOS Interrogation Report No. 267: "The device was designated as L40 and provisions were made for it in the emergency programme. In the testing stage, a torpedo thus equipped was dropped from aircraft flying at speeds up to 720km/h and from heights above 1000m. It was intended to use such torpedoes from the Arado 234. This work was carried out from January 1944 to the end of the war."

In fact, the L40 achieved such good results that "the wings of the L40 device made it desirable to utilise the knowledge gained for the construction of a high speed aircraft. The ultimate intention in this development was to evolve a plane that would approach or even exceed the speed of sound".

Zippermayr stated during his interrogation that the aerodynamics institute of the Technische Hochschule, Hannover, had carried out wind tunnel tests on the L40 design "and passed the opinion that the structure was sound and suitable and could be applied successfully to actual aircraft".

He was then given orders to develop a jet-propelled aircraft using his torpedo wings. "It was the intention to utilise the new principle first in the development of a high-speed fighter. At the same time experiments were to continue to determine the value of the new design in the construction of fast bombers and transport planes. Dr Zippermayr claims that plans were begun to investigate the possibilities of constructing gigantic high-speed airliners, plans which are said to have been successful as far as they were able to progress before Germany's defeat."

Furthermore: "It was decided that the first experimental model was to be a glider that would be released from a tow or carrier-plane at high altitude. Models were constructed and equipped with instruments to register all possible flying and diving qualities. The results of these experiments were then used in the construction of the first full-scale glider model.

"It was with this model about three months short of the first test-flight that work stopped with the end of the war. This model, about three-fourths complete, is now stored at the Hagen carpenter shop in Lofer. After test-flights of this model were completed work was to begin on a jet-propelled craft. Dr Porsche, located at Schuttgut near Zell-am-See had already been assigned the task of supplying the jet-units."

Zippermayr claimed that his Pfeil Flugzeug or 'Arrow Aircraft' would have several clear advantages over more conventional designs: "Most outstanding, of course, is its tremendous speed. If jets of sufficient power can be devised its speed potential, it is claimed, would approach and possibly exceed the speed of sound. The small, but extremely strong wings have much less drag than the conventional variety, making it possible to realise a much greater efficiency from the engine thrust.

"The craft is expected to be extremely stable, especially on the transverse axis, making the plane easy to control. The torpedo prototype flew without any automatic steering device and even at speeds of 80 to 200m per second was perfectly stable. Even at an incidence angle of 52 degrees the torpedoes showed no tendency to stall nor were there any irregularities in the flight direction.

"It is also claimed that the wing loading for such a craft is much less than for conventional types. It is therefore expected that the landing speed will be reasonably low. It is intended that the highest speeds will not be attempted at less than 10,000m to take advantage of the lesser air density. It is expected that the construction of the plane should make mass production even more economical than that of present day craft.

"Materials required for completion: The full-scale test model is complete except for the construction of the tail assembly. Panel instruments and other instruments to record the test-flight data are also required. If these things are obtainable, Dr Zippermayr claims that the first test-flight could be made in about three months' time. A carrier plane would also be required. It is Zippermayr's hope that American aviation authorities will interest themselves sufficiently in the craft to make such a carrier available when the model is declared ready to fly.

"Estimate of test flight performance: it is intended that the plane should be released from the carrier-craft at a height of about 6000-7000m. The test model (without jets) is then expected to dive at terrific speed until it is approximately 1000m from the ground. Here the pilot begins to pull the craft out of its dive until the nose has risen into the air and the angle of approach is as much as 52 degrees. In this position, the plane is expected to maintain its straight line of approach until it is about 20ft from the ground. Here it levels off and makes a regular three-point landing. Zippermayr has two highly competent pilots working with him on the plane, both of whom are anxious to make the initial flight.

"Present condition of project: the nearly finished full-scale model and the plans and drawings required to complete the craft are located at the Carpenter Shop Hagen in Lofer, where they are being guarded by workmen employed by Zippermayr. There are no American guards. Some documents and models have been removed by American agencies. The only name Dr Zippermayr remembers of Americans who have already exploited the target is that of an 'Engineer Bramford of SHAEF'. At present, no work is going on, pending instructions from American authorities as to disposition of the work already accomplished, and of the plans, drawings and models."

Zippermayr's work on the Pfeil Flugzeug came to nothing and his original design drawings have never resurfaced but may well still exist in American archives. ●

ABOVE: This photograph purports to show the mock-up of Zippermayr's Pfeil Flugzeug. Its unusual shape is such that it is not at first obvious in the picture. It is in fact the framework behind the man's head, with the cockpit on the right hand side of the image and the very deep but also very short wing stretching from the upper rear part of the cockpit towards the tail end, to the left of the image.

Good vibrations

Zeppelin pulsejet fighter

When a scientific breakthrough solved the problem of destructive vibrations from pulsejet engines, Zeppelin set to work on designing a cheap twin-pulsejet fighter capable of attacking bomber formations en masse...

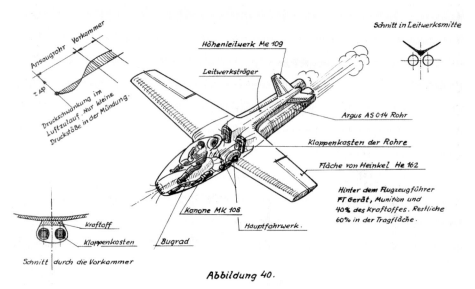

Abbildung 40.

ABOVE: The Zeppelin pulsejet fighter as it appears in Ulrich Hütter's report.

Less well known than the DVL, the AVA or the LFA, the Forschungsanstalt Graf Zeppelin (FGZ) or 'Graf Zeppelin research institute' was nevertheless a reasonably large and well-equipped organisation which carried out numerous experiments in aerodynamics and other areas of aviation research.

Not to be confused with Luftschiffbau Zeppelin, the airship maker, the FGZ grew out of the Flugtechnischen Institut of the Technischen Hochschule Stuttgart in 1937. In the beginning, it consisted of just six people but by January 1944 it had 400-500 staff including four professors, 17 doctors and 22 qualified engineers.

Its primary areas of interest were bomb aerodynamics, parachutes, underwater blast physics, take-off and landing aids, and the aerodynamics of aircraft with additional exterior structural units – such as troop-carrying pods attached to the wings of Junkers Ju 87 Stukas.

During the early part of 1944, the FGZ worked on launch ramps for the V-1 flying bomb and became intimately familiar with the workings of its powerplant, the Argus As 014 pulsejet.

The As 014's main drawback was that it generated destructive vibrations which made it unsuitable for manned aircraft or indeed any aircraft required to do more

than make a single one-way trip. The pulsejet had originally been intended as the powerplant for the Messerschmitt Me 328 light bomber – but when no solution to the vibration problem could be found, the aircraft was cancelled.

However, while the FGZ had been working on its ramps, the nearby Forschungsinstitut für Kraftfahrwesen und Fahrzeugmotoren Stuttgart (FKFS) had been solving the pulsejet problem.

According to a postwar report produced by Ulrich W Hütter, who joined the institute in early 1944, the FGZ and FKFS had worked closely together during the autumn of 1944 on "an anti-aircraft device consisting of an unmanned missile with explosives controlled from the ground via fine steel wires towards approaching enemy formations. The drive was two Argus As 014 pipes.

"In the FKFS, experiments had shown that when these pulsejet tubes were run in parallel operation, so that the inlets of both tubes were parallel and only a small distance from each other, the operation became calmer and smoother than when a single pipe was operated on its own".

Evidently the key to cancelling out the As 014's vibrations was simply to operate a second one right next to it. Hütter said that where a BMW 801 with propeller and other auxiliary machinery took 8000-9000

man hours to build, two As 014s took just 500-600 man hours. If a simple fuselage could also be used, the saving in terms of both time and cost would be considerable.

However, the FKFS also discovered that two tubes running side by side only produced a little more thrust than one tube on its own. Aerodynamic drag was blamed for this anomaly, and it was thought that a suitably shaped cowling to cover the engines' front end would result in big performance gains. This was where Zeppelin came in – its aerodynamic experience was applied to the problem and a fuselage was designed which could house "large amounts of fuel, the explosive, a control system, the large cavities for the intake of the two tubes and the attachment point for the wings".

The FGZ built a test rig and "the double pipes ran quite satisfactorily on the stand, even with large plywood sheaves in the shape of the projected fuselage nose".

There were concerns that the pulsejet missile's guidance system might be difficult to procure, so a manned version was studied in parallel. But "the design difficulties were considerably greater, since the landing gear, radio equipment, weapons etc. had to be accommodated with a larger fuel supply". The aircraft was to have an all-up weight of two tons and a top speed of over 900km/h in horizontal flight at 6000m.

Hütter noted that several attempts had previously been made to power an aircraft with pulsejets including a "manned Fi 103 with enlarged wings, Junkers 'Lilli' device with 500mm tube and DFS/Messerschmitt 235 with two free-floating As 014 pipes". The latter appears to be a reference to the Me 328, since Hütter goes on to say: "However, they repeatedly failed because neither man nor the more sensitive parts of the aircraft are able to cope with the heavy vibrations that occur during tolerable periods of time. There is damage to clothing and skin, to control parts and instruments, the pilot's canopy glazing becomes hard to see through and memory and concentration of the pilot seriously suffer."

Diagrams appended to Hütter's report showed the Zeppelin pulsejet fighter with wings taken from an He 162 and tails surfaces from an Me 109 arranged in a V at the end of a stubby tail boom above the twin As 014s. It was to be armed with a pair of MK 108 30mm cannon and had a tricycle undercarriage.

Work on the fighter was suspended when it became clear that the He 162 was eating up all available production capacity and it would not be possible to make the Zeppelin pulsejet the "fast solution" required. In addition, there were still question marks over the vibrations produced by the jet tubes at high airspeeds – though with a tuned diffuser "and fully elastic suspension of the entire engine, it is conceivable that these difficulties may have been mastered. Until then, however, a lot of development work was still required". It never happened. ●